Praise for *Sacred Acts*

The articles gathered in *Sacred Acts* edited by Mallory McDuff bring me back to reflections on the possible evolutionary roots of ritual as sacred acts. That is, their emphases on taste, leadership, burial, intersections of birds and advocacy, money and mountains, immigration and justice remind me of the intentional and attentional character of sacred acts. In our emergence, we humans stood up, perhaps as much as we were raised up, and we continue to look for that deeper intention in our actions, that attention to an abiding sacred in our world. *Sacred Acts* is a reader for this work.

—John A. Grim, Senior Lecturer and Research Scholar,
Yale School of Forestry and Environmental Studies
Yale Divinity School
Yale Department of Religious Studies.

As Protestant privilege wanes in America, churches are renewed as they respond to the pressing spiritual and environmental needs of our time. The essays in this fine book indicate that some faith communities are doing just that. Their witness challenges us all. I am filled with hope.

— Bill J. Leonard, James and Marilyn Dunn Professor of Baptist Studies
Professor of Church History and Religion
Wake Forest University

sacred
acts

How churches are working to protect Earth's climate

Mallory McDuff
FOREWORD BY BILL McKibben

new society
PUBLISHERS

Inquiries regarding requests to reprint all or part of *Sacred Acts*
should be addressed to New Society Publishers at the address below.

To order directly from the publishers, please call toll-free
(North America) 1-800-567-6772, or order online at
www.newsociety.com

Any other inquiries can be directed by mail to:

New Society Publishers
P.O. Box 189, Gabriola Island, BC V0R 1X0, Canada
(250) 247-9737

New Society Publishers' mission is to publish books that contribute in fundamental
ways to building an ecologically sustainable and just society, and to do so with the
least possible impact on the environment, in a manner that models this vision. We
are committed to doing this not just through education, but through action. The
interior pages of our bound books are printed on Forest Stewardship Council®-
registered acid-free paper that is **100% post-consumer recycled** (100% old growth
forest-free), processed chlorine free, and printed with vegetable-based, low-VOC
inks, with covers produced using FSC®-registered stock. New Society also works
to reduce its carbon footprint, and purchases carbon offsets based on an annual
audit to ensure a carbon neutral footprint. For further information, or to browse our
full list of books and purchase securely, visit our website at: www.newsociety.com

LIBRARY AND ARCHIVES CANADA CATALOGUING IN PUBLICATION

Sacred acts : how churches are working to protect earth's
climate / [compiled and edited by] Mallory McDuff ;
foreword by Bill McKibben.

Includes bibliographical references and index.
ISBN 978-0-86571-700-8

1. Ecotheology. 2. Church work. 3. Environmental protection.
4. Christian stewardship. 5. Climatic changes — Religious aspects —
Christianity. I. McDuff, Mallory D

BT695.5.S198 2012   261.8'8
C2012-900038-8

new society
PUBLISHERS
www.newsociety.com

MIX
Paper from
responsible sources
FSC® C016245

To Ann and Larry McDuff

Contents

Acknowledgments

I am thankful for the contributors who gave their time and energy to craft the chapters of this book. Each organization and congregation featured in the book involves people of faith passionate about justice for all. I am humbled and inspired by their authentic work in this world.

Several people provided feedback on the overall structure and content of the book: Lyn O'Hare, Lorrie Jayne, the Reverend Brian Cole as well as students in the 2011 Environmental Education Methods and Materials class at Warren Wilson College, including Rachel Cairatti, Amelea Canaris, Elena Canaris, Emmet Fisher, Grace Frankenburg, Melissa Hahn, Madeline Kenny, Cella Langer, Lindsay Loftin, John McDermott, Mikel Oboyski, Rachel Rasmussen, Jacquelyn Roshay, Christina Torquato and Kimberly Worthington.

I am grateful for Andy Reed in Asheville, North Carolina for his mentoring and copyediting skills. Many thanks to managing editor Ingrid Witvoet and the staff at New Society Publishers for their appreciation of the connection between faith, sense of place and sustainability.

Lastly, I thank my daughters Maya and Annie Sky for their willingness to participate in church services, talks and presentations at home and in travels to other communities.

Foreword

by Bill McKibben

I can remember the time when there really wasn't a religious environmental movement. In fact, many people of faith tended to view environmentalism with suspicion. Among conservative traditions, it was seen as a way station on the road to paganism; among liberal congregations, as a luxury to be addressed once we'd checked a few small items like war and poverty off the list.

By now, as this book makes clear, that has changed: climate change, in particular, is now a topic as fit for theologians as for chemists. And rightly so—as followers of a scripture that begins with creation, and whose first command is that we keep and dress this planet we've been given, there's really no way for churches to duck the issue.

Painful as this crisis is, in some ways it's been wonderful for faith communities that have really gotten involved: it is redemptive in so many ways to remind ourselves that God's world extends far beyond the boundaries of our human settlements. We're finally starting to understand the (awe-ful) meaning of that "dominion" over the planet we were given—a responsibility that so far we haven't lived up to.

Churches have also had an impact on the environmental movement. I remember when there were only a few nascent beginnings: Earth Ministry, Episcopal Power and Light, Religious Witness for the Earth, Shomrei Adamah. Many people were working on the tiniest level, one congregation at a time—convincing sextons to turn down thermostats, lobbying boards of deacons to buy more insulation. By now, these have all grown into a very real force with very deep political understanding.

In the summer of 2011 I was helping organize a large-scale civil disobedience action in Washington, DC, in an effort to block a proposed ruinous pipeline from the tar sands of Alberta, Canada. My colleagues asked if I thought there would be faith communities willing to get involved. Within a couple of days, hundreds of people of faith signed up to risk arrest. It moved me immensely to see such commitment.

Of course, it's not yet clear that we're doing enough to turn the tide; in fact, the science of climate change has grown steadily darker. We're clearly not going to "stop" global warming—we've already heated the planet enough to melt the Arctic Ocean's ice cover each summer and trigger an ominous spike in extreme weather. No, at this point all we can hope for (and work for) is a world that still works at least a little, a planet something like the one we were born on. That's a hard truth for some to hear, but perhaps those of us used to sitting in the pews can deal with it more easily than some. We know that our best efforts will be matched by a force greater than our own—we know that, having done all we can, we're allowed to take some things on faith.

● ● ●

BILL McKIBBEN is the founder of the organizations Step It Up and 350.org, a grassroots campaign to raise awareness of global warming. He is the author of more than a dozen books, including *The End of Nature*, *The Comforting Whirlwind*, and *Eaarth*. He is a scholar in residence at Middlebury College in Vermont and has taught Sunday school in the United Methodist Church.

A Pentecost Moment
of Change

Mallory McDuff

T HE CLOCK SAID 8:45 AM, which meant we had fifteen minutes
to make the ten-mile drive to church. We might miss the first
hymn but would arrive before the Gospel reading. Getting to
church shouldn't result in a racing heart or a speeding ticket, I told
myself, glancing at the speedometer and settling into the rhythm
of shared time with my daughters, Maya and Annie Sky.

I turned on the radio as a report broadcast grim statistics about
global warming—ice caps melting, habitats disappearing, floods
destroying communities. For a second, I considered changing stations to *American Top 40 with Ryan Seacrest*. "Is that guy saying that
the Earth is getting hotter?" asked Maya from the back seat. "Is that
going to be a problem?" It was 8:55 AM—five minutes until the
church bells rang. I searched for clear language to describe climate
change to my middle-school daughter, knowing her younger sister
was listening too.

This was my dilemma as a mother, teacher and person of faith:
How could I talk to my children about something that seems complex and downright scary? Could I translate the science of climate
change into opportunities for empowering action rather than par-
alyzing despair?

I believe that moral values of faith communities are key to harnessing collective acts to confront climate change. So I decided to
explain the basic science of climate change but also illustrate religious actions to address global warming. This conversation didn't

happen in five minutes (we made it to the church on time). Instead
the discussion has been incremental, explaining a news story about
food scarcity and climate, participating in a weatherization project
at church and joining an interfaith protest against the expansion of
a coal-fired power plant.

When I was Maya's age, I watched the apocalyptic film *The Day
After* at school and became convinced a nuclear winter was coming
to my hometown of Fairhope, Alabama. I don't want my children
to feel alone and powerless against the impacts of climate change,
because they aren't. Much is being done.

Diverse faith communities — Muslim, Jewish and Christian —
are working to love their neighbors as themselves through sacred
acts of justice: installing solar panels on mosques and temples,
tilling church gardens, conducting energy audits on low-income
homes, lobbying against mountaintop removal and supporting
reforestation projects in countries on the front lines of climate
change. These acts reveal a shared moral mandate to care for God's
Earth, especially since climate change will have a disproportionate
impact on the world's poor.

Our religious traditions teach us that it is a sin to unjustifiably
cause human suffering, and almost every faith tradition has issued
a public statement calling for climate solutions. Yet we need to
share and replicate the range of actions that congregations can take
to convert communities to a low-carbon future.

The contributors to this book include a farmer, a climate scientist, teachers, clergy, academics, activists and directors of nonprofit
organizations. They are practitioners doing the work of climate
justice from a variety of faith backgrounds: Episcopalian, Roman
Catholic, evangelical and United Church of Christ, among others.
Though many of the organizations described in this book, such as
Interfaith Power & Light and GreenFaith, are nonsectarian, this
book focuses on the acts of Christians confronting climate change.

People of faith have been instrumental in societal changes such
as the abolition of slavery and the civil rights movement. We live in
a time with enormous capacity for grassroots mobilization based

on justice. This movement to protect Earth's climate is built on both joy and love for the world God created and called good.[1]

The Greatest Moral Crisis of Our Time: Climate Change 101

Several years ago, I attended a workshop called the "Climate Leaders Initiative," organized by the National Council of Churches Eco-Justice Program.[2] The participants wondered aloud how churches would mitigate and adapt to climate change, given its impact on core ministries such as work with disaster relief, immigration and food security.[3] I recalled my daughter's inquiry about climate change and posed my own question: "What is a simple way to explain climate change? What's the elevator speech?"

Without hesitation, staff member Tyler Edgar grabbed a marker, turned to a flipchart and drew a picture of a globe. "When I'm speaking to an adult Sunday school class, I use this simple drawing," she said, sketching the sun and a smokestack and writing "atmosphere, heat and greenhouse gases (CO_2 and CH_4)." In her presentations, she explains that since industrialization, our Earth has been warming; scientists have documented this rapid pace of global warming due to actions taken by humans. Climate change is caused by the release of greenhouse gases in the atmosphere, with carbon dioxide the most common gas.

History provides some additional context for understanding our warming planet. Carbon dioxide in the atmosphere reflects infrared radiation and warms the planet, bringing about what we know as the greenhouse effect,

A drawing illustrates the basics of climate change at a training for faith leaders organized by the National Council of Churches Eco-Justice Program. Photo by Mallory McDuff.

which maintains the Earth at a livable temperature. A British physicist named John Tyndall discovered the role of carbon dioxide in the late 1850s. We now also recognize that methane is another gas with strong greenhouse properties.[4]

In the 1950s, Charles David Keeling measured carbon dioxide levels of 315 parts per million (ppm) in winds off the Pacific Ocean. We know that 350 ppm is the maximum number we can reach and still keep the Earth's temperature from rising further, yet today the level has reached 390 ppm.[5] The higher concentration of carbon dioxide and other greenhouse gases in the Earth's atmosphere is primarily the result of our burning fossil fuels at increased rates.

With the rising gas concentrations, we have seen an increase in average global temperatures of more than one degree F. The warming has caused significant changes such as melting of Arctic sea ice, rising sea levels and increased floods.[6] The National Research Council of the National Academy of Sciences has stated that the risks of inaction outweigh the risks of action, in terms of damage by climate change to Earth's life-support systems.[7]

Despite the overwhelming consensus among scientists, climate change has been imbued with political agendas. Powerful lobbying by the fossil-fuel industry has stalled efforts to consider federal climate legislation in the United States. The stakes are high: ExxonMobil, for example, made more money in 2009 than the recorded profits of any company in history.[8]

While the science reflects the urgency of climate change, many choose to ignore the evidence. It turns out that rational thought does not always guide decision-making, as emotions and values play a significant role in human choice.[9] We need to achieve a low-carbon future, whether people "believe" in climate change or not. In the film *Carbon Nation*, an Alaskan man asks, "Do I believe man is causing global warming? No. But that doesn't make any difference. I want clean water and clean air."

Ultimately, climate change is only a symptom of the difference between our own human interests and the natural world. Wendell

Berry maintains that if we were given a limitless supply of cheap, clean energy, we would continue our destruction of the world by agricultural erosion, chemical poisoning and other forms of "development."[10] He calls us to come into conformity with "the nature of places" on a local scale. Nowhere is this role of values and place more apparent than in our congregations.

A Conversion: Churches Responding to Climate Change

Across the globe, the Christian community has called for climate solutions based on justice. In the United States, the Evangelical Climate Initiative was released in 2006, stating that the moral beliefs of evangelicals demanded a response to climate change. The US Conference of Catholic Bishops declared that destruction of the atmosphere by climate change dishonored God and creation. In 2008, Southern Baptist leaders released a similar public statement that Christians must be held accountable for our actions that harm the environment.[11] The Evangelical Environmental Network launched a campaign called "Creation Care: It's a Matter of Life," which emphasizes the connection between creation care, climate change and the poor.

Translating words to actions, Georgia Interfaith Power & Light (IPL) leveraged $400,000 in federal stimulus money for matching grants to weatherize houses of worship and save 20 percent of their

The Evangelical Environmental Network launched a campaign entitled "Creation Care: It's a Matter of Life." Photo courtesy of Evangelical Environmental Network.

congregations' energy budgets. Georgia IPL has completed 76 energy audits, 11 of Jewish schools and synagogues, with 200 additional congregations in the pipeline.

St. Patrick's Episcopal Church in Atlanta reduced its $36,000 annual energy bill by 15 percent, due in part to energy-efficient upgrades at Malachi Storehouse, one of the largest food pantries in the city. Georgia IPL has collected data from 56 participating congregations, revealing an average annual savings on energy bills of $2,593. These conservation measures have resulted in savings of 4,238,139 pounds of CO_2, the equivalent of taking 377 cars off the road.[12]

This growth of religious environmentalism comes at a time when religious institutions are seeking ways to make faith relevant to modern audiences. Harvey Cox, author of *The Future of Faith*, asserts that Christianity needs to return to its roots and become spiritually fluid, less hierarchical and more countercultural, willing to criticize power structures.[13] For many faith leaders, the calling to address climate change has increased the relevancy of their ministries. Pastor Carol Jensen of St. John United Lutheran Church in Seattle, Washington, notes that new people come to her church because the environment is part of the church's identity.[14] A conversion to reduce a congregation's carbon footprint might also bring more people walking through the church doors.

Four Strategies for Religious Action to Address Climate Change

The authors in this book speak from diverse theological and political perspectives; indeed, many hold conflicting views on issues such as gay marriage or abortion, topics that typically divide believers. Yet their writings reveal overwhelming support for confronting the climate crisis, a powerful force if we can hold our differences in creative ways.

We don't have the option to stay within our religious comfort zones. There is no time for caricatures of each other's religious beliefs, which will squander our collective power to revision our communities on higher moral ground. We need all voices, all sacred acts. This book uses a framework of four avenues for climate action: stewardship, spirituality, advocacy and justice. Within each of the four themes, contributors provide concrete examples of their own efforts to live out religious values of climate justice.

Stewardship

As faithful stewards of God's creation, we recognize that the natural world belongs to God, and our stewardship will protect creation for future generations. Promoting connections between food and faith is one action taken by Christians heeding God's call. In Chapter 1 Ragan Sutterfield, a farmer in Arkansas, highlights the work in church gardens and kitchens to foster healthful food whose production conserves natural resources. Through stories of congregations in Chapter 2, the Reverend Fletcher Harper of GreenFaith challenges churches to decrease their carbon emissions and conserve financial and energy resources. Conservation of land is another way to address stewardship, and in Chapter 3, I examine the role of natural burials in connecting the faithful to the natural world.

Spirituality

Many people have their most profound spiritual experiences in nature: God's creation inspires reflection and our inspiration to care for the Earth. In Chapter 4, Dr. Katharine Hayhoe, a climate scientist and an evangelical, explains the science of climate change and shows how science and our Christian faith can support each other in our protection of God's world. Dr. Norman Wirzba of Duke Divinity School reflects in Chapter 5 on how we can live the Good News in a changing climate by considering God as a gardener. The Reverend Brian Cole turns to scripture and challenges us in Chapter 6 to rethink sermons about the natural world amid the anxiety of climate change.

Advocacy

God calls us to be witnesses to our faith, and Christians are advocating for policies and practices that protect the climate. Religious environmental advocates achieved a major legislative victory with the Coal-Free Washington bill, as described by LeeAnne Beres and Jessie Dye of Earth Ministry in Chapter 7. On the forefront of a green economy, Michele McGeoy, executive director of Solar Richmond, illustrates in Chapter 8 creative partnerships with churches to provide green jobs for youth in Richmond, California. Father John S. Rausch in Chapter 9 examines the decade-long work of churches to advocate for the people of Appalachia impacted by mountaintop removal mining.

Justice

The impacts of climate change, such as increased natural disasters and food insecurity, fall most heavily on the poor and vulnerable across the globe, an injustice given that the United States has been the world's largest contributor of greenhouse gas emissions over the past century.[15] One consequence of climate change is increased immigration, with a new category of migrants called climate refugees. In Chapter 10, Jill Rios describes the work of her church, La Capilla de Santa Maria, in North Carolina, to confront the injustices of a broken immigration system in the context of global climate change. Environmental justice leader Peggy M. Shepard of West Harlem Environmental Action, Inc. (WE ACT) chronicles in Chapter 11 the collaboration with churches to address environmental health issues linked to climate change. And lastly in Chapter 12, the Reverend Mitch Hescox, with the Evangelical Environmental Network, relates his experiences with people of faith on the Gulf Coast after the British Petroleum oil spill.

The Momentum of a Pentecost Moment

We may not think it's politically viable to create public transit, community gardens and renewable energy sources in our landscapes, dominated as they are by Walmart, CVS and Burger King. But the Christian faith asks us to imagine a world that does not degrade God's resources or harm His people. We can bear witness to prophetic voices, not the politics of the practical. Ten years ago, no one could have imagined that a religious environmental organization, Earth Ministry, would be the lead organizer for legislation to transition the state of Washington off coal-fired power.

The prophetic becomes possible because churches are grounded in place with physical addresses. In my home of Asheville, North Carolina, Oakley United Methodist Church created a church garden to serve its local community. First Congregational United Church of Christ installed 42 solar panels as a public witness in the neighborhood. The church is no stranger to radical acts of justice, rooted in place.

Our challenge reflects the question of Pentecost: How will God's spirit move in our lives? Pentecost marks the seventh Sunday after Easter—50 days after the death of Jesus—when the Holy Spirit descended to the disciples. As humans, we may feel threatened by the mystery of the Holy Spirit in our lives today. With climate change, our stability has been interrupted. We face a true Pentecost moment.

In the Acts of the Apostles, the coming of the Holy Spirit is marked with winds, tremors of the earth and fire, but people from all nations come together. As a youth, I remember entering St. James Episcopal Church to find flames of red, orange and yellow construction paper hanging from the ceiling. Pentecost Sunday marked the end of the Easter season, with Lent a memory from early spring.

In our family, my parents would sometimes give up practices, such as driving, for Lent. One year, my father bicycled the 30 miles to work each day, showered in the basement of his office, put on a suit, and then changed his clothes to bike home each evening. On Sundays, my mother insisted on driving him to church, as she didn't approve of attending church in sweaty clothes. Our friends found my father's Lenten discipline both entertaining and per-plexing. I now realize that he was practicing an act of redemption, a Pentecost moment.

God's work of redemption is a mystery, but it happens in a community of people; the Holy Spirit is made incarnate in human experience. We must be ready to become transformed, and in turn, transform our communities. Our congregations are the testing grounds for conversion. Let us imagine and act together.

stewardship

The Lord God took the man and put him
in the garden of Eden to till it and keep it.

Genesis 2:15

For the Lord is a great God,
and a great King above all gods.
In his hand are the depths of the earth;
the heights of the mountains are his also.
The sea is his, for he made it,
and the dry land, which his hands have formed.

Psalm 95:3–5

CHAPTER 1

Food, Faith and a Catechesis of Taste

Resisting the Junk Food of Empire

RAGAN SUTTERFIELD

Hey there! All who are thirsty,
come to the water!
Are you penniless?
Come anyway—buy and eat!
Come, buy your drinks, buy wine and milk.
Buy without money—everything's free!
Why do you spend your money on junk food,
Your hard-earned cash on cotton candy?
Listen to me, listen well: Eat only the best,
Fill yourself with only the finest.

Isaiah 55:1–2 (*The Message*)

THE PROPHET ISAIAH, taking on the role of a street vendor, calls from his stall, giving away the good, nutritious abundance of God in the midst of a Babylonian market selling the junk food of empire. He is inviting God's people to a free feast, a filling, tasty and healthful meal that won't leave them hungry. And yet many walk by, unwilling to accept the abundance offered, preferring to pay for junk food instead of accepting the delicious food and drink prepared by a loving God.

In our own age we find ourselves in a not-too-different predicament. All around us are the offerings of a global food system that increasingly dominates and homogenizes our food choices—under the illusion of more choice. This food system is built upon the same extractive economy that is fueling the rapid and troubling changes in our climate.

We now rely on a bigger-is-better system of agriculture. Machines have replaced human hands in doing the work of farming, and these machines run on fuels that contribute increased carbon dioxide to the environment. The soils they plow are laid bare and compacted by them, compounding desertification—a process by which life-giving soil is turned into infertile ground. With this desertification comes a release of carbon dioxide that is normally sequestered in soil filled with living organisms.

Our animal agriculture system, too, has been transformed from the art of husbandry (care of animals in or close to the home) into the more abstracted "animal sciences." With this transformation we have moved from a pasture-based grazing system that was healthful for both the animals and the Earth to an industrial system that feeds them grain crops like corn and soybeans—crops that quickly add weight to animals but prove so destructive to them that antibiotics must be regularly used to keep them from falling ill.

The animals themselves are no longer treated as animals—literally beings with life-spirits—but as protein sources. Cargill, one of the largest producers of pork and a major supplier of animal feeds, describes its company as providing "protein solutions" (what the rest of us call "meat"). Because the animals are now "protein," they are denied their place as living creatures and are no longer treated humanely, in a way fitting for human beings to act. In the end, both the animals and their keepers—we ourselves—become degraded. We give up our common reality as sentient creatures sharing the breath of life, and we are relegated to playing roles in an economic system that works through abstractions.

The result of this "protein-production" system has been the ravaging of rural economies, the Earth and ourselves. Most farmers have been forced to work in terrible conditions, able to make ends meet only by getting big or getting out. The Earth has been depleted, with fertilizer running into our rivers and down to the Gulf of Mexico, creating a "dead zone" that stretches for hundreds of square miles—a huge bacterial bloom where the oxygen is literally sucked out of the water. In my own state of Arkansas, runoff from chicken farms is poisoning the rivers of neighboring states with substances such as arsenic, a lethal poison used in low levels in some chicken-feed formulations for antibiotic purposes. And because we are eating the highly processed and homogenized food produced from these farms—often merely reshaped forms of corn and soybeans—our bodies are reacting with hormones sent out of balance. Epidemics of both type II diabetes and obesity are part of the price we pay for the unnatural food chain we now rely on.

This industrial agricultural system has promised that for all its economic and ecological tradeoffs, it is the only form of agriculture that can feed a growing global population. And yet this carbon-intensive form of farming is contributing to a climate catastrophe that is rapidly leading to drought, desertification and famine. According to Oxfam, a major global relief organization, food prices, particularly for staple crops like wheat, will more than double in the next 20 years.[1] This cost increase will largely be the result of climate change. Gerald Nelson, an economist with the International Food Policy Research Institute, says, "Agriculture is the sector most likely to be affected by changes in climate of all sectors of society."[2] Our diet of empire junk food not only destroys our bodies and the Earth, it serves to devastate our neighbors, particularly those in the global south, as areas already facing food shortages are further stressed and exploited.

All of this and God is calling to us—come and eat! There is free and abundant food, ready and waiting. As my mentor in agriculture once told me, only one acorn is needed for another oak tree, only a little honey for bees to live off for the winter, yet both create more than they need. God has provided us with a natural economy of abundance, yet that gift is not enough. We have *chosen* instead

lives of scarcity rather than abundance—like indebted people unwilling to save, living on one source of credit and another until,
eventually, bankruptcy comes. Unfortunately, these choices are not
individual ones: some have made their neighbors suffer the brunt
of their debts, the poor suffering for the borrowed profits of the
short-term rich.

So how are we to live in abundance and eat the free food and
drink the free drink of God? How are we to move beyond the junk
food of empire? How are we to tell the difference?

Learning How to Taste

For many of us, the true appreciation of good cheese or beer or
wine or even vegetables is an acquired taste. We must be educated
to like good food, and with time and experience, we feel appalled
that we could ever have even swallowed the stuff that we once
found most pleasurable.

Fortunately, taste can be educated, and with that education our
minds and palates are broadened, our capacity for pleasure deep-
ened. I have had the opportunity a few times now to attend the
Salone del Gusto, a world food fair in Italy put on by the organization Slow Food. The event features aisle after aisle of artisan
food producers—sausage makers and cheese makers, vintners and
brewers, bakers and chefs. Walking those aisles and sampling that
food, it is easy to become amazed at the great variety and genius
of the world's food traditions. But I can also imagine taking some
of my high school students, brought up on fast food, to the event
and being met with more than a few disgusted gestures. It would
require an education in taste—a slow changing of the taste buds,
even the neural circuitry, through the practice of eating well every
day, at every meal—for someone accustomed to a fast-food diet to
truly enjoy an event like the Salone del Gusto.

An education of taste is exactly what we need if we are going to
eat faithfully and avoid the junk food of empire. It is through this
catechesis—both the act of teaching and the knowledge gained—
that we can move from the world-destroying food of the industrial

food system and enter into the flourishing abundance of a creation God called good—opening our eyes to the miracles of the tiny seed that grows through a season to become a tomato, of the two perfect round leaves that burst from the ground and reach toward the sun to become a bean plant. Through this catechesis, we enter into a whole community of beings that each play their part in the amazing dance of life that takes place in the soil beneath our feet—networks of fungi as complex as small cities, incredible bacteria that emit electrochemical pulses drawing plant roots deeper into the soil, nematodes and protozoa that hunt beneath the soil and leave behind rich digested nutrients for plants to use.

This is a community of life that thrives beneath the soil, stretches along the branches of trees, reflects in chloroform the energy of stars and culminates at our tables when we eat together what was grown together. When we come to realize even a hint of this reality, the junk food of empire appears less and less as inexpensive, low-quality convenience and more and more as a desecration.

Our churches have always been places of catechesis—of training Christians for living in the sacred sphere of God's kingdom rather than in the desecrated places of empires. As the poet Wendell Berry reminds us, "There are no unsacred places; there are only sacred places and desecrated places."[3] Perhaps, along with prayer and scripture reading, we need to learn together the art of eating meals—meals that might prepare us for the banquet that God promises to set before us.

In our lessons on the meaning and symbols of the communion rite, we should also teach the many communions that lead to the bread and the cup: the communion of soil and seed, of farmer and crop, of vintner and vine. Yet this learning would be dangerous, as it would ask us to not only explore esoteric questions about the mystery of Christ's presence in the elements but also practical questions of how the wine that we call Christ's blood came to be. Was it made with the help of chemicals that poison the land and animals and people? Were those who picked the grapes paid a wage that would honor what Christ taught us about the care of our neighbors?

Surely danger lurks in any true catechesis, but perhaps a catechesis of taste is indeed the only way for us to ensure that the Eucharistic table—which Christ established and to which he invited us—is a place of thanksgiving rather than of violence. This may seem like strong language, but I believe that what is at stake in this catechesis of taste is ultimately what is at stake in our souls: it is the question of whether or not we are going to live, fully and completely, in reality.

Everything from the climate crisis to the industrial food system has been the result of living in an illusion, a determined denial of what is real. We have ignored the facts of our limits, choosing to grow our food in ways that outstrip the capacity of the land, borrowing time by replacing depleted natural nutrients with fertilizers that are, all too often, dependent on nonrenewable resources. We have convinced ourselves that we could release pollutants, chiefly carbon dioxide, into the atmosphere without limit and without consequence. We have lived in these illusions and many more because we have chosen to live in a state of pride—what theologian Dietrich von Hildebrand has characterized as "value-blindness."[4]

The answer to pride, in classical Christian thinking, is humility: living fully in touch with the earth (humus) and in the full reality of our humanity. We must rediscover reality by being brought, day in and day out, to the fact of our limits. To do this we must seek to live in a world that is unmasked and direct, a world where we do not hide from reality.

I see this almost daily on my commute to work. Most days I ride my bike, and the route includes a steep hill. As I come to the hill I shift into my easiest gears, and even then the cadence of my pedaling slows as I use all my strength to make the climb. On my bike I am fully aware of the energy output needed to overcome the hill—my understanding of that reality is concrete. When I take the same route in my family's car, with its powerful engine and automatic transmission, I don't *feel* anything: we just go over the hill without any evidence of the difference in grade. Though more energy is used and more gasoline burned, the reality of the hill is masked from me.

We can surely think of endless examples of ways in which reality is masked from us through technologies or by values skewed by limited frameworks such as money. This is not to say that these things are wholly bad, but they certainly are not neutral. We must answer these masks of reality with practices and activities that help us to see the world more closely as it is. Just as practices like fasting help us form our desires and our ability to discipline them, we must find ways to live in reality through practices that serve as anchors. St. Bernard of Clairvaux taught us that "the way is humility, the goal is truth."[5] Perhaps, then, getting close to the humus should be our first step in entering the real.

Humiliations

Digging into the humus is exactly what Cedar Ridge Community Church, just outside of Washington, DC, did when the congregation began to wonder about the reality to which God had called them. A church deeply involved in serving the community, Cedar Ridge realized that part of feeding the poor was growing food for them. A large field on the church campus offered the perfect opportunity to provide good, fresh fruits and vegetables rather than the processed, canned and packaged fare available in most food pantries and served in most shelters.

A group of church members took up farming — reading, watching and asking neighbors for help as they began the hard work of learning how to grow things. Within their first year they grew more than 1,200 pounds of food; the next year they grew more than a ton.

Instead of simply distributing the food far and wide, the church focused on three particular shelters — one that feeds meals to the homeless several times a day, one a shelter for young single mothers, and the third a home for neglected foster boys. The joy of providing and eating fresh, abundant food has been contagious, and some of the ministries that have received food from Cedar Ridge have begun to cultivate their own gardens.

Melanie Griffin, a church member and former Sierra Club staffer, says, "Celebrations have been key to the life of the farm." The church celebrates the beginning of the growing season and the harvest, and many groups gather throughout the year for work parties that mix weeding with potluck suppers.

The farm has served as a place to rekindle the agrarian virtues of neighborliness as well. When there is a surplus of a certain crop such as zucchini, church members take the excess home and bake zucchini bread to give away to neighbors—some of whom have even decided to join the church. What Cedar Ridge Community Church has done with its small farm is an example of what other churches can and should do. The church grew more than a ton of food on a little more than half an acre, an amount of land that many churches have at hand.

What if churches followed the movement that has started in many suburban neighborhoods, and which one book has made into a slogan: "Food not lawns"? That doesn't mean churches should simply tear up grass and turn it into rows of corn. Instead, the church's landscaping could be transformed into a place filled with perennial vegetables and beautiful flowers through permaculture gardening. The book *Gaia's Garden: A Guide to Home-Scale Permaculture* provides a road map that can set churches on their way by teaching a form of gardening that attempts to pattern the garden after nature, emphasizing layers of vegetation such as forests have, rather than just a bare patch of dirt with annual vegetables planted in it.[6] Imagine a beautiful garden, filled with food-bearing plants that would require less watering, no mowing, and simple maintenance that could involve all ages—and would serve as a place for both harvest and prayer.

The work of gardening can also be more than simply a way of growing food for ourselves and our neighbors. A garden can be a staging ground for a new kind of economy—for job skills and economic development. This is what Common Ground Community Church is doing with its Goodness Grows mission in North Lima, Ohio. North Lima is a declining suburban town in the midst of the Rust Belt, only 12 minutes from Youngstown, one of the most economically depressed cities in the Rust Belt—an industrial wasteland abandoned by the economic powers that built it. Derelict housing, crime, unemployment—Youngstown has it all.

When Common Ground Pastor Steve Fortenberry was looking for a location for his fledgling church, he found an abandoned nursery with greenhouses that would serve not only as a place for the church to build, but also as a staging ground for an agricultural ministry. The nursery became a base for Goodness Grows, a ministry working to build community gardens, teach job skills to youth and operate agricultural businesses such as a subscription-based vegetable program. Goodness Grows helps a variety of organizations around Youngstown imagine how agriculture could help them bring the kingdom of God to their place of service. The staff at Goodness Grows provides support, planning and critical gardening supplies such as cardboard and mulch for weed control to organizations ranging from GED programs to community development corporations.

New in the works for Goodness Grows is a program to supply companies with fresh vegetables directly at the workplace. This will include collaborating with companies that have wellness programs to establish Community Supported Agriculture (CSA) partnerships and community gardens on company campuses. Through this work Goodness Grows hopes to bring about a redemptive witness for how the employee-employer relationship can be changed for the better.

Seedleaf, an organization working in Lexington, Kentucky, is doing similar work. Seedleaf was founded out of the Communality church community, a group of Christians who have joined together to live intentionally among the poor in Lexington. Ryan Koch, a member of the community, had an interest and vision for community gardens throughout Lexington that would serve as both a place to grow food for the poor and a place for communities to organize and come together. But many community gardens lacked the resources to operate consistently, and new groups wanting community gardens lacked the knowledge to start them. Seedleaf is now meeting these needs by offering expertise and management for community gardens so that more gardens can thrive throughout Lexington. The Communality church made a significant difference in its own community by helping one of its members express his vocation as a gardener. Creating work, organizations and businesses that care for the soil is among the most important work churches can undertake.

Learning to Eat Together

We do not have to get our hands into the earth to participate in the humus — we do that consciously or unconsciously, justly or unjustly, every time we eat. But to truly honor the humus, to honor the work of farmers and the abundant creation of which we are all a part, we must change our role from passive consumers of food to coproducers.

This means that we must learn to cook, mold, knead and chop. We must come to understand the differences in oven temperatures and the black arts of substitution and improvisation when our ingredients do not meet the instructions laid out for us in a recipe. We must become cooks and dishwashers — we must own, once again, the processes of our life as productive members of those processes.

I can think of no better example of a church that has taken on this role of coproducers than Englewood Christian Church in Indianapolis, Indiana. Englewood is an unusual church — a traditional Christian congregation mixed with what they like to call an "un"-intentional community.

Over its 100-year history the church had slowly become a commuter church as members moved away and the neighborhood around the church began to change. But God had different ideas for the church. Over time several member families felt called to rehabilitate abandoned houses in the neighborhood and move there.

Now several church families live right around the church, sharing in its ministries, which include a day care for low-income families, a Community Development Corporation and an online and print book review, *The Englewood Review of Books*.

Englewood is also a church that shows great hospitality. During each of the last several years they have hosted one or two conferences on topics ranging from immigration to the new monasticism. Two conferences focused on sustainable agriculture, and both did something remarkable—they served the kind of food the conference was advocating. I have been to many gatherings high on the virtues of good food, but few of them have been able to pull off the logistics of serving locally grown food that was raised while caring for the Earth.

The task of serving local food wasn't an easy one for Englewood, but they did it by planning ahead, growing vegetables in the church's community garden, and canning and freezing produce for the fall conference. Several church members also keep chickens in their backyards, some for meat and some for eggs, and these too served as part of the food for the conference. The food was wonderful, and we didn't have to feel guilty when lunchtime came after valuable discussions on such topics as changing the farm system or living faithfully in a time of climate change. Most significantly, the food was grown, preserved and prepared at the church or in partnerships with farmers the church members knew. Going beyond the good intentions of serving organic food grown sustainably but brought in by an outside caterer, this was food produced in and by and for the community.

Parishioners at Englewood Christian Church in Indianapolis, Indiana, make applesauce together in the church kitchen. Photo courtesy of Ragan Sutterfield.

What Englewood presented at this conference was only an example of what was already being built in the everyday life of their community. Members of the congregation had already been learning the skills of gardening, canning, raising chickens and butchering them. Englewood was able to offer such delicious food, in a way other conferences often cannot, because the church was already moving beyond the merely consumptive model to one of coproduction.

What Englewood also models is the need for a community to form around the skill-based education required to enable us to escape from eating the junk food of empire. As various members of the church took on new skills such as canning, they shared them.

The sharing of skills is an essential practice that all churches must take up if we are to become coproducers, and churches are perfectly situated for just this task. We have the resources of people, of knowledge and, more often than not, of a common space. What if we invited older members of our churches to teach the younger members the lost arts of canning? What if a family that has taken

Harvesting wheat in the urban garden near Englewood Christian Church provides an intergenerational experience for members of the church. Photo courtesy of Ragan Sutterfield.

up raising chickens in its backyard can guide other church members into the care of laying hens? The possibilities are many and varied—and necessary.

The church kitchen is a great resource in this work. Some members of my own church use it on Sunday afternoons during the late months of summer to can large batches of tomatoes. When they do this with other families in the church, it becomes joyful work—mixed with steaming pots, tomato skins, stories, music and laughter.

Christ Church Little Rock, an Episcopal church that sits conveniently downtown, has even opened its kitchen to serve as a bi-weekly pickup point for an online farmers market organized by the Arkansas Sustainability Network. Market members order food online during the week; farmers deliver it; and volunteers help distribute the produce. Around this market, a community has formed as market members linger to drink a cup of coffee or buy a pastry provided by The Root, a local-foods café.

Christ Church has also opened its kitchen, which is health-department-certified for commercial use, to small sustainable food businesses that do not yet have the money for certified kitchen space of their own, thus serving as a kind of incubator for sustainable business. This is a model that would be easy for other churches to replicate, encouraging the production and processing of good, nutritious food.

Buying food from the market at Christ Church or working with friends in a steamy kitchen to process a bumper crop of summer tomatoes, I am reminded of another important role the church can play in recalling us to the healthful and delicious food of God. The church has long been a place where food is best enjoyed in community. Whether a regularly scheduled church meal, a potluck on a feast day or a Pentecost cook-off, the church is a perfect place for us to learn to eat together.

In the world of fast and convenient food, prepackaged and nutrition-extracted, eating and shopping and preparing food have become lonely acts. We go to the grocery store, buy a can of tomatoes packed thousands of miles away and check out with an automatic system that requires only the knowledge to find a bar code. We can go through the whole process without any human encounter. This has come to appear normal to us, but to the Babylonians of Isaiah's day, a market that held no more human interaction than an "excuse me" in a crowded aisle would have seemed strange. The market was once the center of public life, and still is in many parts of the world. It was the market, the *agora* of Athens, that gave us the foundation for democracy and the discourses of Socrates. We have lost all of that. With the privatization and consumption-oriented marketing of food, we have also lost a good deal of our public life — a life that will be more necessary than ever if we are to think and work together to face the realities of the climate catastrophe.

The Supper of the Lamb

We must prepare for a great feast by learning the good from the bad, recognizing the difference between the delicious food of God and the junk food of empire. That feast is the Supper of the Lamb — the final banquet in which God welcomes his own to the fullness of his kingdom. It is a common image in many Jewish apocalyptic texts, Isaiah included, and it might serve for us as a final picture of what this concern for learning to eat well is all about.

When I think of such a banquet I think of old movies about kings and queens, princes and princesses. Often in such movies there is a culminating scene, a Cinderella-type ball or banquet in which everyone comes to feast together. But before the great event there is a long preparation people go through to reach the ball — to be able to dance, and look and eat in a way appropriate to the celebration.

This is how we might think of ourselves as we prepare for the Supper of the Lamb — the banquet feast of God (a feast that is already beginning). As we learn to eat together in community, to become coproducers of food, as we gain the humility of working with the soil, we are changing ourselves so that we will be ready to enjoy that final meal that will be set before us.

We may ask ourselves, if God were to have this final banquet as a potluck, what would we bring? Would we buy the sorts of food offered in the grocery store, or would we be more careful to buy the kind of food we know was grown with care for God's Earth? Would we bring meat, and if so, what kind? How would the animals that were killed for that meat have been raised and slaughtered?

Imagining our meals as fitting in with this divine potluck is a helpful tool, for me at least. The key is to pay attention while we eat: to think about what we know of our food, to guess at what we don't know, to imagine its life before the plate—a suffering pig in a small pen or a happy one roaming a pasture until the day it died. It is easy to scarf down a burger without thinking much about it, but when we begin to pay attention, to think about what we are eating and how it was raised, we should begin to wonder if our meal is a fitting one for people on their way to the Supper of the Lamb.

Through this attention we begin to honor our food in a way that we can give a proper thanksgiving to the God who provided it, but this process begins far before the eating. I have chef friends who believe that cooking badly dishonors every creature and plant and plot of soil that came in the chain of preparing it. Conversely, there is no better way to honor someone, or the entire chain of work and being that went into the ingredients of a meal, than to cook it well.

A good meal is a sacred thing, and when shared in abundance and joy it can overcome a multitude of sins. The film *Babette's Feast* is perhaps the best picture of the reconciling power of food cooked well. The movie follows Babette, a French woman taking refuge in a small, puritan village in Denmark. She is taken in by two sisters who put her to work making a tasteless fish soup, which the sisters take to the sick and hungry in the community. It is a tightly knit fishing village, where over time many grudges have festered, many small disagreements have grown large. Then one day,

Babette learns that she has won the lottery. Now rich, she tells the people of the village, whom she has come to love, that before she leaves she will cook a feast. Babette, it turns out, is an accomplished chef, and the meal that she prepares is on a scale that they have never seen. The villagers arrive with their grudges, disagreements and ill will, but during the course of the evening, as they eat one delicious dish after another and drink such wine as they have never tasted, their petty disagreements begin to disappear. The village is united again in reconciled love.

Babette's Feast is a beautiful picture of the reconciling power of a meal. Food is our most daily and intimate connection to the creation of which we are a part, and good food can change us for the better. As we face the challenges of a climate thrown into catastrophic change, we must remember this power of a good meal. If we eat it and grow it and prepare it with care and attention, if we become coproducers with the creation, if we open our table to all who want to join us in savoring its goodness, then perhaps it is a meal that will save us. Our task now is to be ready for it.

○ ○ ○

RAGAN SUTTERFIELD is a writer, gardener and teacher living in his native Arkansas. He has written about popular culture, sustainable agriculture and the theology of creation for publications that include *Spin*, *Books & Culture*, *Men's Journal*, *Fast Company*, *Gourmet* and *Plenty*.

CHAPTER 2

Beyond Belief

Effective Religious Leadership on Energy and Climate Change

THE REVEREND FLETCHER HARPER

*Every morning, millions of Hindus say a prayer
to Mother Earth when they get out of bed,
apologizing for any pain they may cause her
by walking on her during the day.*

Writer and scholar Pankaj Jain

WHEN HE ARRIVED in the United States from India, the first thing Pankaj Jain noticed was the cars. "I'd never seen so many of them in India," he said. "The cost of running them all, the air pollution—I couldn't imagine how it was possible." Over time, he was inspired to change his career from software engineering to studying the link between Hinduism, Jainism and the Earth. Now he's an author, a professor at the University of North Texas and a rising Hindu environmental scholar.

In my own work during the past decade with the organization GreenFaith, I have met Christian, Muslim, Jewish and Hindu leaders like Pankaj who are highlighting these connections between their faith traditions, energy use and climate change. Based in New Jersey, GreenFaith is an interfaith environmental coalition that works with faith communities nationwide to help them integrate the environment into their ministries. Among our many

GreenFaith works with congregations from all faith traditions to promote renewable energy. Photo by Rev. Fletcher Harper.

programs, we have conducted dozens of energy-conservation workshops for religious audiences and carried out more than 100 energy audits at religious facilities. I have watched hundreds of congregations address issues related to climate change, from installing solar panels on churches to improving energy efficiency at synagogues. This level of activity is a welcome and marked change from past decades, when energy conservation and environmental advocacy were low priorities in religious circles.

But in the midst of this increased activity, I have witnessed many missed opportunities — opportunities for savings, for involving a wider range of congregants in energy issues, and for making energy leadership within the church more than a rhetorical exercise. This chapter offers reflection on religious leadership around climate change and shares stories of four religious leaders who represent the potential of holistic Christian action on energy and climate change.

Let the Preaching Begin

The past decade has brought increased religious discourse on the moral and spiritual dimensions of energy use. Christian groups including liberal Protestant, Roman Catholic, Eastern Orthodox, and Southern Baptist leaders have denounced our current patterns of energy use as sinful and called for repentance in the form of individual and national commitments to energy conservation and renewable energy. Energy and climate change have made it onto the educational and advocacy agendas of more houses of worship than ever before.

From the election of President Barack Obama through 2009, momentum grew in support of federal legislation that would commit the United States to reducing its greenhouse gas emissions. In 2009, the US House of Representatives passed the American Clean Energy and Security Act (ACES), with support from many religious groups. Legislative victory seemed to be a real possibility.

In December 2009, however, the United Nations Climate Change Conference at Copenhagen failed to reach any binding commitments. And in 2010 the political climate in the United States shifted. It soon became clear that the US Senate would not take up climate legislation, eliminating the possibility of any legislative action on climate change before 2013.

This legislative defeat has important implications for church-based efforts on climate change. Through much of 2010, most religious action on energy issues lay in the area of education and advocacy on climate change. But the legislative defeats, coupled with efforts to defeat or roll back climate legislation at the state level, have made it clear that the battle for comprehensive climate legislation requires cultural support that is both broader and deeper than currently exists. I believe that churches, along with other faith-based institutions, have an opportunity to help create this cultural change by implementing efforts on a wide scale to cut energy use, reduce greenhouse gas emissions, save money and engage new members in their congregations.

A modest number of religious institutions have done exactly this and have offered an important public witness. They have invested in energy conservation and efficiency and have seen substantial financial benefits. These houses of worship have created cultures among their members in which smart energy use becomes a point of pride and a congregational norm. The challenge now lies in replicating the success of these pioneers and making responsible energy management and advocacy a priority across denominations. The logic behind this is simple and the self-interest of congregations powerful.

Hidden in Plain Sight

The potential for energy savings at church is substantial. This is especially critical when church budgets are under pressure from the economic recession or from static or declining membership and pledges. The US Environmental Protection Agency (EPA) reports that if the estimated 370,000 houses of worship in the United States cut their energy use by ten percent, the savings would amount to more than $300 million.[1] The money saved could support outreach to those who are hungry, homeless or out of work; it could fund education, evangelism and mission-related work; it could be reinvested in retrofitting buildings in ways that would lower the energy use of religious institutions even more.

These savings represent found money — the biggest single source of available revenue to American religious institutions. Investments in energy conservation and efficiency offer congregations the chance to reduce operating expenses without cutting programs, while also offering an important witness for the Earth — a priority for many young, unchurched families. For churches, there is no better opportunity than energy conservation to promote organizational growth, public witness and financial gain at the same time.

In the face of this potential windfall, however, most churches still do nothing to manage their own energy use or concern themselves with energy issues — except pay their monthly bill. A disconnect exists between the theological statements of most denominations, the opportunities for energy conservation and financial savings, and the behavior of most congregations. How can we understand this disconnect? And what are the characteristics of churches that have connected climate change, energy and theology?

Growing numbers of Americans believe that taking care of the Earth is a religious responsibility. The 2006 National American Environmental Values Survey found that 81 percent of all respondents—not just people of faith—affirmed that "taking good care of nature is part of our duty to God," while 87 percent believed that "the beauty of nature is a gift from God."[2] A nation of believers, we appear to also believe that God wants us to protect creation.

While people find the idea of caring for the Earth appealing, most have yet to integrate care of creation into the pattern of their lives. This isn't all bad—verbal assent often precedes meaningful action. But if action is the goal for religious communities on energy issues, then belief is not enough. Quaker educator Parker Palmer coined the term "functional atheism" to describe religious leaders or communities who profess to believe but whose behavior shows no evidence to support that belief. This metaphor is relevant to religious action addressing energy and climate.

Getting It Done

What enables certain congregations to reduce their energy use and address climate change? Their leaders usually possess three qualities: they are invested in the congregation; they are committed to the environment; and they function effectively within their houses of worship. Having earned the respect of their church's members and clergy, these leaders get things done in their congregations.

(1) Committed stewards of the faith community

Many effective energy leaders in religious institutions are motivated by their desire to see their congregations—their spiritual homes—steward their economic resources. "When I see these boilers go on, I see money coming right out of our collection plate," said one leader. "That's what motivates me." These faith leaders are aware of the potential for savings represented by energy conservation and mindful of the value of the pledges that support their church. Often long-time members of the community, they work consistently to reduce their church's energy use because they believe it is the proper way to run their church.

(2) *Committed stewards of the environment*
Another quality of effective energy leadership in churches is a commitment to the environment. Some leaders demonstrate their commitment through frugality and restraint, the belief that being wasteful is wrong. Others voice a concern for future generations. One leader told me that he wanted his church to cut its energy use because he loved to fish, and acid rain from power plants was killing the fish in his favorite streams. The fact that their congregations' energy use is inconsequential on a larger scale is insignificant to these leaders because they are motivated by doing their part and being an example to others.

(3) *Effective congregational leaders*
The third characteristic of these leaders is that they know how to achieve concrete outcomes within their congregations. They are able to build consensus around action on energy, organize volunteer efforts and mobilize human and financial resources.

This represents the keystone of all congregational efforts focused on energy and climate change. If a congregation does not have a trusted leader—frequently a lay leader—who can organize a multi-pronged effort that impacts finances and building management, it will be difficult to address energy issues with any success. If this leader cannot listen, build consensus, manage the often divisive nature of energy and climate discussions, and persevere in the face of inertia, little will get done.

I have observed these three characteristics in successful energy efforts in churches, and I offer stories from congregations in New Jersey that describe these leaders in action. Their examples are the best resources we have to help our churches become "not just hearers of the Word, but doers" when it comes to energy and climate change.

Measured Passion in an Historic Space

A clear-spoken man with a calm and diplomatic temperament, Bruce Daggy served as the point person for a GreenFaith energy audit of Morristown Unitarian Fellowship in New Jersey. The congregation's members are rightly proud of this historic building constructed in the early 20th century. Before the audit began, Morristown Unitarian Fellowship's members had internalized the Seventh Principle of Unitarian Universalism—"respect for the interdependent web of all existence of which we are a part"[3]—and had conducted education and advocacy on these issues.

The question for Morristown Unitarian Fellowship was not whether to conserve energy, but how to do so and yet remain consistent with the care of the historic facility. The fellowship's energy audit was completed by Andrew Rudin, an experienced energy auditor and founder of the Interfaith Coalition on Energy.[4] The audit report recommended a range of changes, many of them small items that could be conducted in-house, resulting in $4,000 in annual savings.

Andy Rudin, founder of the Interfaith Energy Coalition, conducts energy audits for congregations in collaboration with GreenFaith. Photo by Rev. Fletcher Harper.

In a measured yet determined way, Bruce took concrete actions to ensure that the fellowship implemented the recommendations from the report, such as organizing work parties to insulate
and weatherstrip the facilities. He reprogrammed and regularly
checked the thermostats, as some areas of the building were being
heated to 80 degrees. Bruce worked to replace more than 50 bulbs
in a stunning chandelier in the grand entrance to the building, a
change that required numerous conversations and meetings with
congregational leaders to ensure that the replacement bulbs met
the building committee's aesthetic criteria. He pursued a range of
additional conservation activities, many of them time-consuming
and unglamorous. As a result, the fellowship reduced its energy use
by 15 percent within one year.

Bruce's story demonstrates several important characteristics
of effective energy leadership within congregations. First, he was
a committed member of his congregation, willing to volunteer
many hours to organize work parties, convene discussions and
engage various constituencies within the congregation—at a time
when he worked full time. Second, Bruce believed in the importance of environmental stewardship and worked hard to put his
environmental beliefs into action.

Third, Bruce built consensus on a number of energy-related
items that raised concerns for those committed to the fellowship's
beautiful facility. How would weatherstripping and insulation
affect the appearance of the lovely wooden sliding doors? How
would compact fluorescent lights look in the 50-bulb chandelier?
Addressing such questions may lack the high moral purpose described by many religious environmental advocates, but this attention to detail represents a hallmark of effective religious leadership
on energy. If the devil can sometimes be found in the details, the
energy savings can be too.

Old Church, New Solution

United Methodist Church of Red Bank, New Jersey, is an old facility and, as with many churches, its membership has decreased in

recent years. "While the numbers of our congregation's members have declined, our activities are increasing," said George Schildge, an active lay leader in the congregation. The congregation faces the problem of occupying a large old building designed for a thousand members but having a current membership of 400. "We've got lots of space that costs money to maintain, and this takes money away from our mission," he said. "That was our motivation."

The church had an additional environmental motivation, as the congregation had entered GreenFaith's Certification Program, so the energy-related project could become a hallmark of the congregation's greening efforts. As a part of GreenFaith's two-year green leadership program for houses of worship, participants integrate the environment into their worship, religious education, facilities management and advocacy.[5]

George wondered if United Methodist Church of Red Bank could "go solar," given its large, unshaded roof. A successful businessman and respected member of the congregation, George had led both stewardship and capital campaigns for the church. Using those same skills, he researched options for solar energy and saw an opportunity. He learned that by raising the capital for a solar array from members of the congregation, he could finance the church's solar project, generate an acceptable return and tax benefits for the project investors and create immediate energy savings and a significant long-term benefit for the church. It could be a win for the church, the investors and the environment.

George approached the church's pastor, the Reverend Myrna Bethke, and the board of trustees, which had completed a capital campaign that included several energy efficiency and conservation features. The board approved the concept with the agreement that any solar project would need to be cost-free and risk-free to the church.

Collaborating with a fellow congregant with technical expertise, George approached 20 members of the congregation to invest in the project with the understanding that the church would purchase the electricity from the owners. The owners, who would form a limited liability corporation (LLC), would also benefit from a federal tax credit, further tax benefits related to the solar equipment's depreciation and from the sale of renewable energy credits — the intangible commodities created through the generation of renewable energy.

Seven members of the congregation expressed interest. As an expression of their support for the church's mission, the member-investors paid for part of the church's roof repair project as part of their investment in the solar project. After seven years, when the value of the tax-related credits had been fully utilized, the investors would pass the system on to the church at no cost — a generous gift.

Working with a sample agreement provided by a solar installer, George fashioned the legal documents required for the project and reviewed these with church trustees. The agreement addressed issues such as the LLC's responsibility for the costs of installation, maintenance and insurance, the cost of electricity, access to the church's roof and other customary issues. After minor modifications, and with the trustees' approval, the Greater New Jersey Annual Conference of the United Methodist Church approved the project.

George and his technical partner then reviewed proposals from four solar panel installers. "We decided not to go with the lowest bid, but used it instead to negotiate a lower price with the installer with whom we wanted to work," he said. Because of this strategy, they were able to reduce the price of the array by close to 20 percent.

The solar array at the church was installed in the fall and early winter of 2010 and commissioned soon after. It now generates more than 30 percent of the church's electricity, and serves as a sign of the church's extensive environmental commitments, which have included worship, education and advocacy — all with an environmental focus. George's commitment to his church and to the environment, coupled with his project-management skills, created an impressive achievement for his church — one that will generate tens of thousands of dollars in revenue while cutting the church's carbon footprint by nearly a third.

For Cleaner Air and a Community in Need

Shiloh Baptist Church in downtown Trenton, New Jersey, has been a pillar of strength in its community and an active voice for the needs of the African American community for decades. The Rev. Darrell Armstrong grew up in Los Angeles's Watts neighborhood, a ghetto where educational and economic survival might seem to crowd out an environmental consciousness. That was not the case for Pastor Armstrong:

"I grew up in south central LA," he said. "I was Baptist, and I must have sung 'How Great Thou Art' a thousand times by the time I was twelve. Then, that summer, my Boy Scout troop organized a trip to climb Mount Whitney. It was a very difficult, challenging climb. I had never had to work so hard physically as I did to get to the top of that mountain. But when I did and when I looked around at the hundreds of smaller peaks that fanned out below where we were standing—then, for the first time, I could say 'How great thou art' and mean it."[6]

When Pastor Armstrong arrived at Shiloh in 2002, he was only in his early thirties, yet he possessed an environmental awareness that combined a sense of the presence of God in the outdoors, an awareness of the disproportionate impact of pollution on most African American communities and a belief that the environment represents an opportunity for economic empowerment. Acting on these beliefs, he commissioned an energy audit with GreenFaith within the first year of his ministry.

The audit revealed opportunities for energy savings in Shiloh's 40,000-square-foot facility. Programmable thermostats replaced the manually controlled models that had regulated the temperature inside Shiloh for decades; this produced a savings of $4,000 within the first year alone. New lights in classrooms, offices, the sanctuary and outdoor flood-lamp fixtures—installed by a retired electrician and Shiloh member—produced additional savings of $3,000 per year. No detail was too small: disconnecting the lights inside the church's drink machine yielded $200 in annual savings. The result was a church that was far more comfortable to use, with more than

$7,000 in annual savings. Soon after the audit, Shiloh hosted an energy-conservation workshop conducted by GreenFaith.

The energy audit was just a start. Pastor Armstrong was aware of the church's unshaded flat roof and saw an opportunity for a solar project. In consultation with GreenFaith and three other area churches that had implemented solar power, Shiloh secured a proposal from a solar company. Church leaders managed the project with efficiency, securing feedback on the proposal from several sources and support from the state's innovative Clean Energy Program. In the fall of 2010, Shiloh celebrated the installation of a 38-kilowatt solar array, dedicating the system at worship on a Sunday morning.

In later remarks, Pastor Armstrong demonstrated his understanding that air pollution affects not only the natural world but also the health of his community. "We are trying, with other organizations," he said, "to give a very clear and definitive message about what it means to create health in our environment, health in our bodies, health in our spirits, health in our souls."

In 2009, as the recession drove unemployment rates into the double digits in urban communities across the United States, Shiloh Baptist hosted a press conference to announce interfaith support for policies to support the growth of green jobs. Pastor Armstrong spoke about the moral imperative to create jobs that would sustain both people and the planet, while reducing the burden of pollution shouldered by too many African Americans. The event drew press coverage statewide and highlighted the holistic nature of his understanding of energy issues.

Franciscan Values in Action

An energetic Franciscan priest, Father Kevin Downey often walks around the campus of St. Mary's Catholic Community, interacting with the church's diverse ministries, which include its school, health ministry to the uninsured and outreach to the hungry in Pompton Lakes, New Jersey. His infectious, even bawdy humor masks his passionate commitment to ministry to those in need, a hallmark of the Franciscan charism. An avid outdoorsman and hunter, he demonstrates a commitment to the Earth with an engaging style, speaking with unmistakable relish about the physical rigor of his hunting trips in the northern Rockies.

In 2006, Father Kevin convened a team of leaders at St. Mary's to develop a strong environmental ministry for the parish. Team members, who were excited by the challenge, included respected leaders within the parish — leaders from St. Mary's building and grounds, education, school and social justice committees. An energy audit, again coordinated by GreenFaith through the Interfaith Coalition on Energy, identified opportunities for annual energy savings of $10,000.

St. Mary's response to the audit recommendations was well-organized and systematic. An energy team that included parishioner Ray Keating and buildings and grounds director Christine Macemon issued detailed reports about their ongoing response to the audit recommendations over a period of a year. The reports, which included year-to-year comparisons of energy use along with notes about the implementation of various recommendations, documented thousands of dollars in savings for St. Mary's.

Educational outreach supplemented the findings from the audit. The parish's social justice ministry hosted a screening of the film *An Inconvenient Truth*, educating more than 200 members of the parish and the broader community about global warming and encouraging them to take action. In collaboration with an energy efficiency project called Project Porchlight, hundreds of parishioners also received free compact fluorescent light bulbs.

St. Mary's School hosted a meeting of representatives of Catholic schools in the region and invited GreenFaith staff to present information about ways in which schools could become involved in environmental leadership efforts. Regular updates in the weekly parish bulletin kept parishioners informed on St. Mary's efforts — a vital success factor in a parish where more than 1,500 people worshipped every weekend. In all communications, St. Mary's emphasized the Franciscan values that motivated their efforts.

With initial momentum established, St. Mary's environmental efforts continued to grow. Parish members took part in Green-Faith's Environmental Justice Tours, learning about the environmental health threats faced by communities of color and low-income communities. They conducted advocacy on issues ranging from climate change to land conservation. Father Kevin and members of St. Mary's youth group participated in the filming of a CBS special on GreenFaith, broadcast to more than one million viewers. And in 2009, St. Mary's celebrated the installation of solar panels on its new Carnevale Center, a project financed through state rebates and parishioner contributions.

Keys to Success

What can we learn from these four success stories that can benefit other congregations addressing energy and climate change?

1. Communication about energy is important but quickly loses value if not accompanied by action.

To date, much religious leadership in the environment has taken place at the rhetorical level—through preaching and teaching. While valuable as an introductory stage of engagement, public speech alone is insufficient. My friend Eitan Grunwald once wrote an article about the importance of effective management within nonprofit institutions. The article was titled, "You're Right. So What?" This question is relevant to religious efforts on energy that require more than "right" words. It is notable that all four congregations profiled in this chapter moved quickly from rhetoric to action, and spent little time engaged in political wrangling or moral handwringing. They were uncomfortable stating a belief and failing to follow up in measurable and substantive ways.

2. Strong leaders make success possible.

All four stories involved strong leaders who mobilized resources from the churches' membership and the wider community. Bruce Daggy built consensus and mobilized significant volunteer resources at the Morristown Unitarian Fellowship, creating connections between energy auditor, Andrew Rudin, and the congregation's members. George Schildge took on the complex challenge of private financing for a church-based solar array. He identified leaders within his church with the skills and resources to offer support for this concrete action. Pastor Darrell Armstrong used the pulpit to educate his congregation about the importance of clean energy to the African American community and to God. He then mobilized leaders within Shiloh Baptist to carry out energy-conservation efforts and identified leaders within Shiloh and beyond to enable the church to go solar. Father Kevin Downey convened well-respected leaders within St. Mary's Catholic community to create a detailed and comprehensive approach to energy and environmental issues. The team members produced measurable results and reported publicly to the parish community.

In two of the four successes, ordained leaders played the central role; in the other two examples, lay leaders were the point persons. This sharing of leadership between clergy and laity holds true across all areas of religious environmental leadership. It is important for the ordained leader to voice public support, but clergy need not be the leaders for the overall energy effort—unless they feel called to play a leadership role and are equipped to do so.

3. Engaging energy issues represents an opportunity to strengthen the church—from financial, moral and leadership perspectives. Successful faith leaders recognize this potential and take advantage of it.
Addressing energy concerns represents a multifaceted challenge that includes issues of communication, facility management, financing, advocacy and education. Taking on such a challenge requires a church to commit a significant amount of its most valuable resource—the time and attention of its members. For a church to decide to invest these resources, it is important that these efforts result in dividends not only for the environment but also for the church.

To this end, effective congregations that engage energy issues frame their successes as responsible stewardship of congregational funds. They view their efforts as creating a positive public identity for their church that can attract new members and serve as a public witness in response to climate change. These churches involve new members of their congregations and help them step into leadership roles. By addressing this seemingly intractable issue on a modest scale, they offer hope that we can address climate change on a larger scale with sound policies and collaborative efforts. Successful energy efforts in congregations reflect a healthy interest in the well-being of the church itself as well as an interest in the well-being of creation.

4. A well-organized, comprehensive approach to energy issues may facilitate broader participation in climate-change advocacy.
My own observations with GreenFaith suggest that by reducing energy use, involving church members in these efforts and communicating the financial and environmental benefits, faith communities can increase the percentage of their members who are willing to engage in climate advocacy. When congregations involve people not normally inclined toward advocacy in energy efforts that benefit their congregation, they frame energy efficiency as part of people's religious identity, not as a political or ideological statement.

Climate change is an issue that generates political gridlock and ideological conflict. If a more holistic engagement of energy issues increases support for policies to fight global warming, the comprehensive approach described in this chapter may offer an important guide for future efforts to build support for national climate legislation.

The four leaders described in this chapter, and the hundreds of others who have carried out similar initiatives in their own congregations, represent a vitally important resource on climate change for churches and the Earth. Replicating these patterns of energy leadership in congregations can promote strong connections between energy use and the church, interrelationships studied by faith leaders such as Pankaj Jain from India. The time has come for religious leaders to partner with faith-based nonprofits, public utility commissions and renewable energy companies to transform these hope-filled models into the norm for energy use across hundreds of thousands of religious institutions across the country and the world.

* * *

THE REVEREND FLETCHER HARPER is the executive director of GreenFaith, a national interfaith environmental coalition. He served as a parish priest for ten years before becoming GreenFaith's leader. During his tenure at GreenFaith, he launched the Green-Faith Fellowship Program, an interfaith environmental leadership program.

CHAPTER 3

Life is Changed, not Ended
Natural Burial, Conservation and Climate

MALLORY McDUFF

Through Jesus Christ our Lord; who rose victorious from the dead, and comforts us with the blessed hope of everlasting life. For to your faithful people, O Lord, life is changed, not ended; and when our mortal body lies in death, there is prepared for us a dwelling place eternal in the heavens.

Commemoration of the Dead, *The Book of Common Prayer*[1]

Families are digging the grave, preparing the body and shroud, transporting and lowering the body, and filling the grave. People want to do more than simply stand by, weep, and write a check when they are grieving.

Robert "Hutch" Hutchinson,
Prairie Creek Conservation Cemetery

ONE MONTH AFTER my mother's sudden death in a bike accident, my father requested that his grown children return to our hometown for a family meeting. At the gathering, he presented a one-page plan for his burial: no embalming or concrete vault, a linen tablecloth as a shroud, a pine casket, a pickup truck to transport the casket, his bluegrass band at the gravesite and shovels for his family and friends to fill the grave.

My siblings and I exchanged quick glances. We weren't prepared to discuss the funeral for our healthy, 62-year-old father, but we affirmed his plan, recognizing that his life companion had just died. My father wanted to build his own casket and even had a prototype—the size of a jewelry box—that he had carved years before. As the ultimate pragmatist, he had asked a friend, Jeff Lowther, to build the casket in the event of his sudden death.

We exhaled collective relief as the conversation ended. My father then placed the paper in a filing cabinet in an upstairs bedroom.

Two years later, he was killed in a hit-and-run bike accident, a mirror image of my mother's death. We sat in that same living room, assuming that we couldn't keep our promises because his body was at the coroner's office, rather than in his bed, where he had hoped he would die at a much older age.

"Let's start by doing one thing on the list to honor his plan," I said. We called his friend Jeff, who built the pine casket in 24 hours, using sailing lines he found in our basement for rope handles. After that one action, the "plan" gained momentum: it became easier to follow his wishes and check off items on the list, from the transport of the body to the music at the gravesite.

By the next day, my father's body was at Wolfe-Bayview Funeral Home in a cooled room for the two days until the funeral. He was not embalmed. For my mother's burial, my father had negotiated with the local cemetery so she could be buried without a concrete vault if he maintained the site. He, too, would be buried without a vault.

The day before the service, my sister and I took two of my mother's linen tablecloths to the funeral home. We sang to him, covered his body and lifted him into the pine casket. After the funeral home staff transported his body to the church, they left the premises, following my father's explicit directives against dark hearses outside the church or green carpeting at the gravesite.

At the church, we walked into the sanctuary as almost 700 people sang the processional hymn "All Things Bright and Beautiful."

After the worship, Jeff's pickup truck transported the pine casket to the cemetery, where we sang gospel songs like "I'll Fly Away" and "Let the Circle be Unbroken." Then children and elders alike took shovels and filled the grave.

The last person shoveling dirt was Phil Strinste, the tall and humble gardener who ran the organic farm that was my father's destination when he was killed. Phil had brought my father's weathered gardening boots to place beside the grave. He continued shoveling with his face bent toward the soil, doing the hard work of grief, returning my father's body to the earth, where life is changed, not ended.

At the time, I didn't realize that my father's burial in Fairhope, Alabama, had anything to do with global issues like climate change. I thought the scale of his burial involved our family, a circle of friends and one congregation. Yet actions of mitigating climate change and adapting to its impacts occur at local and regional scales, as well as national and international levels. Households and congregations take actions every day that either increase or decrease greenhouse gas emissions. Local communities and religious institutions make land-use decisions that fragment habitats or conserve land. Our worship and rituals have the power to influence our relationship with the land around us.

Religious leaders and faith communities often provide the first point of contact when someone dies, and our religious traditions reflect how we care for the dead and the Earth. In this country, our current model of caring for and burying the dead wastes enormous resources and separates the living from the natural cycle of life and death.

In a new movement of natural burial, however, people of faith are returning to more sustainable burial practices. These natural burials consume fewer natural and financial resources and promote involvement of family and friends.[2] Natural (or green) burial addresses climate change in three distinct ways: (1) reducing the environmental impacts of greenhouse gas emissions and other toxins, (2) protecting land as a conservation strategy and (3) creating a

spiritual connection to the Earth. The stories of two natural cemeteries in Conyers, Georgia, and Gainesville, Florida, illustrate the
power of worship on stewardship and climate change.

Reducing the Environmental Impacts of Greenhouse Gas Emissions and Other Toxins

Scientists have documented the rapid pace of global warming
and the role of humans in climate change. We know that climate
change is caused by the release of greenhouse gases into the atmosphere, with carbon dioxide as the most common gas.[3] It is
daunting, however, to realize on a practical level that many of our
everyday tasks—driving our cars, heating and cooling our homes
and transporting our food—involve the burning of fossil fuels that
release carbon dioxide and other gases, such as methane, that trap
heat in the atmosphere.

The United States produces more carbon dioxide per capita
than any other country in the world.[4] For most of human history,
the amount of carbon dioxide (CO_2) in the atmosphere was 270
parts per million (ppm), a number that represents the ratio of
CO_2 molecules to other molecules in the atmosphere. With rapid
industrialization, that number has risen to 390 ppm. Scientists
such as Dr. James Hansen of NASA have reported that 350 ppm
is the safe upper limit in the atmosphere for human and environmental health.[5] According to climate activist Bill McKibben,
getting the level back down to 350 ppm will involve transformative change and a "thousand different solutions," rethinking everything from the products we consume to the energy policies we
legislate.[6]

The true cost of American death

Conventional burials in the United States generate inordinate environmental costs, especially from the release of greenhouse gases
produced by the manufacturing and transport of expensive caskets,
chemicals for embalming and concrete vaults. These products are
not legally required but have become standard practices for the

funeral industry that buries the dead and the religious institutions that plan the funerals.

Each year in the United States, conventional burials require the production and transport of 104,000 tons of steel, 2,700 tons of copper and bronze, 1.6 million tons of concrete, and 1.6 million gallons of formaldehyde.[7] In addition, caskets are often made of endangered or imported hardwoods. While 32 percent of the US population chooses cremation, often for environmental reasons and cost, this practice requires fossil fuels to produce high temperatures of 1,400 degrees F for two hours, and it releases greenhouse gases and pollutants such as mercury and dioxin.[8] As Mark Harris states in his book *Grave Matters*, "For all their landscaping aboveground, our cemeteries function less as verdant resting grounds of the dead than as landfills for the materials that infuse and encase them."[9]

Embalming is an invasive process of preserving a corpse: it involves draining the blood and replacing it with a formaldehyde-based preservative, puncturing the body's organs and vacuuming up fluids and then flooding the area with a preservative.[10] Embalming was not common until the Civil War, when families wanted to transport the bodies for burial.[11] Refrigeration at a funeral home and dry ice at home are two other viable options for caring for the dead for several days until burial.[12]

As defined by the Green Burial Council, natural burial grounds require the adoption of practices that conserve energy, minimize waste and do not use toxic chemicals. Natural burial grounds prohibit the use of concrete vaults, embalming and burial containers or shrouds that are not made from natural materials such as pine or cotton.[13] Conservation burial grounds go one step further and protect land in perpetuity for conservation through voluntary agreements such as conservation easements that limit development on their land. Some conventional cemeteries, especially historic or old town cemeteries, also offer the option of burial without a vault or embalming and accept burial containers like cardboard caskets and shrouds.

Reducing these environmental costs also decreases the financial burden of burials for families. Sixty-seven percent of families in the United States earn less than $45,000 a year, yet the average cost of a conventional funeral in this country is $10,000.[14] A natural burial costs as little as half that amount and often much less. Eliminating the consumption of unnecessary resources makes both economic and environmental sense and reclaims the simplicity of burials practiced by humans for thousands of years.

A conservation cemetery at a monastery: Honey Creek Woodlands

Modern images of Trappist monks are found in the writings of the contemplative Thomas Merton, Trappist ales and the film *Of Gods and Men*. Only 300 Trappist monks remain in the world, and 40 of them live at the Monastery of the Holy Spirit in Conyers, Georgia, the site of Honey Creek Woodlands.

Leaving the skyline of downtown Atlanta, I took US 20 heading east and passed the sprawl of Publix grocery stores, Walgreens, churches and subdivisions. About 30 miles from the city, tall magnolia trees lined both sides of the road to the monastery. In mid-March, the redbud and pear trees were in bloom, their fuchsia, pink and white blossoms announcing the end of winter.

The welcome center for the monastery is a white-gray brick building with a green metal roof and a cross on top. Behind the welcome center stands the retreat house and chapel, an impressive structure that reminded me of cathedrals in Europe. In 1944, the monks built the monastery by hauling concrete in wheelbarrows: one wheelbarrowful added only a quarter inch of height to each tall white pillar inside the church.

About 100 yards past the monastery, down Susong Road, a small wooden sign marks the entrance to the burial grounds, Georgia's only conservation cemetery. A one-room building houses the office of Joe Whittaker, burial manager. On a bulletin board inside the office, a poster describes green burial with three words: simple, natural, affordable.

When I arrived at the office, I noticed a pine urn for ashes on a table, surrounded with yellow and black clip-art logos of the Pittsburgh Steelers. "I'm doing a little arts-and-crafts project," said Joe, sporting a black-and-gray goatee, an easy smile and an engaging manner. He was preparing for the funeral of a sportswriter and Steelers fan whose family wanted to celebrate his love of the team. A Catholic priest presided at the funeral that afternoon, but the family was able to personalize and participate in the service.

Honey Creek Woodlands includes 78 acres as a parcel of the 2,200 acres of the monastery grounds. Of the total acreage at the monastery, 1,000 acres are protected from development in conservation easements. The cemetery is located on a former clear-cut, about one-and-a-half miles from the office. That afternoon, Joe drove me, in an electric golf cart, down a gravel road to the site, where we passed two men planting trees for a stream-bank mitigation project that involved planting 40,000 hardwood trees.

The cemetery includes three locations: a woodland, a meadow and a hilltop area. Flat circular stones the size of a handprint identify the gravesites with inscribed names—Victor Sanchez, Barbara Fox—and the dates of birth and death. Walking between the gravesites felt to me like walking through the woods, rather than through a manicured cemetery. Stakes in the ground mark spots reserved for future burials—white ones for cremation and yellow ones for natural burial. Each stake has an aluminum tag with a number corresponding to the person who will be buried at the site.

"Natural burial is a perfect zero-waste system," Joe said. "Once something dies, it is only dead momentarily. It becomes a part of other life after burial. Your body lives on in the soil and the trees." Joe believes that conventional burial places physical barriers of concrete vaults and metal caskets between the body and the Earth. "Modern burial goes against God's will," he said.

Joe often speaks at churches to explain natural burial to parishioners and ask them to consider a funeral arrangement plan that reduces the environmental impacts of burials and protects God's creation. Putting money and resources into the ground is not a wise investment, he said. "Whether you buy a ten-thousand-dollar metal casket or a twenty-five-dollar cardboard casket, my job is to throw dirt on it." The cost of a burial space in the meadows area at Honey Creek Woodlands is $2,500, which results in significant savings to families. Joe draws on his corporate background, ironically in market research for the junk-food industry, to help families save money.

An Episcopalian and avid outdoorsman, Joe always told his wife he wanted to be buried in the woods, although he didn't know how to make it happen. In 2005, he was listening to National Public Radio in the parking lot of a Bi-Lo grocery store, and he heard the end of a story on green burials. He assumed the narrator was describing a cemetery in some progressive community of Portland, Oregon, or Seattle, Washington, but the story featured Ramsey Creek Cemetery in Westminster, South Carolina, the first green burial site in the country. He started volunteering in October 2007 with Billy and Kimberly Campbell and learning the business.

Family and friends shovel dirt to cover the grave at a service at Honey Creek Woodlands on the grounds of the Monastery of the Holy Spirit in Conyers, Georgia. Photo by Joe Whittaker.

The monastery had contacted the Campbells for consultation about starting a natural cemetery in Georgia and asked them to recommend someone to manage the cemetery. When the abbot of the monastery called him to manage the cemetery, he answered. In 2008, Joe quit his job to commute twice a month for ten days straight, digging graves in the woods and helping families participate in the work of grieving.

Monasticism, the Earth and burials

Trappist monks lead a cloistered life devoted to contemplation; they belong to the Order of Cistercians of the Strict Observance. When I met the abbot of the monastery, Father Francis Michael, he defied my stereotype of monks in long white robes and black scapulars. He spoke with a strong Philadelphia accent and wore Wrangler jeans, a dark green fleece jacket and a blue baseball cap. A self-trained expert in butterflies and dragonflies, Father Michael has lived at the monastery since 1974. A few minutes after we met, he announced that he'd rather talk while we were looking for butterflies. We climbed into a red truck after he moved his binoculars, camera and three field guides from the passenger seat. "Today, we are looking for a butterfly called a falcate orangetip," he said. In the past ten years, he has identified and photographed 52 species of dragonflies on the monastery grounds.

The monastery is one of the largest green spaces in the metropolitan Atlanta area. Under Father Michael's leadership, the monks have brokered partnerships in conservation with nonprofits like the Georgia Piedmont Land Trust and the Arabia Mountain Natural Heritage Area.

As we drove in search of butterflies, Father Michael reminded me that burying the dead is a corporal work of mercy, one of the seven practices of charity toward our neighbor, such as feeding the hungry and providing shelter to the homeless. Traditionally, Trappist monks were buried in shrouds or only in their habits. So this natural cemetery at Honey Creek decreases the environmental impact of burials by connecting to Trappist traditions. (Monks are buried in a cemetery behind the church, rather than at Honey Creek, and paradoxically, some of their family members insist on embalming.)

"For a long time, we've been quoting scripture that the Earth is ours to master and subdue," Father Michael said. "But all of creation is the body of Christ, not just humans." He stopped the truck to show me the site of a former slave cemetery on monastery grounds. We walked in silence past the gravesites, marked only by weathered cement stones. No doubt these slaves were buried in shrouds or simple pine boxes, much like people now buried at Honey Creek.

Protecting Land as a Conservation Strategy

Land conservation is critical in the face of a rapidly changing climate. The EPA estimates that public and private lands in the United States remove nine hundred million metric tons of carbon dioxide from the atmosphere each year.[15] The loss and fragmentation of forests, grasslands and agricultural lands reduces the capacity of these natural carbon storage systems or "carbon sinks." Thus land conservation strategies can help to mitigate carbon emissions.

As we adapt to warmer temperatures and higher sea levels, land conservation also protects and connects intact landscapes, while maintaining the integrity of habitats within landscapes. Ecologist Reed Noss writes, "Land conservation on a vast scale is our best hope for adapting to climate change."[16] Fragmented landscapes make it difficult, if not impossible, for many species to disperse and adapt to changing climatic conditions.

Promised land and climate change

Because of their landholdings, many faith communities can address climate change through land stewardship. Denominations own the property on which churches are located, as well as additional tracts of land. The United Methodist Church, for example, has created three green cemeteries at camp and conference centers.

Many of the lands owned by faith communities are under threat, however, due to financial pressures and alternative uses for development or extraction of natural resources. Jewish summer camps in the Poconos and Catskills, for example, are being approached to lease their land for natural gas drilling. Many of these camps have 200 acres of land or more, and a lease could bring almost a million dollars. The long-term risks from this extraction process called "hydrofracking" include pollution of water, land and air.[17]

Natural burial represents one strategy for promoting land conservation, especially through cemeteries that involve partnerships with environmental organizations that hold conservation easements. In these cases, funds that go toward burial can promote the purchase of additional property for long-term land stewardship.

Land conservation at Prairie Creek Conservation Cemetery

Robert "Hutch" Hutchinson became interested in natural burial as a way to generate money for land conservation. As the executive director of Alachua Conservation Trust and a former county commissioner, Hutch has 25 years of experience in land conservation. Opened in 2010 with 78 acres, Prairie Creek Conservation Cemetery lies adjacent to Prairie Creek Preserve, between Paynes Prairie

At Prairie Creek Conservation Cemetery in Gainesville, Florida, natural burial includes the use of pine caskets without concrete vaults. Photo courtesy of Prairie Creek Conservation Cemetery.

State Preserve and the Lochloosa Wildlife Management Area near Gainesville, Florida.

The mission of the nonprofit Conservation Burial, Inc., which operates Prairie Creek Conservation Cemetery, is to promote natural burial practices that conserve land and reunite people with the environment. The Alachua Conservation Trust (ACT) serves as the fiscal agent for the cemetery, which will ultimately buy back the land with funds acquired from burials.

In the future, every cemetery in Alachua County will have a green burial option, Hutch predicted. "Just like organic food and solar energy used to be avant-garde and expensive, green burial will become another option out there," he said. Orthodox Jews, Muslims, Baha'i and some traditional Christians already honor these natural burial traditions.

The cost of a burial at Prairie Creek is $2,000. A portion of the burial fee goes into a perpetual cemetery management fund, but all remaining funds are used to pay for the land and to purchase and restore more land in the future. The cemetery's plans for ecological restoration include planting native trees, removing invasive and exotic plants and protecting threatened and endangered species. Prairie Creek expects to bury 300 people per acre, compared to 1,000 per acre at modern cemeteries. The cemetery may also decide to expand before reaching this number to "spread bodies as thinly across the landscape," in order to conserve land, as Hutch maintains.

For individuals on the board, this cemetery has taken on deeper meaning beyond land conservation since three board members experienced deaths of loved ones. Hutch's own stepson was killed last year in an arbitrary street robbery in Nicaragua, and his ashes were buried at Prairie Creek.

Another board member of Conservation Burial, Inc., Susan Marynowski, brings a diverse suite of skills as an herbalist, musician and environmental educator to the creation and implementation of the cemetery. From her perspective, the overall goal of conservation cemeteries is to conserve land in its natural condition with outcomes that range from conserving wildlife habitat to carbon sequestration. She noted that money for land conservation is drying up across the country, but natural burials can lead to a business model that supports conservation. In Florida, land costs $5,000 to $10,000 an acre. "Imagine that we bury one hundred people per acre," she said. "If each burial generates one thousand dollars after expenses, the value generated per acre is one hundred thousand dollars."

For Susan, this work with Prairie Creek created a new paradigm for cemeteries where you can have a picnic, walk the trails and see birds. "God is in everything and everybody," she said. "Recycling our body into the body of God is the perfect way to be in the body of God." Susan lost her father when she was young and never got to see his body or attend his burial. "I experience the acceptance of death at every single burial," she said.

In the fall of 2010, the board held a blessing ceremony facilitated by a Catholic priest, a United Church of Christ minister and a Unitarian Universalist minister. At the ceremony, each minister blessed one aspect of the cemetery: the workers who had initiated the cemetery, the people buried there and the land itself.

Creating a Spiritual Connection to the Earth

The stories of Honey Creek Woodlands and Prairie Creek Conservation Cemetery reveal the power of burial to create deep connections between people and places. As Allan Moynihan, a Baha'i board member of Conservation Burial, Inc. said, "The economic aspect of the cemetery supports conservation, which then allows people to connect spiritually with the land." Much as natural birthing returned the birthing process to mothers, natural cemeteries have connected families to the natural cycles of life and death.

This desire to reclaim these connections surprised those like Hutch, who had been in land conservation for decades. "Families are digging the grave, preparing the body, transporting and lowering the body and filling the grave. People want to do more than simply stand by, weep and write a check when they are grieving.

The work of natural burial can be cathartic and spiritually meaningful, especially when connections to nature are made in the unique and beautiful ceremonies we have witnessed," he said. To that end, people have the opportunity to work through their grief in both physical and emotional ways.

Local environmentalist Kathy Cantwell was the first person buried at Prairie Creek, and her friends collected all her environmental T-shirts and sewed them into a shroud. One man was buried in a Mexican poncho and a US flag to symbolize his heritage. During an Orthodox Jewish funeral, everyone passed around scissors and cut a piece of their clothing to bury with the person.

As an environmental educator, Susan Marynowski recognized that reconnecting people to the land creates the awareness necessary to build support for conservation. "Prairie Creek is a place where all faiths can meet around the Earth," she said. She described the burial of a Unitarian Universalist Iranian woman married to a Jewish man, as well as the funeral of an African American man whose family members now want to be buried at Prairie Creek.

At Honey Creek Woodlands in Georgia, the burial manager has witnessed this same connection to faith and place. Joe Whittaker believes that the physical acts of shoveling dirt or lowering the casket provide healing and a demonstration of love. He described meeting a man in his thirties named Benjamin Womack, who was dying of cancer but didn't have any family or savings. Benjamin died the next week, and his band members raised the funds necessary for the burial, even donating additional funds to the monastery.

Wrapped in his grandmother's purple and yellow quilt, Benjamin's body rested on a piece of plywood with rope handles on a table. Flower petals were strewn around the gravesite with three wooden slats laid over the grave. When it came time to lower the body into the grave, Joe whispered instructions to friends who held black webbing laced through the rope handles. Several of the parents of Benjamin's friends who attended the service decided that they too wanted to be buried at Honey Creek Woodlands.

Looking Toward Natural Burial: Lessons for People of Faith

Addressing climate change through natural burial is not as simple as changing an incandescent light bulb to a compact fluorescent, but the impacts of natural burial on the climate are long lasting and multi-generational. On a practical level, everybody will die. Burials that protect the Earth can impact all people of faith.

For faith communities, creating a natural cemetery on a parcel of land held by a denomination may be a logical first step. To this end, consider the following strategies gleaned from the experiences at Honey Creek Woodlands and Prairie Creek Conservation Cemetery:

1. Partner with a local land trust or conservation nonprofit with experience in land conservation. Prairie Creek Conservation Cemetery collaborated with Alachua Conservation Trust, and the Monastery of the Holy Spirit partnered with conservation groups such as the Georgia Piedmont Land Trust. Ensure that you have partners or board members with ecological experience, as conservation cemeteries contribute to ecological restoration, increase carbon sequestration and support biodiversity conservation.

2. Recruit board members who are passionate about natural burial for a variety of reasons, from land stewardship to religious values.

3. Get legal advice from a board member, a law clinic at a local university or a willing pro bono lawyer. Prairie Creek used the Conservation Clinic at the University of Florida, where law students compiled information on the Florida statutes and made recommendations. Laws differ in every state, so legal advice is crucial.

4. Get advice from other conservation cemeteries and the Green Burial Council, which certifies natural burial grounds.

5. Remember that natural cemeteries require start-up time before a steady revenue stream begins. Prairie Creek involved three years of meetings, organization and research before the cemetery was licensed and operating.

6. Plan for efficient, low-cost maintenance. Honey Creek's location one-and-a-half miles from the main road resulted in unanticipated costs such as road maintenance. Try to use existing personnel to staff the cemetery if possible, to keep overhead low.

For individuals interested in green burial, these lessons provide some guidance:

1. Document your wishes for a natural burial with specific instructions about caskets, embalming, vaults and location of burial.
2. Look for a place for green burial in your region. Also ask at older "town" cemeteries in smaller towns or rural areas, which often do not require vaults and provide inexpensive options for burial.
3. Ask your conventional cemetery to consider burial without a vault. Suggest the establishment of a vault-free "green" corner that would not require mowing.
4. If you consider cremation, explore the possibility of spreading ashes at a nature preserve or an existing green burial ground.
5. Research the options, from home funeral to natural burial, through books such as *Final Rights: Reclaiming the American Way of Death* and *Grave Matters*, as well as websites such as the Funeral Consumers Alliance.[18]
6. Ask for what you want. As more people ask for it, green burial will be provided.

On Reflection

After visiting Honey Creek Woodlands, I couldn't stop talking about death. At a mother-daughter tea party, I talked about green burials. While teaching, I connected content about conservation to cemeteries. One student said, "Mallory, I think you're spending too much time on death."

In my forties, I realized that my friends and I had not thought about the connection between our death and the Earth. We were too busy finding childcare, making beds and grocery lists and working for environmental causes in our jobs.

Like many people, I become overwhelmed by the actions I should take to confront climate change. On a given day, I feel that I should advocate for renewable energy policies, raise funds for solar panels in the public schools and dry my clothes on the line in the winter. (Sometimes in response, I drive to the Shell station down the road for a Diet Coke and a *People* magazine.)

I will die only once, and I have a choice. I can choose a burial that protects God's climate and invites my children to engage in physical and emotional ways. Perhaps by the time I die, all Episcopal camp and conference centers will have a space for green burial. My middle-school daughter Maya was six years old when my father died. She speaks with clarity about one act at his funeral: shoveling dirt at the grave.

Life is changed, not ended. On a philosophical level, I get it, but in reality, my father and my mother are gone from my daily life. Even my younger daughter Annie Sky said to me, "I wish your mommy was here, so I could know her." My mother will never sew a quilt for my children. My father will never sing a gospel song at their bedsides.

Yet their burials connect us to God's creation. The pine casket, the soil and their bodies became a part of a natural landscape. And all of it is sacred.

●　●　●

MALLORY MCDUFF, PH.D. is the author of *Natural Saints: How People of Faith are Working to Save God's Earth*, published by Oxford University Press. She teaches environmental education at Warren Wilson College in Asheville, North Carolina, where she lives with her daughters Maya and Annie Sky.

spirituality

For you shall go out in joy, and be led back in peace;
the mountains and the hills before
you shall burst into song,
and all the trees of the field shall clap their hands.

Isaiah 55:12

But ask the animals, and they will teach you;
the birds of the air, and they will tell you;
ask the plants of the earth, and they will teach you;
and the fish of the sea will declare to you.
Who among all these does not know that the hand
of the Lord has done this?
In his hand is the life of every living thing
and the breath of every human being.

Job 12:7–10

CHAPTER 4

At the Intersection of Belief and Knowledge

Climate Science and our Christian Faith

KATHARINE HAYHOE

God has not given us a spirit of fear,
but of power and of love and of a sound mind.

2 Timothy 1:7 (NKJV)

SOMETHING UNUSUAL is happening to our planet. Across much of the world, average temperatures are warming. Summer heat is coming earlier, with heat waves that are stronger and last longer. Unseasonable melting of snow and ice is occurring from the Arctic to the Alps. Many of the rains we used to count on are becoming increasingly unreliable. Plants and pests, bugs and birds are moving toward the poles, into new regions where they have never been seen before, unhindered by cold winter temperatures that used to keep them at bay.

Before we can talk about solutions, we need to understand the cause of the problem. There is no doubt that the climate is changing, but how do we know what is causing this change? If climate change is natural, we only have one response: adapt. But if it is human-induced, and our actions can halt these changes, then we have another option: fix the problem that is driving these changes.

Which is it, and how do we know?

The Root of the Problem

To definitively attribute our changing climate to human causes, we must first eliminate all other natural suspects. In the past, most large-scale climate warming has been driven by gradual, long-term changes in the amount of energy the Earth receives from the sun. These changes are amplified, or increased, by natural feedbacks within the ocean-atmosphere system. Temporary changes in regional climate have also been caused by internal changes, or natural cycles, in the way heat and energy are distributed around the world by the ocean and atmosphere. Could either of these be responsible for the warming we've seen today?

During the first half of the 1900s, the amount of energy the Earth was receiving from the sun gradually increased. This increase would—and did—contribute to a warming of the Earth's climate but accounted for only a relatively small fraction of what was observed over that time.[1] For the past three decades or more, energy

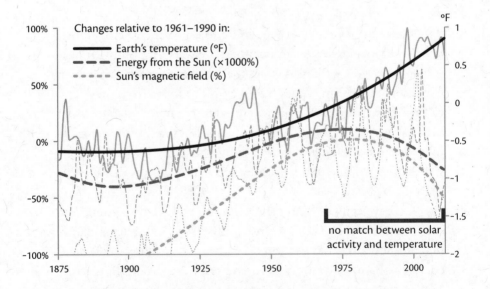

During the first half of the 1900s, increases in energy from the sun occurred at the same time as the planet was warming. Since the 1970s, however, our planet has received less energy from the sun, even as it has continued to warm. Image courtesy of Dr. Katharine Hayhoe.

from the sun has been *decreasing*. So if the Earth's climate were being primarily controlled by the sun now, as it was in the past, it would have steadily cooled over the past 30 years. Instead, we have seen the opposite: a warming that is completely inconsistent with a solar control on climate.

Let's look at the other natural cause mentioned earlier. Climate constantly changes as a result of natural shifts in the distribution of heat in Earth's climate system. However, physical laws regarding conservation of energy demand that, if it is getting warmer in one place, it must be cooling in another. This time, that is not the case. Warming is taking place worldwide: over the oceans and the land, in the tropics and at the poles, at the Earth's surface and throughout the lower atmosphere.[2]

Even if the sun or natural cycles can't be responsible for today's change, why do the large majority of scientists think humans are the cause? To answer this question, we need to establish a clear connection between human activities and climate change.

Natural Trend or Human Interference?

Earth's temperature is regulated by a natural marvel called the greenhouse effect. The atmosphere naturally contains certain levels of heat-trapping gases: water vapor, carbon dioxide and methane. These gases trap some of the heat given off by the planet inside the atmosphere, instead of allowing the heat to escape to space. This heat-capturing system prevents Earth's energy from being lost to space too quickly. At natural levels, these gases keep our planet at a comfortable average temperature of 59°F, nearly 60°F warmer than it would be otherwise.

Enter the Industrial Revolution, when humans began to dig increasing quantities of fossil fuels (coal, oil and eventually natural gas) from the Earth's crust to power the enormous technological advances of the day. When burned, fossil fuels produce carbon dioxide. Carbon dioxide is one of those heat-trapping gases that naturally occur in our atmosphere; however, humans are altering the balance of the system.

During the 1700s, we produced an average of 10 million metric tons of carbon dioxide each year. Today, we produce 32 *billion* metric tons per year; and that number is going up every year.[3] That's nearly five tons per person, more than 50 times an individual's body weight. About one-third comes from industrial factories, one-third from car exhaust and one-third from heating and cooling homes and other buildings.

Some of the carbon dioxide we produce ends up in the ocean, and some is absorbed by plants; but on average, 45 percent remains in the atmosphere, where it continues to build up, year after year.[4] Through our increasing use of fossil fuels, we have artificially increased atmospheric levels of carbon dioxide by 40 percent, and methane levels by 250 percent.[5] When it is artificially enhanced, the greenhouse effect traps even more of the heat energy given off by the Earth inside the atmosphere, rather than releasing the heat into space.[6] This is what is heating our planet.

The best science available tells us two things. First, these increasing levels of heat-trapping gases are the cause of most of the changes in climate we have already observed. And second, future change will far exceed anything we humans have experienced so far.[7]

Why Climate Change Matters

"Weather" describes how conditions change from day to day, and even year to year. "Climate," on the other hand, is the average of weather statistics over multiple decades. Although weather is very changeable, climate can be quite predictable. Unlike weather, climate is not inherently chaotic. It is driven by changes in the energy balance of the Earth. If we know what causes changes in Earth's energy balance—and we do—then we can predict climate.

Of course, temperatures have always gone up and down from year to year: that's how weather works. But on climate timescales of decades, global temperatures over the past 150 years have increased by 1.3°F, with nearly half of that increase occurring in the past 30 years.[8] The decade of the 2000s was the warmest on record, with the 1990s and the 1980s second and third warmest, respectively.[9] The year 2010 tied with 2005 for the warmest year on record, and stands alone as the wettest year on record as well.[10]

If temperature continues to increase at the same rate observed over the past 30 years, it will take only four more decades to double the warming that's occurred so far on our planet. A temperature increase of a degree or two may seem like a relatively small change. It is, in weather terms—but not in climate terms. That's the key difference.

Past changes in the energy balance of the Earth, such as the Little Ice Age of the 1700s or the warm period over Europe during medieval times, were driven by changes in energy from the sun, enhanced by natural feedbacks within the ocean-atmosphere system. These changes were relatively small compared to what this century may bring. Even so, these relatively small energy imbalances had enormous impacts on the societies and civilizations of that time.[11] Why?

Our societies are built on the assumption that the climate will remain stable. The underlying structure of our food supply, our water resources and the design standards for our homes, our roads and our industries are all based on this premise. For example, if you live in a cool, wet climate, you will build a house that can withstand heavy rain and snowfall, not one that can be kept cool in a hot summer. Farmers in your region will plant crops that thrive in cooler, damper conditions, and local plants and animals will be adapted for survival in that climate. Water-supply structures will be based on the assumption that water sources and supplies will remain largely as they are today. Although many societies have an emergency plan for fires, floods and heat waves, there is an underlying assumption that such events will be the exception rather than the norm.

Today, climate change threatens our notions of stability and security. Constants we used to be able to count on are becoming increasingly inconstant. Within our children's lifetimes, for example, a typical summer in Illinois could become like one in Texas;[12]

winter snowpack in the Sierra Nevada Mountains, a primary water source for California's Central Valley, could shrink by 90 percent;[13] and certain areas of the world, such as the western United States and southeast Australia, could be at great risk for more frequent and severe wildfires.[14][15]

The Impacts of a Warming World

Many changes in recent years are consistent with our picture of a warming world. These include the warming in northwest Canada and Alaska, where temperatures have increased at more than twice the rate of the rest of the continent over the past 50 years.[16] These warmer temperatures are melting the frozen ground that anchors buildings and roads throughout the Arctic.[17] More than 200 Alaskan towns and villages are at risk as their foundations crumble and their buildings topple and fall.[18] One community has already been forced to abandon its homes.[19] The US Army Corps of Engineers has estimated it will cost between $150 million and $400 million to move just one town like this one out of immediate danger.[20]

The Arctic isn't the only place where ice is melting. Nearly every mountain glacier in the Himalayas, Andes and Alps is receding.[21] Drinking water and hydroelectric power for the nearly nine million inhabitants of Lima, Peru, are currently supplied by water from glaciers that are likely to disappear within just a few years. More than one-sixth of the world's people depend on meltwater from glaciers or winter snowpack for their water supply. In 2008, the president of Peru announced plans to begin desalination of ocean water to at least partially make up for disappearing glacial resources.[22] California's Central Valley farmers depend on melting snow in the Sierra Nevada Mountains for much of their water supply. In 2005, the governor of California issued an executive order mandating the reduction of heat-trapping gas emissions, citing as one of his reasons that "increased temperatures threaten to greatly reduce the Sierra snowpack, one of the state's primary sources of water."[23]

The enormous ice sheets of Greenland and Antarctica are also losing mass.[24][25] All this melting ice ends up in the oceans, accelerating the sea-level rise already underway from ocean warming and subsequent expansion. It's estimated that over the next century, sea levels may rise an additional one to five feet.[26][27] Today, 10 percent of the world's population, nearly 650 million people, and more than 3,000 cities are located in low-elevation coastal areas around the world.[28] Most are in developing nations, where few resources are available to hold back the rising water. In New York, a sea-level increase of three to four feet would mean that what used to be the "100-year flood" could occur once every four years.[29] For the nation of Bangladesh, the same amount of sea-level rise would be enough to flood 17 percent of the entire country.[30]

Finally, plant and animal species, particularly those limited to areas with suitable temperatures, are on the move. For some, these changes raise the specter of extinction. The polar bear is perhaps the most famous example; its habitat is disappearing as Arctic sea ice melts. Today, 5 of the 12 documented bear populations are already in decline.[31] For other species, warmer winters are a boon, allowing mountain pine and bark beetles to proliferate throughout the western forests of North America, killing millions of acres of trees in a single outbreak.[32]

As unsettled and changeable as current conditions are, the future promises much worse if we continue to rely on our old, outdated ways of life, ways of life based on a quick, cheap and easy supply of polluting fossil fuels. Heat waves would become a way of life, with months, not days, per year of daily highs over 100°F across much of southern and central United States.[33] Extreme drought would threaten as much as one-third of the world, taking over many agricultural areas and leading to mass migrations of "environmental refugees."[34] (See Chapter 10.) Changing conditions could doom more than half the world's species to extinction.[35]

There's no denying that this is very discouraging news. But it doesn't have to be that way. Today, more than ever, we need the courage to change the things that should be changed, so that we can continue to prosper on this planet.

The Response to Climate Change

The dangers of climate change have been documented in scientific and popular literature for more than a century.[36] Since Dr. James Hansen's testimony before the US Congress in 1988,[37] global warming has become a household term. So how have we been doing over the past 20 years or so? Have we taken this threat to heart?

During the 1990s, global carbon dioxide emissions increased at an average of 1 percent per year.[38] Since 2000, carbon emissions have increased at an average of over 3 percent per year worldwide, even through the economic slowdown of 2008.[39] At some point, the world *will* run out of easily accessible fossil fuel resources. But there remains a vast, untapped resource of unconventional fossil fuels, enough to power the world for centuries to come.[40] It is false hope to anticipate that the fossil-fuel age will end, without too much damage done, because we will soon run out of fossil fuels.

It might be true that our global actions don't demonstrate concern for climate change. However, much of the increase in carbon dioxide emissions has come from developing countries with emerging economies. In many of these nations, a 2011 survey revealed, climate change lags behind other serious concerns, such as air and water pollution.[41] Is it possible that the majority of people in North America and Europe *are* concerned, but that our positive actions aren't affecting global emissions yet?

Over the past 12 years, Gallup has been asking US citizens whether, according to what they hear in the news, the seriousness of global warming is generally exaggerated, correct or underestimated. The number of those who responded "generally exaggerated" hovered around 30 percent from 1998 to 2002, then began to rise. By 2010, as many as 48 percent of respondents believed the seriousness of global warming was exaggerated.[42] That this change in opinion occurred during the warmest decade — and five of the warmest years — on record clearly demonstrates how public opinion on climate change is becoming increasingly independent of the physical reality.[43]

Not only has public understanding of this issue radically changed over the past decade, but much of this perception, at least in the United States and Canada, now runs along increasingly divided party lines.[44] In other words, political affiliation, rather than scientific fact, is determining public opinion. When the Gallup survey began in 1998, 35 percent of Republicans and 23 percent of Democrats believed news of global warming was exaggerated. By 2011, the numbers for Democrats remained roughly the same, while those for Republicans had climbed to 67 percent.[45] During the 2010 mid-term election in the United States, 49 percent of re-elected Republican representatives publicly and explicitly repudiated the role of humans in climate change.[46]

What really saddens me, however, is how these divisions also run along religious lines. In 2008, a study by the Pew Forum on Religion & Public Life asked, "Is there solid evidence the Earth is warming because of human activity?"[47] People who did not identify with any church or faith group had the highest rate of agreement, at 58 percent. Mainstream Protestants and Catholics came next, at 48 percent. Down at the very bottom of the list were white evangelical Protestants, of whom only 34 percent agreed with this statement. In other words, 66 percent did not.

Unsurprisingly, this divide is also reflected in church leaders. The US Conference of Catholic Bishops stated in 1998 that "care for the Earth is a requirement of our faith," while in 2011 the Pontifical Academy of Sciences released a report calling on "all people and nations to recognize the serious and potentially irreversible impacts of global warming caused by the anthropogenic emissions of greenhouse gases and other pollutants."[48] Similar statements have been issued by Anglicans and Episcopalians.[49] However, a 2011 Lifeway survey of US Protestant pastors asked whether they agreed with the statement, "I believe global warming is real and manmade."[50] Only 28 percent of evangelical pastors agreed with the statement while 52 percent of pastors from mainline churches agreed. As part of the evangelical community, I have spent a long time asking myself: how can there be such a divergence between what science is telling us and what we, as a community, believe?

Why Are Science and Faith in Conflict?

There is no easy answer to the question of why faith and science are in conflict over the issue of human-caused climate change. However, one thing is clear: the reason for this divide does not lie in the basic tenets of our theology about the environment and the planet, where by "theology" I mean beliefs that could or would appear on a statement of faith. In fact, we need to agree on only a few very basic points to be on the same page on the issue of climate change. These points are simply the following:

- **Earth sustains our physical existence, but we can push the boundaries of its bounty.** Almost any human on the planet would agree that the Earth sustains us: it provides the food we eat, the water we drink and the air we breathe. Most of us also acknowledge that, through our actions, we have polluted the air, muddied the water and even limited the food available to our less fortunate brothers and sisters in many parts of the world. As Bono stated in a 2011 CNN interview, "You can blame droughts on God, but famines are man-made."[51]

- **God created the Earth and gave us responsibility for it.** Nearly all of us who identify as Christians agree that—in some way, shape or form—God was involved in creating the Earth, and it is good. We also read in Genesis that Adam was given the responsibility to care for, or steward, creation. Regardless of our views on stewardship and creation care, most would agree that it's important to respect God's creation. After all, if someone you love gives you a gift, one in which they also rejoice and take delight, you do not treat it like garbage or throw it in the trash.

- **It is wise to conserve our resources.** Finally, most of us also agree that it's important to conserve. Moderation in all things may be a value that we do not practice sufficiently. As a human race, though, we all respect the concept of conservation and acknowledge its wisdom. It's just common sense. As the Chinese proverb says, "The frog does not drink up the pond in which it lives."

I would argue that these three points are really all we need to agree on, in terms of theology or beliefs regarding the physical world around us, in order to understand that we need to do something about climate change.[52] Furthermore, it seems that most of us already do agree on these points. So why does the conflict over climate change still run along deeply rooted religious lines?

Part of the problem may be the long-standing distrust between Christians and scientists, a problem whose roots stretch centuries into the past. We could discuss the long-standing divide between science and faith in the United States and the United Kingdom. We could talk about the 1925 "Monkey Trial," the ongoing debate between creation and evolution, and even bring up the sanctity of life. Despite the strong Christian roots of many of the founders of modern science,[53][54] faith and science in western civilization have come into conflict many times over the centuries.[55]

However, here is the essential difference between climate change and other science-based conflicts: *we do not have the luxury of time to resolve the long-standing distrust between faith and science before tackling climate change.* My research, and that of my colleagues, clearly demonstrates that we have only a narrow window of time—on the order of years, not decades—to make smart choices that will enable us to avoid many of the potentially dangerous consequences of climate change.[56]

So rather than talking about general issues, I'd like to offer three reasons for the disconnect between faith and science specific to climate change. My hope is that by identifying these barriers, we can envision how to tackle these challenges in the relatively short period of time that remains to us.

Reason One: The Evidence Is Not Easy to See

Many of the more obvious symptoms of climate change—including melting Arctic sea ice or sinking South Sea islands—cannot be seen in our own neighborhoods. In our communities, the sky is blue; the grass is green (even here in Texas in the summer of 2011, where most continue to draw from our rapidly disappearing aquifer to water their lawns in the midst of the most severe drought on record); and the water coming out of our tap is clear and abundant. Our environment looks pretty good.

Not only that, but the manifestations of climate change that we do see can be unclear, and sometimes even downright contradictory. For example, global warming can lead to *increases* in snowfall. How can this be?

As average air temperature increases, the air can hold more water vapor in both summer and winter. In summer, this leads to more frequent heavy rainfall in some regions. In winter, though, when a storm sweeps through, it picks up the extra water vapor and dumps it as snow—and in larger quantities than would otherwise occur. At first glance, more snow would seem to suggest that the climate is cooling. In reality, though, the increased snowfall can be a symptom of the warming. Compounding this effect is the fact that, as the atmosphere warms, the bands of storm tracks circling the globe that pass over the northern United States and southern Canada are shifting farther north. This shift alters how often these regions have storms, and how large those storms are. Both of these changes have already been well documented and together have been targeted as contributing to the observed increase in snowstorms over the northeastern United States in recent years.[57]

In the summer of 2009, I coauthored a report by the United States Global Climate Research Program that connected these dots, clearly drawing the link between climate change and snowstorms over the Northeast.[58] This report was in no way intended to serve as prophecy, but it turned out to be exactly that: the winter following its publication saw an unbelievable number of record-breaking storms, including those known as "Snowpocalypse" and "Snowmageddon."

I do not mean to imply that this unusual season was a direct consequence of climate change—far from it. Any individual event, and even an entire season of events, is just one of the thousands of statistics scientists need to collect before a formal attribution can be made. However, this winter was entirely consistent with what we would expect as a result of climate change altering the average conditions of winter in the northeastern United States. In no way did it contradict the science of climate change; rather, these events bolstered scientific theories of how climate change would affect winter precipitation in the future.

In public opinion, however, this winter was perceived in exactly the opposite way. One senator famously built an igloo on Capitol Hill and invited Al Gore to move into it.[59] Many more invoked that favorite phrase, "It's freezing outside—where's global warming now?" to show how ridiculous the idea of global warming was, when the entire East Coast was buried up to its neck in more snow than it had seen in 100 years.

How can we explain, simply and clearly, that those snowstorms are consistent with a warming world? Climate change is too complex a science to lend itself easily to the five-second sound bites that is all that many of our channels of communication allow. Evidence for a human influence on all aspects of our climate can be difficult to discern.

Reason Two: Confusion is Rampant

I am the last person you'd characterize as a conspiracy theorist. I don't enjoy listening to friends expound on how secret military experiments are seeding our skies with silvery particles or how pharmaceutical companies are introducing ingredients into vaccines so our children will require drugs for the rest of their lives. But even I can't deny, based on the evidence of my own eyes, that there is an intelligent disinformation campaign at work on the issue of climate science, and much of this effort is aimed at conservative and Christian communities.

Errors are being propagated by sources trusted by many Christians. Conservative news pundits ridicule climate science and scientists on a regular basis. We've already seen how pastors and

politicians can influence our perspectives on climate. And some
Christian organizations actively participate in generating and
spreading false information on climate change and other creation
care issues.[60][61] False claims include, for example, that "there is
no consistent, peer-reviewed scientific research that establishes a
cause-and-effect relationship between increased atmospheric carbon dioxide and higher global temperatures."[62] In truth, however,
there are thousands of studies in the peer-reviewed literature that
document this relationship, and the heat-trapping properties of
carbon dioxide can be easily measured.

Many of those who have the most to lose, economically or ideo-
logically, in breaking our addiction to fossil fuels are doing their
best to ensure that our addiction continues.[63] Substantial efforts
are being made to muddy the waters on climate change, promote
the idea that the science is not settled, actively oppose any legislation to limit emissions and, more recently, discredit or discourage
scientists themselves.[64][65] This approach is very similar to the tobacco industry's attempts to obscure the connection between cancer and smoking, strategies that involved some of the same tactics
and even some of the same players.[66]

One of the key false messages in the climate confusion campaign is that there is no scientific consensus. An example of the
methods used to bolster this myth was a petition from the Oregon
Institute of Science and Medicine that was circulated in scientific
and technical circles a number of years ago. It was claimed that
17,000 qualified scientists had signed this petition, stating that
global warming had no scientific basis and urging the US government to reject the Kyoto Protocol and other agreements to mitigate climate change. In fact, the petition asked if global warming
was *already* causing catastrophic warming. (My own answer to that
would be that for some people, such as native Alaskans, it may be.
For others, not yet.) In addition, *Scientific American* estimated that
only 200 of the signatories held legitimate and relevant degrees.[67]
Other signers were not legitimate scientists, including "Dr. Red-
wine" and one of the Spice Girls.

The truth is that 97 *percent* of scientists actively researching and publishing in the field agree that climate change is occurring, and that most of it is the result of human production of heat-trapping gases.[68]

Another approach is to challenge the credibility of the scientists and the data directly. Over the past ten years or so, for example, several climate scientists have been under attack regarding the legitimacy of the "hockey stick" graph, which uses proxy or natural thermometer records to reconstruct temperature over the past 2,000 years. It's called a "hockey stick" graph because it shows nearly 1,900 years of stable climate followed by a sharp upward "blade": the temperature rise that has occurred over the past century. The implication of this graph is that our current warming is unprecedented in the history of western civilization.

The hockey stick debate was so contentious that it prompted an independent investigation by the National Academy of Sciences, which concluded that the main findings from the research were correct.[69] But the hockey stick debate was just one of a series of increasingly ferocious attacks. In late 2009, for example, academics' computers in the United Kingdom were illegally hacked and emails between British and US climate scientists stolen. A handful of phrases were extracted from more than 10,000 emails and used to allege wrongdoing on the part of the scientists: a serious charge that led to eight independent panels and investigations to probe these allegations.

While the scientists had certainly been less than courteous in some of their conversations, the fact is that *every independent panel*—including the British government's House of Commons Science and Technology Committee, the US Department of Commerce Inspector General and most recently the US National Science Foundation—has vindicated the scientists of any wrongdoing. The last of these investigations, released in August 2011, concluded with this: "Finding no research misconduct or other matter raised by the various regulations and laws discussed above, this case is closed."[70]

Scientists are still arguing, people say. And, of course, we love to argue. But what surprises me most is the remarkable scientific consensus that we *do* see. Statements made by engineers and chemists more than 100 years ago are amazingly similar to what we know today about how climate change is happening, and what it means for our world.[71]

Reason Three: The Truth is Frightening

Climate change is a daunting problem. Even thinking about it can be overwhelming. Doing something about it could limit or constrain goods and rights that many of us hold dear, especially in the United States.

Both psychology and theology tell us it's often easier to deny the reality of a problem than to do something about it. For example, an alcoholic must admit to the illness before he or she can seek help. We need to own up to our unhealthful behavior before we can move forward. And, in God's infinite wisdom, each one of us must confess to being a sinner before we can accept Christ's saving grace.

In the same way, we're addicted to the old, dirty ways of getting energy. We have to admit that addiction before we seek help, and this can be a very frightening step. A 2009 report from the American Psychological Association unsurprisingly identified uncertainty and mistrust as barriers to taking action on climate change.[72] It also revealed, however, that feelings of anxiety, helplessness and guilt were common. People's perceptions of what others were doing (or not doing) were used to justify their own inaction. Lack of control also contributed to a general feeling of helplessness in the face of an overwhelming task.

In the case of climate change, there's no getting around it: the truth is frightening. As a scientist, however, I believe that there is objective truth that can be revealed through the natural world. As a Christian, I believe that that truth can set us free. And as an optimist, I also believe that the more truth we know about a problem, the better chance we have of making smart choices to deal with it.

Fear takes us only so far: sometimes, no farther than the closest pillow under which we can hide our head.

We hear what I call "climate myths" all the time: from Uncle Joe at Thanksgiving, from a colleague in the elevator at work, from a neighbor as he washes his car. Several of the most common myths have already been addressed in this chapter. Many more have been tackled by John Cook, an evangelical Christian and founder of the website Skeptical Science (skepticalscience.com). And I discuss others, including some of our "Christian myths," such as why God would let something like this happen to the Earth, in the book *A Climate for Change: Global Warming Facts for Faith-Based Decisions*, which I coauthored with my husband Andrew Farley, a Christian author and pastor who was himself a climate-change skeptic.[73]

Learning to distinguish between truth and falsehood is a key step toward understanding climate change and why it matters to us. I would strongly encourage all of us to familiarize ourselves with the simple answers to the most common arguments so clearly described by Skeptical Science. We *can* and *should* equip ourselves to actively combat falsehood with truth.

Our Motivation is Love

Science can provide a plethora of information, facts and analysis. But science can do only so much. When it comes to making choices that affect us, our families, our communities and our planet, it's up to our hearts to guide our actions. Why should we care?

Jesus gave us the Great Commandment that we are to love our neighbor as ourselves (Matthew 22:39). In the book of Acts, Paul was asked by the other apostles to do no more than remember the poor, the very thing he was eager to do (Galatians 2:10).

How does this relate to climate change and the disasters it may bring? Let's take Hurricane Katrina as an example.[74] Who was most affected by Katrina? Not the wealthy who could afford to leave and then rebuild when they returned, but the poor, the elderly and the sick. A study reviewing the social aspects of this disaster concluded, "Katrina exposed the consequences of decades of institutionalized

discrimination and inequality, resulting in extreme human suffering, devastation and economic losses for individuals and families
on the lower rungs of the socio-economic ladder."[75]

This kind of suffering reflects exactly what we are seeing today
around the world: it is the people with the fewest resources who
are most harmed by the type of changes we expect under climate
change. The figure on the opposite page powerfully contrasts those
who have contributed to creating the problem of climate change
with those who will be most vulnerable to its impacts. World
Vision International, one of the largest relief and development
organizations in the world, states on its website, "Climate change
will affect almost every aspect of World Vision's work and mission
in the years to come. It has the potential to make poverty much
worse. World Vision's concern for the poor obliges us to address
issues related to climate change."[76]

According to the Global Humanitarian Forum, climate change
is already claiming an average of 300,000 lives annually and cost-
ing more than $125 billion dollars per year.[78] We are pouring relief
money into a bucket with a constantly growing hole in the bottom, and that hole is climate change.

So what can we do? I am convinced, first, that everyone needs
to understand what's happening to our Earth. And it is my hope,
second, that this understanding will make clear the urgent need
for solutions. We need new ways to reduce the impact we are having on our planet and to adapt to those changes we cannot avoid.

The Next Step

How can we quickly, effectively and affordably reduce the effect we
are having on our planet? How can we restructure our economy,
our infrastructure and our society so that it can adapt to coming
change?

We can teach ourselves, our children and our communities to
be good stewards of the bounty God has given us, and in doing
so to care for the welfare of our less fortunate brothers and sisters
around the world.

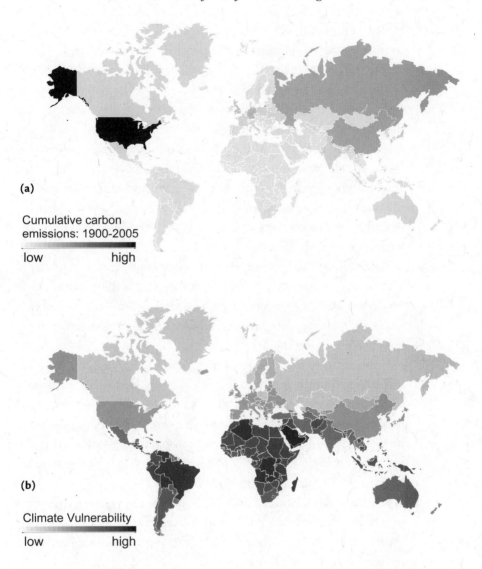

(a)

Cumulative carbon
emissions: 1900-2005

low   high

(b)

Climate Vulnerability

low   high

Nations that have contributed the least to the build-up of carbon dioxide in the atmosphere
are likely to suffer the greatest impacts. (a) Cumulative carbon dioxide emissions by nation
for 1900–2005, compiled by the World Resources Institute; (b) climate vulnerability index by
nation, interpolated from gridded estimates of Samson et al, 2011.[77]

We can prepare for what we can't avoid by conserving the resources we have and making wise decisions to reduce our vulnerability to climate-related change in the face of an uncertain future.

We can limit our own impact on the planet by making responsible choices that improve our quality of life at the same time as they help others. Often we feel that doing something about climate change involves pulling the plug on everything—our televisions, our showers, our air conditioning, even our cars. That's not true. It's about starting with what we have and making it known that we want more options. Many excellent and easy-to-read books, including 50 *Simple Steps to Save the Earth from Global Warming*, offer some excellent ideas to start.[79]

Ultimately, though, we have to support fundamental change. We have to wean ourselves off our dirty, inefficient and old-fashioned ways of getting energy, ways that pollute our air and our water, increase our dependence on foreign energy sources and often fail to invest in the local economy.

Opportunity lies in every crisis. And in this case, we have an unparalleled opportunity to rethink the way we live: to transition from the constraints of coal and oil to the freedom of endlessly renewable, homegrown solar and wind energy; to replace outdated, wasteful technologies with the most efficient state-of-the-art alternatives; and to better our environment and, with it, the welfare of all the inhabitants of this unique planet.

As the apostle Paul reminds us, "God has not given us the spirit of fear, but of power and of love and of a sound mind" (2 Timothy 1:7, NKJV). Too often we allow false fears—of economic hardship, reduced quality of life or even loss of freedom or rights—to control our minds. In doing so, we ignore the call: to love our brothers and sisters who are already bearing the brunt of a changing climate today, to care for the future generations who will inherit this planet and to share in the purpose of our loving God, who carved out from the vastness of space our unique Earth and gave it into our care.

● ● ●

KATHARINE HAYHOE, PH.D. is an evangelical, a climate scientist and a professor in the department of political science and director of the Climate Science Center at Texas Tech University. She served as an expert reviewer for the Intergovernmental Panel on Climate Change and coauthored the book *A Climate for Change: Global Warming Facts for Faith-based Decisions*.

CHAPTER 5

In God's Garden

Living the Good News
in a Changing Climate

Norman Wirzba

God planted a garden in Eden, in the east.

Genesis 2:8

ONE OF MY PRIMARY JOBS as a professor at Duke Divinity School is to help future pastors and leaders of the church see that ecological and agricultural issues are also deeply theological concerns. I want my students to understand that God is not interested only in the salvation of their individual souls. God loves the whole of creation as well as each of its particular creatures. Loving all creatures, God also cares deeply about the fields and forests, the mountains and the oceans, the soil and water, and the air and the sunshine that make their life possible. When friends describe my position to others, they half-jokingly say that I am a theologian of dirt.

I like that job description. If I had my way, all students graduating from seminaries and divinity schools would think of themselves as theologians of the dirt. Why? Because one of the most important truths about God is that God loves soil. Scripture portrays God as a gardener and farmer because God is constantly at work in the soil, holding it, breathing the breath of life into it—all so that creatures can live and be fed. If we read scripture carefully we soon discover that God is the first, the best, the essential and the eternal Gardener. The day God ceases to garden is also the day we all die. I don't hear many theologians or preachers say that, but it is true.

It is hard for us to appreciate this characterization of God as a gardener and farmer because relatively few among us any longer depend on gardening or farming to live. This puts us in a unique and utterly novel position. Viewed historically, most of humanity has been involved in their own food production. Participating in the growth of food, they also understood with the tactile certainty of their hands, tongues and stomachs that food is not a product or "commodity." It is a *vulnerable* gift that has its roots in ecological processes and its life in the grace of God. Changing climate conditions mean there is no guarantee that food will be readily, conveniently or cheaply available. People can fail to exercise appropriate care or they can become exploiters of the land. When they do, the land and its inhabitants will languish.

The people of the Bible, including some of their teachers and prophets, were farmers and shepherds.[1] This means that the God they worshipped was daily encountered as the life-giving power at work in soils, plants and animals. God's love and provision were not abstract but could be tasted in the grain transformed into bread and the grapes fermented into wine. Daily work tending sheep and cultivating crops brought them into intimate contact with God's own farming work in the world. Is it any wonder, then, that God should be described as the Gardener and as the Good Shepherd? Should we be surprised that these people understood paradise as a garden of delight called Eden?

It is bad theology to presume that the only relationship God cares about is the one with humans. From beginning to end, scripture reveals a God who desires that the whole of creation be healthy and well. Though people through greed, sloth and arrogance do much to destroy the Earth, God remains faithful to creatures, promising to turn what we lay waste into fruitful fields and nonviolent life together (Isaiah 65 and Revelation 21–22). God promises to reconcile to himself all things, "whether on earth or in heaven" (Colossians 1:15–20), because everything God has made is good and worthy of our care and delight. This is the "Good News" we need to hear—and then live into—as we address catastrophic climate change and the many other ecological crises of today.

Understanding *Where* We Are

Many of our current ecological problems are the result of our inability to understand the world as God's "creation." We do not see our world as the expression of God's abiding and sustaining love, and so do not appreciate how our ways of living might reflect a refusal or violation of that love. Looking at the world around us, what many see instead is a realm named and narrated as "nature," a realm that has little intrinsic or sacramental value. To understand nature we use the tools of science rather than theology. To live in nature we use the metrics of market economics rather than the theological virtues of faith, hope and love.

The problem is not that we think scientifically or with an economic interest in mind. If we are to live sustainably and well on this Earth, we need good science, just as we need to pay very careful attention to markets and production and consumption practices. The heart of our problem, rather, is that when we look out upon the world we see a stockpile of "natural resources" rather than a manifestation of God's love, provision and concern. We approach the world with an instrumental frame of mind, thinking about it in terms of what it can do for us, rather than with a theological orientation, thinking about how creatures play an important role in God's overarching concern for a healthy and reconciled world.

If we are to live better in this world we need to appreciate that *where* we are is the garden, or farm, of God. If we want to address problems such as climate change, soil erosion, deforestation, desertification, species extinction, the pollution of our waters and the abuse of animals—all problems that spring from the same distorted vision and understanding—then we need to recover a strong sense of God's presence as the Gardener and Farmer of the world. Without this understanding, our temptation will be to think that God has left the world and does not deeply care about what happens in or to it. We may even think that we can do with creation whatever we want. According to scripture (see Psalm 104), however, God is constantly present to and active in creation, en- abling creatures to be and to flourish. To be followers of God is to pledge to be participants in God's life-building ways.

We do not need to go far into scripture to see God's intimate relationship with Earth. The opening creation stories in Genesis communicate a vision of God's creative work as involving crea- tures. In the first story, God separates day and night, land and sky, water and earth. Then God says, "Let the earth put forth vegeta- tion: plants yielding seed, and fruit trees of every kind on earth that bear fruit with the seed in it.... Let the waters bring forth swarms of living creatures, and let birds fly above the earth across the dome of the sky.... Let the earth bring forth living creatures of every kind: cattle and creeping things and wild animals of the earth of every kind" (Genesis 1:11, 20, 24). This is not a picture in which a distant God imposes life and order on earth, as if by force. Genesis 1 shows us a Creator who is in a dynamic, cooperative re- lationship with plant and animal life, enlisting and enabling crea- tures to grow and develop themselves.[2] It shows us a God who delights in the beauty and variety of life, a God who routinely pronounces that the world is good. In a manner quite unlike the neighboring Mesopotamian view, in which humanity exists to feed the gods, the God of Israel is one who provides food for every living creature.[3]

In the second creation story, beginning in Genesis 2, God's intimacy with and concern for creation become even more pro- nounced. Here we are told "God planted a garden in Eden, in the east" (Genesis 2:8). This is arresting language because we know that in the ancient world creation stories often portrayed gods engaged in violent battle. Not so with the Israelite God. God makes the first human being (*adam*) by taking soil (*adamah*) into his hands, molding it, and then breathing into it the breath of life. God does the same with all the plants and the animals. God enters into the ground so that out of it "every tree that is pleasant to the sight and good for food" (Genesis 2:9) can grow. God uses and molds the same ground to form "every animal of the field and every bird of the air" (Genesis 2:19).

It is hard to read this story and not see that God loves soil. God is near to it, working in it, so that the life called creation can flourish and be well. God does not relate to creation from afar. God's relationship to creation is that of a gardener who daily attends to the needs of the garden, making sure that its life is properly nurtured and protected.[4] This story teaches that gardening is profoundly important and fundamental work. Why? Because it is through gardening that life's fertility and growth occur. Moreover, it is through gardening that we learn to calibrate our desires and expectations to the needs and potential of the land we depend upon.

Its importance for us is underscored by the fact that God put the human being in the Garden of Eden "to till it and keep it" (Genesis 2:15). As this story describes it, the goal of all human life is to participate in God's watering, weeding, composting and soil-building life, and then to delight in it and with it in Sabbath rest.[5] When we garden the world, we not only live into our divinely appointed identity and vocation, we also participate in God's creative and sustaining ways with the world. We show that we are made in the image of God the Gardener.[6]

This theological picture of God's intimacy with and care for the Earth is hard to find in today's popular imagination. For many people, the world is simply the random assortment of elements that together function as a warehouse or superstore we can enter to get what we want when we want it. Our primary mode of engagement with the world is not as gardeners but as shoppers.

The story of how we came to this picture of the world as a bundle of natural resources waiting to be used by us is complex.[7] But we need to understand it, even if only minimally, if we hope to address the catastrophe that global warming promises to be. Among its most important elements is the idea that God is irrelevant to how the world is appropriated. According to the position that would come to be known as "deism," though God may have created the world long ago, God no longer matters because nature runs according to its own laws, laws that we can understand through science. And because things in the world do not have their end or purpose in God, the only value they can have is the value we assign to them. Using reason and technology we can engineer the world so that it becomes a place more suitable and comfortable for us. Following the admonition of scientists like René Descartes and Francis Bacon, people were encouraged to use their minds to master the world.

When we consider how much we have altered the face of our planet, for good and for ill, it is easy to see that we have excelled in our mastery. Using the insights of science and the tools of modern technology, we have constructed an industrial complex and a global economy that is rapidly consuming, and in many cases wasting, water, soil, timber and minerals—all through the burning of fossil fuels and the heating of our atmosphere. In our quest for cheap and copious amounts of food, we have created a culture of agribusinesses that destroy land, degrade plants, animals and farm workers, and are a major source of greenhouse gases. Of course, it would be a major mistake to view all the developments in medicine, sanitation, communication and transportation as bad. But when politicians and economists routinely tell us that the overriding goal of societies is to grow their economies because without such growth our high standard of life will come to an end, we need to think again.

Whether or not this "standard" of life is appropriate or justifiable is hardly ever discussed. Meanwhile we continue to pump carbon into the atmosphere, creating climate patterns that will bring devastation to our fields, forests, glaciers and oceans, and that will wreak havoc with our food systems and coastal communities. Regions of the world that currently produce enough food will find themselves facing more pests, droughts and destructive downpours, and less reliable weather.[8]

James Gustave Speth tells us that it took all of human history to build the seven-trillion-dollar economy of 1950. Today, economic activity grows by that same amount every decade.[9] Economies cannot grow at rates like this without exacting a heavy toll on our lands, waters and atmosphere. J.R. McNeill, a leading environmental historian, has documented this toll in terms of more specific indicators: from 1800 to 1990, energy use saw a 75-fold increase, with coal production accounting for a 500-fold increase; human population grew from one billion in 1820 to more than six billion today (and the overall appetite of today's citizen is far greater than it was nearly 200 years ago); world GDP increased more than 100-fold from 1500 to 1990; global freshwater use jumped from 110 cubic kilometers in 1700 to 5,190 in the year 2000, a nearly 50-fold increase; and soil degradation, either through mining or agriculture, has effectively compromised two billion hectares, an area roughly the size of the United States and Canada combined.[10]

These figures are alarming because they demonstrate that we are quickly burning, bulldozing and consuming ourselves out of existence. That we see no limits to what we can take from the world means that we have abandoned the idea that the world is a garden that has only so much and no more. That we see no problem with our often exorbitant desires and standard of life means that we have given up on our gardening responsibilities. What we fail to recognize is that in refusing the gardening requirements of attention and care we also condemn the whole world to a place of desolation and want. We have forgotten the words of the prophets who said long ago that abuse of the land and its inhabitants will bring down judgment in the form of trembling lands (Amos 8:8) and melting mountains (Micah 1:4).

Moving Forward

It is hard to hold onto hope when confronted with the complex and catastrophic effects of climate change. The degradation is systemic and the obstacles to positive change appear immense. Where does our hope reside? How are we to move forward in the context of a warming world that we are systematically degrading?

From a Christian point of view, the answer must be that our hope resides in the God who has not given up on us or on the world. When we take seriously the image of God as the eternal Gardener or Farmer we also discover that God has always been and continues to be present to the world as the source of its nurture and life. God still holds the soil of our lives in her hands, still waters the furrows of our crops and still breathes the breath of life upon all of us. That we are here today, able to grow and enjoy good food, is the confirmation of that. Though we may do much to assault the Earth, God has not ever stopped being a gracious and hospitable host to the world.

The major question, in my view, is whether we will encourage and help each other to be faithful to this God. Will we commit to participate in God's gardening and farming work in the world, and then make this commitment practical by turning some of the grounds of churches, synagogues and mosques into gardens that both feed others and make our neighborhoods more beautiful?[11]

Students from Duke Divinity School work as interns with community members in the Anathoth Community Garden, a ministry of Cedar Grove United Methodist Church. Photo by Norman Wirzba.

Places such as the Anathoth Community Garden at the Cedar Grove United Methodist Church in North Carolina provide models of this ministry, and my own students benefit from summer internships at this garden, where they grow food in a Christian community.

Will we accept our divinely given identity and vocation to "till and keep" the garden that this world is? Ecclesiastes 9:4 says, "Whoever is joined with all the living has hope." Despair is not an option for those inspired by God's love, because in despairing we signal our abandonment of each other. We communicate that the world and its inhabitants are not worthy of our care. Love, however, signals that we value the life of others so much that we are prepared to commit to them and join with them in a shared life. This is what God's love has been from the beginning. Are we prepared to love God by loving the world brought into being and daily maintained by God's love?

In an effort to make this love less abstract, I would like to suggest that gardening may be one of our most important and urgent tasks. I don't mean that everyone must therefore become a professional gardener, though it would certainly be a good thing to have as many people with hands in the soil as possible. Clearly gardening is not an option for all. But I do think that we have a responsibility—precisely because we eat and make food choices every day—to purchase food that reflects a gardener's priorities and cares. In other words, even if we may not garden ourselves, we have the daily opportunity as individuals and faith communities to encourage and support those who grow food in a way that honors God and nurtures the health of fields, plants and animals. When we learn that industrial food production contributes as much as 20 to 30 percent of today's greenhouse gases, we will also see that growing good food in an ecologically responsible way will go a long way toward healing creation.

Gardening is both an indispensable activity and a comprehensive attitude for how we approach the lives of others. It is a fundamental way of being in the world, even when we are not physically in a garden plot, because it shapes how we perceive, receive and engage others. Gardening is among the most intimate and practical (and delectable) ways we know for joining with the living—and with God as the source of life—because it represents our commitment and submission to the needs and potential of creaturely life. When we garden well we have the opportunity to slow down, become patient, pay more attention and perform more exacting and charitable work.

To garden well is to discover the paradoxical truth that self-fulfillment is achieved through our dedication to the life of another. We learn that our life is not something to be controlled but something to be received, nurtured and then shared with others. We experience the deep gospel truth that to save our life we must first learn to give it away (John 12:24, 25). When we do this we join hands with the God who is always seeding, watering, weeding, protecting, harvesting, sharing and delighting in the world. We enter into God's triune life, a life in which the Father, Son and Holy Spirit continually make room within themselves for the other to be.

It will appear counterintuitive, perhaps even quixotic, to recommend gardening in the face of problems like climate change and ecosystem collapse that are clearly global in scope. Does this not amount to a retreat from engagement with the powers that are hell-bent on exploiting and degrading the Earth?

Given the scope and speed at which our ecosystems are being destroyed, and given the unprecedented challenge of meeting the long list of social and ecological problems associated with climate change, there clearly is a pressing need for coordinated efforts among faith communities, nonprofits, scientists, business leaders and governmental bodies. We need international agreements to reduce the emission of heat-trapping gases, just as we need binding commitments to stop the erosion of our soils and the pollution of our waters.[12] These efforts, however, will not find the encouragement they need or be sustained if we do not change the attitudes and expectations that have brought us to this point.[13] We cannot continue to treat the world as an inexhaustible store or warehouse that exists for our own satisfaction. We need to shift our thinking and acting at the most basic levels. I propose that we recover a theological vision that apprehends and engages the world as a garden, and that invites all people to take up gardening affections and responsibilities.

When we adopt a gardening practice and perspective, we will be better equipped to move beyond the abstractions that often accompany our thinking about climate change and other ecological problems. What I mean is that for too many people the prospect of increased storm activity, erratic frost cycles, melted glaciers and the migration of biological pests registers only as a hypothetical possibility. There is little real appreciation for how changes of this sort directly compromise our ability to grow and share food. The problems of climate change remain "out there" and will be worked out "somewhere else."

The more we adopt a gardening way of being, however, the less likely we will see climate change in this hypothetical way. The more time we spend in gardens, or the more we get to know and depend upon those who do, the more we will understand that these global problems always have a local and regional origin and effect. This is another way of saying that the more that we can move into our gardening identity, the greater our attention in the world will be. With this increased attention we will also come to appreciate that the best thing we can do for the degradation that is being worked out all over the world is to refuse to participate in the degradation of the places upon which we stand and from which we draw our food. The healing of the world begins with the healing of the places where we live and the nurture of the soil from which we eat. It is as we learn to love our home places that we will see how precious the diverse home places of the world are. Learning to nurture and protect our own gardens, we will see how vital it is that all the world's gardens be healthy and whole.

Gardening work creates the conditions in which solidarity with all the world's eaters can develop. This is solidarity that begins with our love of the soil and then expands into love for all the creatures that grow out of it and are fed by it. There has never been a time when the need for solidarity was more urgent. There has also never been a time when God did not invite us into the gardening life that nurtures and sustains the world. My belief is that as faith communities grow gardens together they will not only help with the healing and feeding of the world—and thus serve as demonstration plots of God's Good News—they will also become more powerful witnesses to the God who daily sustains, protects and takes delight in creation, and who detests our abuse of it.

I may be a theologian of dirt, but more fundamentally I am an eater of the gifts of soil and sunshine, rain and wind. I am the daily recipient of the gifts of God that are, when closely held and gratefully tasted, as miraculous as the manna that long ago fed the Israelites in their exodus to the Promised Land. Our land and our atmosphere are today in peril. Like the Israelites, we need to hear the Good News that God has not given up on us or on the creation that is both beautiful and good. It is news that has the power to convict us of our irresponsible ways but also convert us into the image and likeness of God the Gardener.

◦ ◦ ◦

NORMAN WIRZBA, PH.D. is the research professor of theology, ecology and rural life at Duke Divinity School, as well as research professor at the Nicholas School of the Environment and Earth Sciences at Duke University. He is the author of books that include *Food and Faith: A Theology of Eating* and *The Paradise of God: Renewing Religion in an Ecological Age.*

CHAPTER 6

The Birds of the Air
Preaching, Climate Change and Anxiety

THE REVEREND BRIAN COLE

No one can serve two masters; for a slave will either hate the one and love the other, or be devoted to the one and despise the other. You cannot serve God and wealth. Therefore I tell you, do not worry about your life, what you will eat or what you will drink, or about your body, what you will wear. Is not life more than food, and the body more than clothing? Look at the birds of the air; they neither sow nor reap nor gather into barns, and yet your heavenly Father feeds them. Are you not of more value than they? And can any of you by worrying add a single hour to your span of life? And why do you worry about clothing? Consider the lilies of the field, how they grow; they neither toil nor spin, yet I tell you, even Solomon in all his glory was not clothed like one of these. But if God so clothes the grass of the field, which is alive today and tomorrow is thrown into the oven, will he not much more clothe you—you of little faith? Therefore do not worry, saying, 'What will we eat?' or 'What will we drink?' or 'What will we wear?' For it is the Gentiles who strive for all these things; and indeed your heavenly Father knows that you need all these things. But strive first for the kingdom of God and his righteousness, and all these things will be given to you as well. So do not worry about tomorrow, for tomorrow will bring worries of its own. Today's trouble is enough for today.

Matthew 6:24–34,
The Word of the Lord for the Eighth Sunday after the Epiphany 2011

The Sermon from the Pulpit, The Cathedral of All Souls, Asheville, North Carolina

A person who watches birds is called a birder. I am not a birder. I am a person who watches birders.

I first began watching birders 20 years ago when my friends Greg and Mark invited me to go bird watching with them. I showed up at the appointed time, wearing my basic relaxed spring uniform — button-down shirt with khaki shorts, baseball cap and clean running shoes. They showed up with the gear necessary for the day — binoculars, bird books, life lists of the birds they had already discovered and those birds they hoped to see at some point on this side of eternity. In my own life, I knew I had seen a cardinal, blue jay, robin, crow, turkey vulture. After that, I was a little fuzzy. I kept this knowledge to myself.

I had imagined we would set up a spot somewhere, and the birds would come to us. I mean they fly and everything, and they do not care to be chased. But instead of waiting for the birds to find us, we tramped through the woods with binoculars at the ready. As we walked, Greg and Mark spoke about bird walks past and what birds we might actually see that day.

At some point, they ceased looking for birds and instead focused on listening for them. It was in this moment that I realized I was way out of my league. My friends, the birders, admitted that they had recordings of bird sounds, which they listened to on occasion to sharpen their skills in the woods.

I pictured my friends, each in his own room, listening as a kind, sympathetic public radio-style voice introduced the warbler before it began to warble or the bluebird before it blew. For them, birds were not simply color and beauty to behold but also sound and song to listen for.

Once they began describing the bird sounds, I realized then and there I was a watcher and listener of birders and not birds. The world my friends were describing, where people paid close attention to small dashes of color or sounds of song without ever spying the singer, was a world I had never ventured into before.

"Look at the birds of the air."

Jesus invites us to look at birds, to a practice of seeing beauty and the kind of care God is able to extend to the things we can too easily ignore or fail to see altogether because we are busy, worried or anxious about things we are unable to control anyway. We confuse worry and anxiety with taking life seriously. But Jesus is clear that anxiety and worry do not constitute the life God intends for us.

In the ways we try to name the various images of Jesus for us, we include the confession of Jesus as healer, as the One who causes blind eyes to see and raises the dead and cures the leper. In the New Testament Gospel accounts, we are told Jesus does these acts without ever having Jesus walk us through exactly how to cause the blind to see or the lame to walk.

But in this passage from the Sermon on the Mount, Jesus shows us how to cure the anxious and the worrisome. Look at birds. Consider the fields. In other words, move the focus from you and the anxiety that you have made into a mountain, and go instead to an actual mountain. Go to a field, to a place where birds can be found, and for a time look upon them and not your own worries, which will not add to your life.

Along with looking at birds and considering fields and the beauty found in fields, Jesus instructs us to seek the kingdom of God as an antidote for anxiety and worry. Again, look beyond yourself; look into a landscape made by God, where God's justice reigns, where the virtues abound, where the teachings of Jesus are the native tongue.

When I consider anxiety and the kingdom of God, I am reminded of W.H. Auden and his poem "For the Time Being: A Christmas Oratorio," which includes in its chorus the lines, "He is the Truth. Seek Him in the kingdom of Anxiety. You will come to a great city that has expected your return for years."[1]

Auden's poem was written in 1942, in a dark time of war, and expressed a hope for God's enduring presence in the world, a world that would not be sustained by a sentimental God but only by the

God who has known death and overcome it. Only then could the One who lived in the shadow of the cross ask us not to worry, not to be anxious.

We live, as Auden has noted, in a kingdom of anxiety. We are making progress against a variety of diseases once considered fatal. We can communicate across the globe through wireless technology. Yet anxiety and worry seem to gallop along as always, reigning over us and marring our ability to strive for God's kingdom, because the land of anxiety distracts our vision and keeps our view collapsed in upon ourselves.

In the midst of the land of anxiety, there is a path to God's kingdom, to a place where we are invited to see beyond ourselves and to look upon all that God has made and has blessed as worthy of God's care and delight.

God delights in the bird, in the field, in the beauty that holds no dollar value, that cannot be bought or sold and that calls out for our allegiance to the God who is the true source of life and security. Anxiety will always be the false steward of our lives, robbing us of the *now* that God has given us. The theologian Stanley Hauerwas reminds us that when we seek first the righteousness of the kingdom of God, that which we seek is given to us, not achieved.[2] Anxiety and worry invite us to strive on our own, to wage a battle where we stand alone against all that causes us to fear.

At first glance, the words of Jesus about not being anxious seem like simple, comforting words, the kind of message you might find in a good self-help book or in any issue of *The Oprah Magazine*. But the words of Jesus directed to his disciples—to not worry, to not be anxious—reflect a deeper meaning when we remember who said them. Jesus is not simply saying to breathe deep, count to ten, look at a bird and remember a happy memory.

Jesus is inviting us to look at the birds, to consider the fields, and then to realize that the birds and the fields are not simply birds and fields. They are doorways into another land; they are exits from the land of anxiety. Those birds and those fields are the way in to God's kingdom.

When we look beyond our own anxiety, we can remember that Jesus came to save and to offer life that is real and abundant, life that serves and seeks the good of the other. Then we begin to see our own healing and to live as if Jesus has healed us, because he has.

Each month, the Cathedral of All Souls offers shelter and meals to women who would otherwise be homeless and on the streets. It is not enough for us to say to them, "Don't worry." When we look beyond ourselves, we can see them, the women who enter our community, and we can be reminded that in Christian communities, we are called to bear the burdens of one another.

When we look beyond our own worries, our own attempts to provide the security that ultimately only God provides, then we can begin to live without fear and walk through anxious places. We can offer Good News that is truly good because the source of the news is trustworthy; it has overcome death and invited us into another land, where our return has been expected for a long time.

In Isaiah, we are reminded that God has not forgotten us, the people who have been in exile, who have lived in anxious lands. God reminds us that our names have been inscribed on the palms of God's hands. God is inked up, in other words—with our names upon the hands of the Holy One.

And God awaits our return, reciting our names as prayers, waiting, waiting, for us to search for the bird in the field that takes us deep into the landscape of God, where we have not been forgotten, where our true home has always been.

Amen.

On Reflection: Preaching when the Climate is Changing

I preached this sermon at the Cathedral of All Souls, where I serve on the clergy staff. I include it in this book on churches and climate change because I believe those who preach in this anxious time need to reflect on how climate change has shaped Christian faith and how Christians hear sermons about creation from the pulpit.

The pulpit at the Cathedral of All Souls, Asheville, North Carolina. Photo by Wesley Duffee-Braun/Wesley Photography.

I once heard Wendell Berry speak in a seminary chapel. Before he began his remarks, he mentioned that he was always uncomfortable in front of, or behind, a pulpit. It was a witty remark and immediately captured Berry's feelings about the location of the lecture.

In contrast, I am at ease in a church, both before and behind a pulpit. Having grown up Baptist, with worship and church attendance an almost daily occurrence during childhood, I have heard countless sermons in my life. Today, as an Episcopal priest, I spend a great deal of time preparing to stand in a pulpit and to proclaim the Good News found in scripture.

I expect something important to happen in a sermon. I have been deeply moved, and also deeply offended, by sermons, but I continue to believe that the sermon is a vital way for Christians to understand how the story of God informs our own stories and how God's time shapes our time.

Those who listen to sermons and seek them out for a comforting word are often trying to find a way for the church as an institution to support their attempts to live out their faith in the world. The preacher about to preach needs to be aware that the young environmentalist in the pew is listening.

There is an often-cited quotation attributed to the 20th-century theologian Karl Barth that challenges us to read with holy scripture in one hand and *The New York Times* in the other. The image suggested by Barth is that we hear the story of the Bible in the context of the times in which we live. While in the Christian tradition we speak of Jesus Christ, the same yesterday, today and tomorrow, the way we respond to Jesus is deeply informed by the particular-ity of our own age. In our time, *The New York Times* is filled with stories about climate change, and the news is worrisome.

As a preacher, I am aware that the people who listen to my sermons do not hear them in a vacuum. They hear them alongside the stories of their own lives, their own hopes and dreams and their own understanding of the world in which they live. (As they listen to my sermons, they might also be scanning *The New York Times* with their iPhone apps.)

With each preparation of a sermon, at some point I begin to consider particular listeners and how they will hear the sermon next Sunday. Will the sermon on hope ring hollow to the woman whose husband just died after a long illness? Will the sermon on forgiveness honor the difficulty of forgiving a person who abused another? Will the sermon on contemplative prayer sound ridiculous to the young mother who is juggling children and work?

I am also aware that people listen to sermons with their own boundaries of what they believe constitutes a sermon. Sermons that address important social issues such as race, poverty, war and peacemaking can sometimes be accused of being political and not biblical. There is the old saying that the preacher stopped preaching and went to "meddling."

As an earnest seminarian many years ago in Kentucky, I spent some time in a farming community, attempting to explore how Christian congregations could support family farmers in a time when many farms were being lost at a rapid rate. As a part of this project, I surveyed several family farmers in Bath County, Kentucky, asking what role the local church played in their lives and vocations.

One question pertained to the role of preaching and whether clergy should preach on topics related to family farming and the economy. The responses to this question were divided between a desire to hear the topic of family farming addressed in sermons and the belief that clergy should stick to the Bible in their preaching.

What held the responses together was a strong belief that preaching should be rooted in scripture. The farmers who wanted to hear themes related to family farming in sermons saw their vocation related to themes of the care of land in the Bible. One woman stated she believed farming was the holiest vocation, after the ordained ministry, because the work took place outdoors in God's creation. She saw her life in the Bible.

The farmers who did not want farming mentioned in sermons were obviously family-farm advocates, yet they did not see their life and their work addressed in the Bible. Everyone wanted the sermon to be biblical. What was biblical, however, differed according to each farmer's understanding of what is contained in scripture.

The goodness of creation and the anxiety of distress

The story of the Bible is set in a world that was created by God, who recognized creation as good. Even though scripture admits that the natural world carries wounds of human brokenness within its life, the Christian tradition continues to note that the world of creation confesses God's goodness.

With a changing climate, when human activity has brought into real question the future viability of life on our planet, we must see that our actions have marred something God has made good. Climate change is both a scientific and a theological problem in light of God's work in the world.

Climate change has influenced the way we think about the natural world. I believe strongly that Jesus speaks a timeless truth about worry and anxiety and the human desire to control what cannot be controlled, and urges us instead to see daily life as a gift from God. But the invitation to consider the lives of birds and the flowers of the fields, instead of being a sign of comfort, might instead show us another opportunity for distress with the loss of biodiversity and avian populations and the dramatic sacrifice of farmland and green space to development and suburban sprawl. In other words, consider the birds and the field, and add to your sense of alarm!

Does anxiety concerning climate change eventually lead individuals to paralysis, to a sense of hopelessness? I know enough about climate change to know that we are no longer living in a time of avoiding it but rather, at best, managing how we live with and adapt to the measurable changes in Earth's climate. If we refuse this task, then the potential of climate collapse could cause many to choose denial rather than action; knowing our actions are coming too late can easily make denial more attractive than adaptation.

But the Christian who is motivated to act because of climate change might be especially well suited to the task *even if our work appears hopeless*, because the life and teachings of Jesus are given to us not with any expectation that we will be successful but rather that we will be faithful. If the Christian life is devoted to following the way of Jesus, then the way, we are told, involves walking toward death, *trusting that life is found on the other side*. We keep moving when some would seek to avoid pain or make scapegoats out of the behavior of others.

In the letters of St. John, we are told that perfect love casts out fear. In considering birds and fields, we are asked to see things that God has made, that God has loved. If we admit that Christians believe that God loves us in spite of ourselves and that we are invited to love as God loves, then our love of God's creation is not conditioned on its health and sustainability. If we love as God loves, then we love the bird and the field, even when they are distressed and under siege. If anything, our love and our care matters more when the life we are called to love is in need.

While Jesus' words remain timeless in this lesson, we might now hear them not simply as a call to let go of worry and anxiety in light of creation's beauty but also as a call to seek justice because something that God has made has been mistreated. Consider the bird and the field and then love them the way God loves them. Our love can motivate us to seek their protection, even if our attempts are potentially futile.

In this way, we end up bearing the burden of the natural world, of seeking its good, not out of our own self-interest that our actions will return us to some sort of "Garden of Eden" moment, but in order to walk in the way of Jesus, who bore burdens for others because of love.

Words that motivate love, not sentimentality

This sermon on the birds of the air also treated the natural world as timeless in the same way that Christians consider Jesus' teachings to be timeless. The world that I referenced in the opening story about bird watching assumes a perfect natural world, where beauty is encountered and all creation is wholesome and filled with grace.

While I would prefer to live in such a world, the listener to this sermon might prefer the world as we know it, not the world as I desire it. What would I find today if I went back to those same woods near Louisville where I first went bird watching with my friends? Has suburban sprawl expanded east into the county? Would we have to walk farther and listen more intently to see and hear the same number of birds?

Most sermons run the risk of becoming sentimental, of harking back to some golden time when it was easier to be faithful, when Sunday schools were full, when the world as we knew it (or interpreted it) seemed to work. In a time when chaos and uncertainty appear in abundance, the sentimental sermon can bring comfort, though it is a false comfort. Tell us about the good old days. Bless our postures of denial.

But sermons can also motivate instead of placate. Flannery O'Connor once said that you will know the truth and the truth will make you odd. We live in an age with warfare and misguided energy policies, with corporate, governmental and personal choices all reflecting unwise assumptions about our ability to manage God's creation forever without sacrifice. Choosing to live in this era with eyes open to all that denies life requires a strong willingness to be odd, to pay attention while not losing hope, to act without confusing right action with preferred outcome.

Sermons have often been used to motivate believers by feeding fear and anxiety, which is a gross distortion of the Christian gospel. If perfect love casts out fear, if love can motivate us to open ourselves up to others, especially the strange other that is the bird or the open field, then the larger effort to combat climate change might discover something essential about how to disarm fear and anxiety from the Christian tradition.

Regardless of who attempts to use fear and anxiety to motivate others, be it the evangelist in a street revival or the environmental group writing a letter to Congress, fear and anxiety are not sustainable for creating a permanent vision of how to live, of how to be in a world made by God, filled with beauty and hope and justice and grace. The call not to worry, therefore, is not an invitation to live in denial, to unplug from the world's needs.

Rather, acting out of love of God or love of bird or field is a wise choice, a sustainable choice, a choice that can be made again and again, regardless of how distressing or encouraging the next round of environmental news might be. What motivates us is not an avoidance of the fear placed before us, but rather the essential goodness of the life we share in this world. That is the vision that marks and motivates our actions.

Bringing the biblical world to our changing planet

For those who preach in the age of climate change, I would encourage us to make a home in the expansive world of the biblical story as we are given it, rather than the narrow spaces we have carved out for what we believe constitutes biblical preaching. Too often, biblical preaching translates into a disembodied conversation about spiritual matters, while leaving the natural world, the economies that shape our lives, and matters of war and peace to the realm of politics and public policy, better discussed by experts from somewhere else.

Churches often believe they are taking environmental concerns seriously when they hold a worship service outside. As someone who sunburns easily, I don't look forward to those Sundays. Also, such moves, if done in isolation, end up trivializing the very concerns we want to address.

Instead, allow the natural world to come "inside," to figure prominently in prayers and litanies and hymns and sermons. The biblical story is not simply a story of theological conversations between fellow humans or between humans and God.

The biblical world we encounter in scripture is a whole world, a flesh-and-blood place where nothing in life or the created world exists outside of God's concern or the vision that God gives to humanity. The care of the natural world is an ongoing concern of God and God's people. Preaching that does not engage the natural world has to go to great lengths to ignore the central place of creation in God's story.

In preaching, we are not trying to offer only a glimpse of that biblical world for selfish use in our own world. In preaching, we are attempting to collapse those two worlds, to allow the biblical world to completely encounter our own. Just as the children enter into Narnia through a wardrobe in C.S. Lewis's tales, so the sermon can be a door into another world, a sacred landscape that explains the world in which we live in the here and now.

Thus the threat of climate change is also an opportunity for Christians to correct our distorted view of the proper place of biblical preaching. By restoring the whole world of God's story to interact with our own, in both its pain and its grace, we give a more accurate picture of the true landscape of God's story. As congregations care for creation in the midst of climate change, we offer a whole vision of God's call for us to love and serve as Christ loved and served.

In my own tradition of Anglicanism, the Anglican Communion has promoted the Five Marks of Mission, which have guided mission work since the mid-1980s. The five marks are

To proclaim the Good News of the Kingdom
To teach, baptize and nurture new believers
To respond to human need by loving service
To seek to transform unjust structures of society
To strive to safeguard the integrity of creation and sustain and renew the life of the earth[3]

All these marks are interrelated and need to be understood as a whole approach to the mission of Christ given to us. We are not encouraged to say, "I prefer the first and the third mark." The marks are woven together. For Anglican preachers, the call to "sustain and renew the life of the Earth" has been lifted up by the wider communion for emphasis in preaching and mission.

To preach a hopeful vision of God's natural world in the face of climate change has precedent in America's civil rights era and the Black church tradition. The preaching of the Rev. Dr. Martin Luther King, Jr., and of countless other Black preachers whose names are not known to us, was preaching that acknowledged the realities of racism, of the violence done to African Americans and the need for the American society, and especially Christian congregations, to acknowledge our failure to live by our high ideals and principles, stated in the Constitution and upheld in a theological vision based in scripture.

But the preaching did not stop there. The preaching of that era also held up a vision of hope, of a time when the racial divide would be healed. Despite all the evidence to the contrary, African American preachers refused to cheapen their vision of what was possible, what was achievable, what was the vision of God's reconciling way.

"A tree gives glory to God by being a tree." This is how Thomas Merton begins an essay, "Things in their Identity," in his book *New Seeds of Contemplation*.[4] Merton goes on to say, "For in being what God means it to be it is obeying Him. It 'consents,' so to speak, to His creative love." Merton sets a vision, a vision that needs to be rightly proclaimed, that creation gives glory to God by being what God intended it to be.

If we, in our actions, prevent God's creation from achieving its true identity, we, the people of God, are culpable of silencing the message of the Good News. Considering the bird and seeking its protection and restoration allows us to seek God's kingdom while preaching without need of pulpits.

In Wendell Berry's novel *Jayber Crow*, we are told the story of a man living through the 20th century in rural Kentucky who serves

as a witness to the changes and chances that impact the fictional
town of Port William. Jayber, who once considered a vocation as
an ordained minister, instead becomes a barber and also a janitor
of the Baptist church in town. He occasionally attends worship
services and remarks on the young preachers who quickly pass
through the pulpit in Port William and their inability to know the
place where they are preaching: "They had imagined the church,
which is an organization, but not the world, which is an order and
a mystery. To them, the church did not exist in the world where
people earn their living and have their being, but rather in the
world where they fear death and Hell, which is not much of a
world."[5] Now is the time for pulpits to be places where we imagine
the church and the birds and the fields as all signs of God's presence and grace. Whether in front of or behind a pulpit, the Good
News needs to include all of creation again.

● ● ●

THE REVEREND BRIAN COLE is the sub-dean of the Cathedral of All
Souls in Asheville, North Carolina. He grew up in Hayti, Missouri
and attended the Southern Baptist Theological Seminary. An Episcopal priest, he serves on the Executive Council of the Episcopal
Church.

advocacy

You are my witnesses, says the Lord,
and my servant whom I have chosen,
so that you may know and believe me
and understand that I am he.
Before me no god was formed,
nor shall there be any after me.

<small>Isaiah 43:10</small>

How does God's love abide in anyone
who has the world's goods and sees a brother or sister
in need and yet refuses help? Little children, let us love,
not in word or speech, but in truth and action.

<small>1 John 3:17, 18</small>

CHAPTER 7

From Church Sanctuaries to the Steps of the Capitol

Faithful Advocacy for a Coal-Free Washington

LeeAnne Beres and Jessie Dye

*We all individually can do our part to slow climate change
by driving less, changing light bulbs and [carrying out]
other energy-saving efforts in our homes and churches, but
until we address climate change in a systemic manner—
such as passing a federal climate bill or phasing out coal—
we will always be treating the symptoms,
not finding a cure.*

The Rev. Brooks Berndt, Vancouver, Washington

ON FEBRUARY 14, 2009, Seattle University student Bryson Nitta had a dilemma: the 20-year-old environmental studies major didn't have a date for Valentine's Day. He saw an announcement for Environmental Lobby Day at the Washington State Capitol on February 14, and as an aspiring law student, he imagined that lobbying and environmentalism would be a good pairing—and take his mind off his romantic problem.

At this lobby day, Bryson learned about Earth Ministry and the faith-based environmental movement. "I went to Catholic schools all my life, and we learned about caring for creation," explained the tall, curly-haired Bryson. "But I had no idea that people of faith were actually lobbying on behalf of the environment—it totally blew me away." Because he needed to do a service-learning internship to graduate from college, he called Earth Ministry the following January and spent a semester putting both his faith and education into practice.

Founded in 1992, Earth Ministry was one of the first organizations in the country to link Christian faith with environmental stewardship. Today, it is a national leader in training people of faith in advocacy skills and in providing opportunities for religious voices to be heard in public-policy decision-making. At the time of Bryson's epiphany, Earth Ministry, through its Washington Interfaith Power & Light (IPL) project, had launched a campaign to phase out coal-fired power in Washington State.

As part of this ongoing campaign, Earth Ministry reaches out to congregations to educate members about the environmental and human costs of coal and the available alternatives. Bryson helped set up town hall meetings around the state on faith, climate and coal during his spring 2010 internship. His job was to contact local

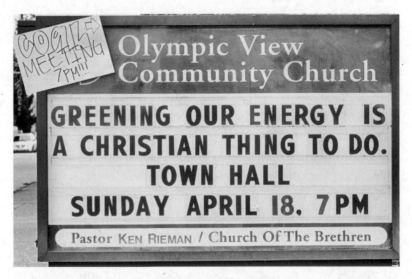

Earth Ministry hosted five "Beyond Coal" town hall meetings with congregations around the state to educate religious communities about the moral imperative to end coal-fired power production in Washington. Photo courtesy of Earth Ministry.

church leaders to let them know about these town hall gatherings in the lead-up to Earth Day in April.

"Hundreds of people came to the town halls in every corner of the state," Bryson recalled, "It was a great example of living out Jesus' call to discipleship." Two of the town halls were held in churches, and clergy spoke at all the events, along with scientists, state legislators and community activists. Bryson was especially pleased to set up a meeting in Spokane, his hometown in eastern Washington. Earth Ministry and its local partners hosted a community forum on the campus of Gonzaga University, at St. Aloysius Catholic Church, where Bryson's parents attend mass. Earth Ministry staff shared faith perspectives on climate and coal, and denominational statements on energy and climate change. Attendees viewed the short film *Covenant* on the faith community's involvement in the Texas coal wars, followed by an overview of how transitioning off coal will help meet Washington State's climate goals.

Bryson spoke about his faith journey to this packed gathering of clergy and local religious leaders. Many were from the social concerns committee at St. Aloysius, but they were joined by Quakers, Episcopalians, Lutherans and United Church of Christ members. "In my classes in college, I learned academic theories about sustainability," Bryson told the audience of his elders. "But riding over here tonight, I saw windmills in the Kittitas County fields and realized that this is the future." Bryson talked about the choices facing his generation to create a sustainable world with green jobs and clean energy. "My Catholic faith teaches me to love my neighbor and care about the poor," he said. "There is no better thing we can do for the poor and for future generations than to move beyond coal."

Inspired by his words, the audience put faith into action by handwriting personal letters describing climate change as a moral issue to their state senator, who also happened to be the Senate majority leader with influence over legislative decision-making about coal. In that moment, those 40 faith leaders turned into what are becoming increasingly common: religious environmental advocates.

From Individual Action to Faithful Advocacy:
The Evolution of Religious Environmentalism

Earth Ministry has led the way in caring for creation from a faith perspective since its founding 20 years ago. Earth Ministry's work relies on the strength of three paths to stewardship: individual faith formation, greening congregations and faithful advocacy.

Individual faith formation

To know and experience the sacramental presence of God in the natural world is an experience as old as human history. People can connect with the divine through nature and with God's presence in wild lands and gardens. As the Bible directs, "Stop and consider the wondrous works of God" (Job 37:14). Once the divine face of God is revealed through nature, it is a natural next step to make the connection between faith and care for God's creation.

The great monotheistic religions of Judaism, Christianity and Islam are unified in calling followers to practice stewardship and justice. Earth Ministry's initial programs helped people make the connection between spirituality and the natural world through experiential field trips, inspirational gatherings, lecture series and worship services. Feeling this connection with the divine in creation can help us make individual choices for sustainability, such as driving less, eating local organic produce, installing energy-efficient light bulbs, recycling and more.

Greening congregations

Once we as people of faith decide to honor creation in our own lives, we often seek to express these values with others in community life, worship and liturgy. Earth Ministry's Greening Congregations program asks faith communities to honor the Earth in their communal life. Some churches commit to creation-care language in worship services or educational offerings, and many make significant changes in the operation of their building and grounds.

Other choices include instituting toxic-free grounds care, using china instead of styrofoam, conducting a church-wide energy audit, purchasing energy-saving appliances for the church kitchen and hosting a community screening of an environmental film. Earth Ministry's church-based programs have a multiplier effect as people take what they learn at church into their home, business or professional settings. These programs give congregations the resources to care for creation while building a stronger community of faith.

Faithful advocacy

Individual actions and church commitments that respect God's gift of creation are imperative, yet a single vote by Congress or a state legislature can wipe out a thousand acts of Christian caring. Earth Ministry is now at the forefront of engaging people of faith in environmental advocacy, giving spiritual people the tools and the knowledge to make religious voices heard on such important issues as climate and energy.

Earth Ministry partners with other religious and environmental organizations in Washington State to build a vocal constituency for environmental protection. In 2006, Earth Ministry joined the Environmental Priorities Coalition, a coalition of 24 of the state's leading conservation organizations working to pass proactive environmental bills in the state legislature.[1] Now in its eighth year, the coalition annually selects four priority bills that will protect the air, land, water and people of Washington.

Members of the religious community have a right and a responsibility to make sure that their values are heard by elected officials, especially at a time when those who protect Earth's ecosystems are outspent by those who extract its resources. Nowhere is that moral voice more needed today than in the fight against coal.

Faith, Climate and Coal

Coal-fired power brings up images of the London of Charles Dickens, with the black smog of coal stoves hanging in the chilly Thames fog. A more modern version of this urban horror is the ubiquitous pollution in China, home to 16 of the world's 20 most polluted cities.

But in the verdant Evergreen State, most people are not aware that Washington uses the same coal power that sickened Victorian England and now shortens lives in China. TransAlta, the only coal-fired plant in Washington, is the state's single largest point source of carbon dioxide pollution, producing approximately 10 percent of total greenhouse gas emissions.[2] Carbon emissions from Trans-Alta are the annual equivalent of emissions from 1.8 million cars on the road and contribute to the one-and-a-half billion tons of climate-warming carbon dioxide that American coal plants produce every year.[3]

Mercury from the plant has been shown to cause neurological damage and developmental delays in children[4] and has been found in high concentrations in both Olympic and Mt. Rainier National Parks, the closest national parks to TransAlta.[5] The nitrogen oxide haze of TransAlta, the third worst in the United States for visibility impairment, also contributes to asthma rates in neighboring states.[6]

The largest source of carbon dioxide emissions worldwide is the combustion of fossil fuels such as coal, oil and gas.[7] Carbon dioxide emissions from coal combustion account for approximately 40 percent of global emissions from fossil-fuel use and about 80 percent of emissions from the US electric power sector.[8] In his book *Climate Hope*, Ted Nace quotes climate scientist Dr. James Hansen as saying that ending emissions from coal is "80 percent of the solution to the global warming crisis."[9]

This is not a new argument. In a 2007 letter to Kraig R. Naasz, CEO of the National Mining Association, Hansen states his case: "Cumulative CO_2 [carbon dioxide] emissions, which properly apportion responsibility for climate change, are coal (~50%), oil (~35%), and gas (~15%). Potential emissions from coal are even greater on the long term, given coal's larger proven reserves. As my colleagues and I have shown, the only practical way to bring human-made climate change under control is by phasing out coal use except where the CO_2 is captured and sequestered."[10]

Faced with these sobering facts, faithful advocates from around the country have joined together in a campaign to end the use of coal-fired power. Nationally, the Interfaith Power & Light network of 38 state affiliates coordinates a religious response to climate change, which includes moving beyond coal. In Washington, Earth Ministry hosts the Washington IPL project that spearheads a faith-based effort to transition the state off coal.

To be successful, Earth Ministry is reaching out to people of faith who have never spoken out publicly about faith and environment. By participating in trainings, clergy and lay leaders learn concrete skills to weigh in with state legislators and members of Congress on behalf of creation.

Religious Values and the Move Beyond Coal

All faith traditions teach that we have a responsibility to care for the poor and most vulnerable, the least of these among our human and natural communities. All God's children deserve enough food to eat, clean water to drink and safe air to breathe. We are called to work for justice while caring for the common good. Coal-fired power production runs counter to these deeply held religious values.

Coal destroys creation

As discussed in Chapter 9, mountaintop removal mining has already contaminated 2,000 miles of rivers and could continue to destroy more than 1.4 million acres of forested mountains.[11] Coal burning pollutes water, contaminates fish, rains sulfuric acid on our forests and leaves a legacy of toxic waste. Coal ash, one of the byproducts of coal burning, is a toxic substance often stored in retaining ponds where it can contaminate ground water.

Coal is damaging to human life

Every stage of the coal-fired process is dangerous to human health, from mining and processing to burning and storage of waste ash. Those most often impacted are the most vulnerable members of our communities: the poor, the elderly and the children. The connection between coal-plant pollution and asthma is convincing, but more silent and disturbing are the effects of mercury from coal plants. These toxins are known to cause neurological damage in babies and children. Coal burning is linked to the leading causes of death in the United States: heart disease, cancer, stroke and chronic lower respiratory diseases.[12] Nationwide, the health costs of pollution from burning coal top $2.7 billion per year.[13]

Coal burning is poor stewardship
Cleaner alternatives to coal-fired power plants already exist. Energy conservation alone would eliminate the need for a coal plant in Washington State. Renewable energy from wind and solar power, new ways to store power and smarter electricity grids can help make coal obsolete.[14] A green energy economy is one viable response to the current environmental and economic crises. In Washington, we can buy solar panels manufactured near the shores of Puget Sound and use power from windmills that provide income to wheat farmers on the east side of the Cascade Mountains. These choices support local businesses, provide good jobs for workers and ensure clean air and water for everyone.

Coal is an enemy of the common good
The worst effects of coal-fired pollution are yet to be seen. The impacts of climate change, including droughts and floods across the globe, will intensify over time as a result of a warmer planet with an unstable climate. We are called to work for generational justice and should not steal from our grandchildren what we have inherited from our grandparents.

Becoming a Faithful Advocate for a Coal-Free Future
What does advocacy for God's creation mean? How can people in the pews step out of the church and into the halls of power?

Marcy Lagerloef was initially anxious about making the leap to advocacy, as the thought of calling her legislators was intimidating. A lifelong Episcopalian with a master's degree in biological oceanography, she had retired from a 22-year career with the EPA—yet talking to her elected officials about climate and coal was something she never felt qualified to do.

At the same time, however, she had always seen a connection between faith and environment: "Creation is sacred to me," she said. "As a scientist, I know a lot about the interconnectedness of all life and love to educate and move people in a new direction." She felt energized by greening her congregation through organizing Earth Day services and promoting car-free Sundays at Grace Episcopal on Bainbridge Island near Seattle, Washington.

Through the training of Earth Ministry, Marcy found the confidence to call her legislators. "I realized that I didn't have to get every scientific fact and policy detail nailed down in order to speak to my representatives," she said. "I have a few minutes to share a bit about my faith community, my values and the general direction I want them to take in writing legislation. They were welcoming to me and happy to hear what I had to say. I had no idea it was this easy."

Since then, Marcy has trekked to the state capitol in Olympia several times, participated in organized lobby days and encouraged others in her church to meet with legislators. Because Earth Ministry's staff teach "faithful lobbying" workshops at these events, every newcomer to the legislative process becomes more at home in the offices of elected officials. Marcy has established an ongoing relationship with her elected officials, who remember her from visit to visit. They know her as a woman of faith and someone who cares deeply about her community, her neighbors and God's creation.

Like many people of faith, however, Marcy does not want to provoke conflict. "I'm seeking an alternative path to conflict, polarization, rhetoric and despair," she explained. "That means learning to hold a core of peace despite what is going on, and to operate from that grounding in faith." By relying on a spiritual foundation, religious environmental activists can transcend political divisions and policy disagreements, and focus on shared values.

Marcy isn't alone in making the leap from caretaker to faithful environmental activist. Back in Spokane, the group of religious leaders who listened to intern Bryson Nitta speak about alternatives to coal also felt moved to take their concern to the next level. In August 2010, Earth Ministry organized constituent meetings with two of Spokane's state legislators, Rep. Timm Ormsby and Sen. Lisa Brown, to discuss moving the state beyond coal. Eight religious leaders met with Rep. Ormsby and eleven with Sen. Brown. The group of citizen lobbyists represented five different Christian denominations.

Earth Ministry staff offered specific tips to the faith leaders for a successful meeting with elected officials:

- Introduce yourself as a person of faith by church, denomination or as a member of Earth Ministry.
- Try to find something good your elected official has done recently, and thank her or him for it.
- Pick one, or at most, two issues to focus on at a time. Too many topics confuse the issues and dilute the effectiveness of your comments.
- Be clear about what you are asking the elected official to do. Mention specific legislation by name or number if you can, both at the beginning and again at the end of your meeting.
- Speak from the heart, and emphasize your values. Nobody expects you to be a policy expert on these issues. Tell a short personal story and tell them why you (their constituent) care about this issue.
- Keep it short and simple. Don't be sidetracked by rhetoric.
- Don't be afraid to admit that you don't know an answer to a question. You're there to offer the moral perspective, not to answer detailed policy questions. Remember that your elected official works for you.

Both legislators listened closely to the group from Spokane and even shared their own stories and faith backgrounds. Felicia Reilly, a young mother, brought her infant son with her to the meeting with Rep. Ormsby. She later blogged about her reasons for partici-pating in the meeting: "I learned that the coal plant in Centralia causes mercury pollution that is especially dangerous to pregnant women and babies. As a mother of two beautiful boys, this was an outrage to me. I was aware of the scary statistic that newborns are, on average, born already exposed to over 300 contaminants from pesticides to industrial toxins. I was unaware that among those contaminants were pollutants from things like, you guessed it, coal-burning power plants."[15] Felicia and her son made a differ-ence that day, and people of faith just like her are having a positive impact in their communities too.

Green Energy: A Pastor Superhero

The Rev. Brooks Berndt, a United Church of Christ pastor in Van-couver, Washington, grew up with a father committed to social justice and the teachings of liberation theology, in which God is on the side of the oppressed. Brooks went to seminary at Harvard and received his Ph.D. through the Graduate Theological Union in Berkeley, California. Though politically progressive, he describes his theology as historically anthropocentric, focusing on humanity as the center of it all.

As a pastor, Brooks often makes up stories for the children's ser-mon that continue from week to week. For one series, he created a sequel to *The Lorax*, the book by Dr. Seuss. In developing his ser-mon, Brooks began to realize that care of nature and the sacredness of all life is central to Christian spirituality, and he began to use a theological lens to think about environmental issues.

It wasn't long before Brooks began thinking about climate and coal. From his own reading, he knew that the TransAlta coal plant, located about 100 miles from his church, was the largest contributor of carbon dioxide and other toxic pollutants in the state. Through Earth Ministry, he connected with local Sierra Club activists, and one day he received an email requesting a venue in

Vancouver to host a Coal-Free Washington meeting. Brooks offered his church, and the group that showed up included a mix of religious and secular environmentalists.

Like many pastors, Brooks has to balance competing interests. Two members of his congregation have worked at the TransAlta plant. "One of them has some sympathy toward the corporation, but strives to keep an open mind," he said. "The other has become involved in the coal campaign and is passionate about phasing out coal. It adds an interesting dynamic to my pastoral leadership."

Brooks expresses himself in creative ways using skits, dramatic monologues and comedy improvisation. As part of the Coal-Free Washington Campaign, he helped create a mascot, the Coal Monster, who looks like the old Kool-Aid pitcher. Fighting him would be Brooks' alter-ego: Green Energy.

A member of the congregation sewed boots and a hat to complement the green costume for Green Energy, the nemesis of Coal Monster. The debut of these characters occurred on the morning of a staid hearing at the State of Washington's Department of Ecology on nitrogen dioxide haze pollution from the TransAlta plant. Brooks and about 30 churchgoers and environmentalists held a mock battle between the two foes for a rush-hour audience. "I was in the parking lot dressed as the superhero Green Energy just as a FOX newscaster arrived to shoot footage of me zapping the Coal Monster," he said. The superhero Green Energy helped energize people around this social and environmental issue and preach the gospel in creative ways.

On a more serious note, Brooks often reminds his congregation why religious communities should become involved in social action. He points out that people of faith do good work by volunteering at homeless shelters and food banks, but at some point Christians must deal with the source of the problem—such as providing more help for homeowners on the brink of foreclosure or investing in community mental health treatment. The same is true on environmental issues.

"We all individually can do our part to slow climate change by driving less, changing light bulbs and [carrying out] other energy-saving efforts in our homes and churches," said Brooks. "But until we address climate change in a systemic manner—such as passing a federal climate bill or phasing out coal—we will always be treating the symptoms, not finding a cure."

Legislative Victory for a Coal-Free Washington

In late 2010, the Environmental Priorities Coalition chose "A Coal-Free Future for Washington" as one of its four priorities for the 2011 legislative session. Earth Ministry and its Washington Interfaith Power & Light project and the Sierra Club were the lead organizers of the campaign, which resulted in a bill to transition the state off coal.

As introduced, the legislation had two main elements. The first addressed the fact that the TransAlta plant was grandfathered in when the emissions standard was implemented and therefore did not have to meet the state's existing emissions performance standard, which limits the amount of air pollution from power plants in Washington: the legislation would apply the existing limits to the plant by 2020. Coal burning creates more than twice the air pollution allowed by this health-protecting standard, so TransAlta would have to significantly alter its operations or transition off coal.

The second part of the bill ensured a just transition for workers by requiring the TransAlta Corporation to develop a decommissioning fund to clean up contaminated land and to help Lewis County transition to more sustainable economic opportunities. The governor would appoint a local community board to approve the plan, and financial assistance from the state's economic development funds would provide additional community support.

This authentic concern about the economic well-being of the workers at the plant was a major focus for the public interest community, as TransAlta had laid off 600 mine workers overnight when the company ceased mining operations in 2006. The faith community in particular, driven by Jesus' call in the Gospel of

Mark to "love your neighbor as yourself," wanted to ensure that the transition to a clean energy future would create jobs and a healthy economy for the local community.

In the lead-up to the 2011 legislative session, bishops and pastors wrote opinion pieces for local papers, voicing moral support for cleaner energy and protecting the local community. Earth Ministry helped to organize groups ranging from the United Methodist Women to the Unitarian Universalist Voices for Justice. Churchgoers from districts throughout the state contacted their legislators by phone and email, reminding them that burning coal goes against religious values. Christian clergy and Jewish environmentalists testified at hearings in favor of the bill. Religious leaders went from office to office at the state capitol distributing information about the legislation and the reasons their communities supported it. And last but not least, Bryson, Marcy, Brooks and hundreds of other faithful activists showed up in force to call for a Coal-Free Future for Washington at Environmental Lobby Day on February 15, 2011.

These efforts paid off with a legislative victory and landmark agreement. The bill's progression through the state legislature prompted the TransAlta Corporation and governor's office to enter into negotiations with the public-interest community. In a grace-filled moment, with all the stakeholders at the table, a historic agreement was reached on March 5, 2011 that reflected the parties' shared vision of a coal-free future for Washington.[16] The elements of the agreement included

- a staggered phase-out of coal-burning at TransAlta, with one boiler going off-line in 2020 and the other in 2025 as the plant meets the state's emission performance standard
- pollution controls for nitrogen oxide applied to both boilers by 2013
- a decommissioning plan to clean up the site of the coal plant once it shuts down, and to prepare the land for future economic development
- TransAlta contributions of $30 million to a community invest-

ment fund for energy-efficiency projects and economic development in Lewis County, and $25 million to an energy technology transition fund, which must be spent on supporting innovative energy technologies and companies in Washington State.[17]

The state Senate incorporated the elements of this agreement into the Coal-Free Future for Washington bill (SB 5769) and passed it later the same day with strong bipartisan support. The bill then went to the House of Representatives, where the coordinated efforts of the environmental, religious, health and labor communities, along with support from TransAlta and the governor's office, secured passage in mid-April. It was signed into law by Washington Governor Christine Gregoire on April 29, 2011.

The new law phases out coal burning in Washington, protects residents from harmful air pollution and invests in a clean energy future for Lewis County and the rest of the state. It represents common ground and shared values among environmental organizations, the religious community, labor unions, the local community, the TransAlta Corporation and elected officials — almost unheard of in these polarized times. This historic achievement reflects a model for the nation of how moving from dirty fuels to clean

Representatives from the state legislature, industry, labor, environmental, health and religious organizations stand with Governor Christine Gregoire as she signs the Coal-Free Future for Washington bill into law on April 29, 2011. Earth Ministry Executive Director LeeAnne Beres is on the far right. Photo courtesy of Earth Ministry.

energy can create jobs and build a healthy economy. It is a resounding "Yes" to protecting the gift of God's creation while caring for God's people.

For every group of citizens speaking from their deepest values, there are plenty of industry lobbyists wearing expensive suits rather than clergy robes. But religious advocates have the long arc of history bending toward justice on our side, and we faithfully persevere. Working in community, we came one step closer to a Washington State where children breathe clean air, green jobs strengthen our local economies, energy conservation and renewables provide the bulk of our energy, and our daily lives reflect the values of our faith.

Engaging in policy advocacy is surprisingly energizing and is a necessary next step in our commitment to achieving Jesus' vision of a just and loving society. It also helps to build our faith through the practical application of spiritual discipline. Advocacy requires us to examine and recommit to our deepest values, which are at the core of our religious beliefs. In return, our faith provides us with the inspiration and energy to lead, and to ensure that those values are reflected in decisions made for the greater good of the community.

Yet faithful advocacy is more than just lobbying in the state capitol or sending a letter to Congress. The need to advocate for the least of these among us, whether human or other of God's creatures, is the work of the soul. To be an advocate for all creation is to be part of a movement, a community of people who believe that another world is possible and who are engaged in what eco-theologian Father Thomas Berry called "the Great Work." To be a faithful advocate is to joyfully answer, "Yes!" when responding to Jesus' invitation to discipleship.

*   *   *

LEEANNE BERES is the executive director of Earth Ministry in Seattle, Washington, and its Washington Interfaith Power & Light project. She has 20 years of experience working on energy and fisheries issues with environmental organizations in Seattle. LeeAnne has a master's degree in marine fisheries management and worships at Fauntleroy United Church of Christ.

JESSIE DYE is the program and outreach director of Earth Ministry. She has a law degree and decades-long experience working with faith communities in conflict resolution and mediation, especially with the Catholic Archdiocese of Seattle. Her home church is St. Mary's Parish in central Seattle, and she is the mother of two grown children.

CHAPTER 8

Turning Over
the Money Tables
The Economy, Green Jobs and Congregations

Michele McGeoy

We are committed to being good stewards of the Earth,
and that is not just about caring for nature but also caring
for our neighbors who struggle with the realities
of a challenging urban life.

The Rev. Sylvia Vásquez, Walnut Creek, California

In *THE GREEN COLLAR ECONOMY*, author Van Jones shows how one solution can address our two biggest problems by both invigorating our economy and caring for the planet. He makes a strong case for investing in the training of green-collar workers. "Rather than creating job-training pipelines that put these kids at the back of the line for the last century's pollution-based jobs," he notes, "we need to be creating opportunities for them to be at the front of the line for the new clean and green jobs."[1] Today's economy is built on and powered by oil, natural gas and coal, all diminishing non-renewable resources that contribute to climate change. We need to move out of the pollution-based gray economy and into a healthy new green economy.

In Richmond, California, we have been doing just that—training underemployed and unemployed people to work in the solar industry. At the grassroots organization Solar Richmond, we conduct three-week, hands-on solar installation training sessions in partnership with the city's "RichmondBUILD" pre-apprentice construction training. Each session offers intensive instruction to prepare trainees to work in the solar industry. As part of the training, the students install a two-kilowatt solar-electric system on the roof of a low-income Richmond residence.

In 2007 Van Jones came to the first solar installation completed by our students on an elderly resident's home. The event featured the mayor and other dignitaries, coverage by the media and an announcement by one of the larger solar companies with deep venture-capital backing that it would hire hundreds of people in the next few years.

Then the dust settled. The cameras went home, and we went back to the shop. Three of our graduates had interviews with the solar company, but none of them was hired. In fact they returned from the interviews feeling disrespected by the process. A Latino graduate, Santiago, was asked if he "thinks in Spanish." The interview focused on anger management rather than construction skills, with questions such as, "What would you do if your boss yelled at you or a co-worker dropped a tape measure on your foot?"

From this painful experience for our graduates, it became clear to me that training was only a first step, given the cultural divide between those seeking jobs in a green economy and the companies creating the jobs. A second challenge was getting our graduates enough work experience to compete in the job market. To meet the challenge, Solar Richmond moved the interview process from the desktop to the rooftop. We started a staffing agency to make it easy for companies to try out our graduates. We would cover the risk of the insurance liabilities, and they would hire our graduates for a specific job. And this is where faith-based communities have made a difference in promoting a green economy, as they green their congregations.

Churches have been at the forefront of connecting the environmental movement with social justice. In 1987 the United Church of Christ's Commission for Racial Justice issued the famous docu-

ment, "Toxic Wastes and Race in the United States: A National Report on the Racial and Socio-Economic Characteristics of Communities with Hazardous Waste Sites."[2] In this first national study
correlating waste-facility sitings and race, Benjamin F. Chavis, Jr.
wrote, "This report is intended to better enable the victims of
this insidious form of racism not only to become more aware of
the problem, but also to participate in the formulation of viable
strategies."

The new green economy enables communities of color to take
a proactive position in the greening of our planet. We are called
to care for creation and address the issue of climate change, but as
Christians we are also called to care for the poor. Green-collar jobs
connect people who need the work with work that needs doing.

St. John's Uses Purchasing Power to Create Opportunity

St. John's Episcopal Church in Oakland, California, had raised
enough money to purchase a solar energy system, and the congregation wanted to invest in renewable energy and create opportunities for people in our community. Solar Richmond helped the
church collect and evaluate bids from solar installers who were
willing to try a few of our graduates on the job. The dynamic in
our relationship with the solar companies shifted when we were
able to say, "Here's a one-hundred-thousand-dollar job, and we'd
like to get a bid from you." The church committee decided to hire
Sun Light & Power because of the company's reputation for quality work and its commitment to hire our alumni in the past.

Our graduate, Eliseo Navarro, joined the installation crew for
the week-long job. In that time he proved himself to be a strong
worker and was subsequently hired full time. Not only did the
church's ecology group lower St. John's carbon footprint but it
also used its purchasing power to create a full-time job for a graduate who otherwise might not have gotten this opportunity. Gary
Gerber, president of Sun Light & Power, saw this collaboration as
a win-win relationship. "We get new business and have an opportunity to try out local talent," he said. Bob Davidson from St. John's

Markell Parker and Eliseo Navarro install panels at St. John's Episcopal Church in Oakland, California. Photo courtesy of Solar Richmond.

was grateful for the upfront help Solar Richmond provided in collecting and analyzing data for sizing and design of solar systems. "The service was useful to us at St. John's, and it was consistent with our desire to give back and support our local community," he said.

Changing Larger Systems — Turning Over the Money Tables

At St. John's, one church with a small solar project influenced the career of one of our graduates, but larger change must happen on a systemic level. Getting doors to open for our graduates has proven much more difficult than I had imagined.

Directly across the freeway from the office of Solar Richmond is a manufacturer of one of the most efficient solar-electric panels in the world. The company installed a large system on its own roof, yet we were not able to get a single graduate on the job, despite the fact that one of our board members worked for the company. We made repeated calls asking if our graduates could play some part in the installation but were told that they were on a deadline and could not afford the slightest delay to the project. The company is an efficient organization that, like all for-profit entities, is beholden to investors to make sure that returns are maximized.

Having worked in the solar industry for eight years, I often encounter what I call the "clean conscience" that says, "I'm saving the world by installing solar panels, so I don't have time to worry about race and class issues." While this attitude does create efficient companies, it overlooks the possibility of creating a new economy that will "lift all boats."

Shipbuilding during World War II helped build the economy here in Richmond. Many African Americans moved to Richmond from the South and worked side by side with women entering the workforce for the first time. Kaiser's Richmond shipyards built a total of 747 Victory and Liberty ships for the war effort, more than any other site in the United States. The city broke many records, even building one Liberty ship in less than five days. Richmond grew, seemingly overnight, from 24,000 people to 100,000 people.[3]

In 1945, the shipyards shut down as fast as they had started up four years earlier. Tens of thousands of shipyard workers, many of whom had relocated to California, were thrown out of work. As returning servicemen reentered the workforce, women and minorities were no longer welcome. Richmond entered into a long period of economic decline and stagnation that persisted for decades.[4]

When I started working in the solar industry in 2004, I realized that this new, green economy had the potential to lift Richmond out of its continued dire economic position. In 2005, Richmond had one of the highest poverty rates in the Bay Area and the second highest per capita murder rate in the state.[5] Despite the fact that Caucasians were not the majority of residents in Northern California, the vast majority of employees at the company where I worked were white. As I looked at the racial makeup of other solar companies, this disparity seemed common. Something needed to be done to ensure that our residents would benefit from the green economy.

With the city's high murder rate and the strong presence of Chevron as Richmond's largest employer, the only time Richmond was in the news was when someone was killed in the streets or the environmental community was battling the refinery. The introduction of the solar industry into our community changed both this perception and the reality. Since 2006, Solar Richmond has been recognized as a model green-collar jobs program by the Community Action Partnership and the Oakland-based Ella Baker Center for Human Rights, and the company received the Barbara Boxer Conservation Champion Award. National media, including *USA Today*, *The Oprah Magazine*, *TIME*, *NPR* and *Solar Today*, have featured articles about Solar Richmond's pioneering work.

While Richmond has a unique story, it is not unlike many urban cities in the country. The wealthiest five percent own 63.5 percent of the nation's private wealth.[6] Not only is there a massive wealth divide in our country, but the divide follows racial lines. Four decades after the civil rights movement, African Americans still earn only 57 cents and Latinos 59 cents for each dollar of white median family income. The differential is even starker for net wealth—the total value of investments, savings, homes and other property minus any debt. Blacks hold only 10 cents of net wealth, Latinos 12 cents, for every dollar that whites hold.[7]

Tremendous resources are being invested to address climate change. At this critical juncture, the rich could continue to get richer by exploiting these technologies, or the poor could begin to prosper from them, narrowing the gaps in both income and wealth.

I believe that churches can help to create a new economic system rooted in equity and justice. In the temple in Jerusalem, Christ turned over the money tables and chased out the merchants. We have been unable to do so to the all-powerful financial institutions that created the banking and mortgage crises, but there is still hope that we can transform the economics of energy. As Christians we are called to take care of God's beautiful creation *and* to care for the poor. This new green economy has the potential to create wealth across demographic and racial lines, and the church has the potential to influence that change.

An Alternative to Traditional Finance

A living example of that potential is St. Paul's Episcopal Church in Walnut Creek, California, known for maintaining the town's oldest parish chapel, a sturdy redwood building consecrated in 1891. The parish wanted to install solar panels but lacked the capital to invest; nor could the tax-exempt institution take advantage of the 30 percent federal tax incentive available to for-profit businesses. In spite of that, the congregation now has 135 solar panels on its 120-year-old roof—a formidable achievement that sends a powerful public message to the community.

For years, congregation members talked about going solar but couldn't see beyond the real financial constraints of the upfront costs. In 2007, the church partnered with Solar Richmond to create a solution. Together, Solar Richmond and St. Paul's set up a system that supplies nearly all of the church's energy needs without adding any of the solar initiative's $187,000 cost to the parish budget.

Creative financing for environmental stewardship

Although the 500-member church secured donations for part of the system, the bulk of financing was made possible by investors in the congregation. Led by Dave Mattern, the dedicated chair of St. Paul's environmental committee, parishioners banded together and formed a private limited liability corporation (LLC) to take advantage of available solar rebates and tax incentives. They named their company Sonlight Solar Power.

After securing the investments, a power purchase agreement (PPA)[8] was formed between Sonlight and St. Paul's. Under this agreement, Sonlight owns the solar arrays and provides solar electricity to the parish at a fixed rate competitive with conventional utilities. Funds previously allocated for utility company payments now go to Sonlight to pay back the investors.

Solar Richmond was able to secure pro bono assistance from a San Francisco law firm, Hanson Bridgett LLP, to represent the church throughout the PPA process. "We were inspired by the community benefits of this project," said lead attorney Steven Miller. "The combination of environmental benefits and economic development is powerful and exciting." The investors plan to transition ownership from Sonlight Solar to the church once all tax benefits are realized and their investments are repaid in full.

The array on the roof of St. Paul's comprises 135 solar photovoltaic (PV) panels with a peak-power capacity of 28 kilowatts. The system includes five inverters to convert DC to AC power. Over the lifetime of the panels, the energy generated will prevent more than 1.7 million pounds of greenhouse gas emissions from being released into the atmosphere by conventional power plants, an amount equivalent to the pollution caused by 575 cross-country road trips. According to the US Department of Energy, it takes more than 178 acres of trees one year to absorb this much carbon dioxide.[9]

Lifting up the community

As the environmental team at St. Paul's began shopping for a vendor, they were not willing to compromise on the quality of installation, but they were willing to have the job take a little longer to create opportunities for those from the neighboring community of Richmond. They contracted with Real Goods Solar with the agreement that the company would bring on graduates from the Solar Richmond training program for a portion of the labor. The Reverend Sylvia Vásquez was proud that her parish would be a leader in community change. "We are committed to being good stewards of the Earth, and that is not just about caring for nature but also caring for our neighbors who struggle with the realities of a challenging urban life," she said.

As part of the training, the graduates had installed a small residential system on the roof of a low-income Richmond residence. The installation at the church provided experience for these gradu-

Solar Richmond graduates provide service to the community by installing panels on Richmond Village, an affordable housing project. Photo courtesy of Solar Richmond.

ates on a larger array, working with professional installers from Real Goods Solar. Setting up the system was an opportunity for these graduates to gain experience working side by side with seasoned installers where they could earn a living wage and their technical skills could shine. "I learned to install solar on my neighbor's roof, and now I'm out in Walnut Creek working on a system ten times as large," said Angela Greene, a Solar Richmond graduate who is now working for the City of Richmond's Green Academy.

Moving forward

The system set up by St. Paul's and Solar Richmond, developed and refined over the past ten years, reflects an extraordinary congregation working to create a new model of collaboration between faith communities and businesses. Such a structure encourages multilevel partnerships among churches, nonprofits, for-profit energy companies and individuals. The finances, taxes and legal aspects of the project were complicated and demanded time from members like Dave Mattern, who had the expertise to create the investors' LLC and the dedication to manage it for years to come. Pulling together members of a congregation to invest and start a company is not an easy feat. The path is made easier by such companies as Trinity Solar and Solar City, which offer PPAs or leases to churches, provide the infrastructure and set up all the financing so that the church puts no money down yet realizes savings from the reduced electricity bill.

Another resource for churches is a new start-up company called Solar Mosaic, a web-based platform that enables communities and congregations to pool their members' investments to create financing for their place of worship. Congregants purchase "solar tiles" to fund the project. Then, by receiving annual payments from Solar Mosaic, they get their money back over the time it takes for the solar installation to pay for itself.

Solar Richmond also has created a for-profit entity called Solar-ForAll that can realize the tax benefits and pass them through to the churches via lowered electricity prices. In partnership, Solar Mosaic and SolarForAll can help solarize a house of worship without the congregation putting any money down, and they can also make sure that jobs are created for the disenfranchised. We are currently piloting the offering in the Bay Area and hope to eventually offer this service nationally.

Barriers to Employment

Creating this bold economic shift is not as simple as training people how to find a rafter in a roof or mount an inverter. The realities of living in poverty create many barriers to successful ongoing employment, including lack of decent, affordable housing, transportation, childcare, healthful food and access to education.

A further barrier is the culture gap between decision makers and graduates struggling to move on a pathway out of poverty. I recently spoke with the CEO of a solar energy company who was reluctant to give our graduates a chance. When I explained that not all of our graduates own cars, he replied, "That makes me uncomfortable. The kind of person who doesn't own a car—is that the kind of person I want on a rooftop with a million dollars worth of solar panels?"

Then there are the effects of living amid such a high level of violence. Last year one of our students, Jahon Gadlin, was shot and killed in North Richmond. We brought in a trauma debriefing counselor to help other students process the loss of their classmate. The counselor asked them how many had lost a friend or family member to violence. The tears streamed down my face as I watched all the students raise their hands.

Jahon's parents came to what would have been his graduation. Our staff presented a plaque inscribed with a poem he had written called "I Am." Not only did his parents have the strength and courage to come to the ceremony, but they also spoke and encouraged their son's classmates to persevere and succeed. They thanked us profusely for the transformation they had seen in Jahon in the weeks leading up to his death. Our work is not just about jobs; it is about deep transformation, healing and connection.

Many of our students have lived through or witnessed traumatic events, including shootings, incarceration and violent death, and most have experienced the barriers of race and poverty. Solar Richmond is offering more intensive resources to students to help them cultivate the necessary leadership skill of emotional intelligence, to increase their resiliency in the face of such trauma and to help address residual post-traumatic stress disorder. Because of the impact of early stress, many youth in our community need a specialized curriculum to maximize their strengths.

For example, as a result of traumatic stress, some of the young adults we work with have difficulty concentrating, are prone to suspicion and over-reaction and are vulnerable to post-traumatic reactions to both job-related and interpersonal demands. Research shows that traumatic stress has long-term effects on the nervous system, resulting in heightened sensitivity to stimuli and to criticism and a tendency to become emotionally overwhelmed. To ensure that these young people learn the necessary job skills, we must address their psychological as well as educational needs.

In our training, we teach students how the human brain responds when it feels threatened, so they can recognize the signals when they are triggered. We practice techniques such as deep breathing and repeating mantras that calm the nervous system. Through this holistic training, we believe our graduates will be more likely to lead healthier lives and sustain meaningful and well-paying careers as a part of this new green economy.

Ownership

At Solar Richmond, we are also learning from other green-job training programs across the globe to improve our future programs. To turn the tables on our economic system, we need to think in terms of wealth creation, not just poverty alleviation. It is not enough to just provide training for entry-level jobs; we need to provide a pathway into leadership and ownership.

One model we have followed is that of Ohio Cooperative Solar, a Cleveland-based company that owns and installs PV solar panel arrays on institutional, government and commercial buildings. The Ohio Cooperative Solar provides wealth-building opportunities in order to stabilize their community. The company is 100 percent owned by the workers who live in Cleveland and face barriers to employment.

Another example for our future lies in worker-owned co-ops such as they have in Spain. In 1956, in the town of Mondragon, a Catholic priest named José Maria Arizmendiarrieta founded a corporation that is now a federation of worker cooperatives. This cooperative is now the seventh-largest business in Spain, providing employment for 85,066 people working in 256 companies.[10] At the MONDRAGON corporation, executives never make salaries higher than nine times the lowest-paid workers. This contrasts with the fact that the salaries of S&P 500 CEOs average $10.5 million, 344 times the pay of typical American workers.[11]

Christ spoke out against the imbalance of power in his time, and I can only imagine what he might say today about the wealth gap in our country. In Richmond, we are working toward providing a pathway out of poverty and into ownership for our graduates by creating a worker-owned business modeled after these examples.

In 2010, the number of killings in Richmond fell from 47 to 21 in just one year.[12] The year before, Richmond was recognized as having installed more solar wattage per capita than any other large Bay Area city.[13] While Solar Richmond cannot take the credit for either of these statistics, I do like to think that the work we have done in our community has contributed to both of these successes.

In Richmond and across the world, the impacts of climate change will fall on the poor and most vulnerable. The chair of the Intergovernmental Panel on Climate Change, Rajendra Pachauri, says, "It is the poorest of the poor in the world, and this includes poor people even in prosperous societies, who are going to be the worst hit."[14]

But Proverbs 31:9 (NLT) instructs us, "Yes, speak up for the poor and helpless, and see that they get justice." As Christians, this new green economy is our opportunity to meet our call to care for God's creation as well as our call to care for the poor. The good news is that it's not only Christians who have this call: Judaism teaches the value of *tikkun olam* as the imperative to repair the world, and the Buddha taught his people, "Like a caring mother holding and guarding her only child, so with the boundless heart hold yourself and all beings."[15]

All religious traditions call people to care for the Earth and for the poor. Imagine if every place of worship were to install solar panels on its roof while making sure that the wealth created from the work goes to serving those in need. The faith-based community could make a significant difference in the lives of many by standing up and using its power to build a new green economy inclusive of all.

❖ ❖ ❖

MICHELE MCGEOY is an entrepreneur and the founder and executive director of Solar Richmond, a California-based nonprofit organization that provides training and work experience for young adults in green jobs in the solar industry. She worships at First Congregational Church in Berkeley, California.

CHAPTER 9

The Cross in the Mountains

Mountaintop Removal in Appalachia

FATHER JOHN S. RAUSCH

We of various faith communities assemble to pray with residents of the mountains. These communities live with fear caused by the devastation of mountaintop removal. We pray for renewal of human and ecological communities throughout the mountains and for alternative work to bring greater diversity and choice for employment. We pray by raising the Cross of Christ to remind us that Earth belongs to God by creation and to us by delegation, and ultimately God must rule over all human affairs.

From a prayer read at The Cross in the Mountains
ecumenical service, September 11, 2010

STORM CLOUDS gave the sky a changing pattern of light and darkness and offered some cover from the searing sunlight of the record-hot September of 2010. Seventy-five Christians gathered to pray atop Pine Mountain near Whitesburg, Kentucky. The Cross in the Mountains was designed as an ecumenical prayer service to renew Appalachian communities, with many of the prayers addressing the aggressive mining practice known as mountaintop removal. The four-acre prayer site looked onto Black Mountain, where strip mining was destroying part of Kentucky's highest ridge.

Mountaintop removal lops off the tops of mountains, sometimes as much as 500 to 800 feet, with enormous blasts that loosen

Mountaintop removal mining has devastating impacts on the ecology and health of communities throughout Appalachia. Photo courtesy of Fr. John S. Rausch.

the ground above the coal seam. In this form of strip mining, the loosened earth, called overburden, is then pushed into the valleys below, filling the streams and creeks. The coal is scooped up by front-end loaders and hauled away by trucks carrying more than 100 tons for processing and cleaning.

The price paid by the local residents includes the flooding exacerbated by denuded mountains, water polluted by mine drainage and cracked foundations from blasting. In addition, this mining practice destroys the local ecosystems. Mountaintop removal is the cheapest way to mine coal, but it's also the most destructive.

A Call to Prayer

Research on the economic and environmental impacts of mountaintop removal is available online with a few keystrokes. Only political will and moral outrage against mountaintop removal is lacking, and public prayer provides a vehicle to speak to the heart of people of faith about this issue.

The prayers written for The Cross in the Mountains combined gratitude for creation's beauty with forgiveness for its abuse. The gathering prayers reflected a holistic view of community, including a healthy environment for children, safety for miners, sustainable jobs for the unemployed, best-practice forestry management, clean water and security from flooding and property damage caused by mountaintop removal.

The Cross in the Mountains continued the nearly decade-old struggle to galvanize the faith community around the pernicious effects of mountaintop removal. Grassroots organizations such as Kentuckians for the Commonwealth and the Ohio Valley Environmental Coalition began the campaign on the political front long before religious folks got involved. However, the faith community brought prayer and religious symbols that moved the struggle to a different level.

This chapter examines the historical role of Christians confronting mountaintop removal and uses The Cross in the Mountains service to reflect on the connection between public prayer, mountaintop removal and climate change. By ascending a mountain in prayer, people of faith leave the confines of their church buildings to bear witness to an oppressive social structure. In the process, participants themselves have experienced the embrace of nature and become more committed to the care of creation.

Discovering the Potential of Public Prayer

Beginning in the 1960s, when the mining industry was gouging out mountains with little restraint, people in ministry began listening to the cries of those without power. The Commission on Religion in Appalachia, consisting of 18 Christian denominations, was organized in 1965 in response to the poverty and underdevelopment of the region. This ecumenical group encouraged the pooling of human and financial resources to address problems such as unemployment, housing, health care, labor, black lung, welfare rights and regulations for strip mining.

In 1970, clergy and lay people formed the Catholic Committee of Appalachia, a network of people of faith who began to listen in a systematic way to stories from local residents affected by the power of corporations. The experience initiated a two-year process that culminated, after 100 small feedback sessions, with the first Appalachian Catholic bishops' pastoral letter, "This Land Is Home To Me."[1] The document put church efforts squarely behind creation and the poor, creating a tension between some coal executives and people in ministry.

History provides some context for the contradictions between the wealth of coal and the powerlessness of the people. Introduced in 1964, the War on Poverty legislation failed in Appalachia because its programs were based on the "culture of poverty" theory, which emphasized that people from more traditional cultures lacked the skills and attitudes for success in the modern world. From this perspective, overcoming poverty required changing the personality of mountain people in Appalachia.

Many academics soon realized that the "culture of poverty" theory basically blamed the victims, who were constrained by political and economic structures. Local power structures in the mountains served the interests of absentee corporations that owned the timber and coal resources and controlled the land like a mineral colony.

In a 1981 land ownership study, one percent of owners controlled 44 percent of the land in the 80 Appalachian counties sampled. Of the 13 million acres of surface land in the study, 72 percent was held by absentee owners, as were 80 percent of the mineral rights. Astonishingly, more than 75 percent of the mineral owners paid less than 25 cents per acre in annual taxes.[2] This absentee ownership and inadequate tax base denied community services and opportunities for residents of the mountains. The powerlessness of the people came from the social, economic and political structures that surrounded the coalfields.

One of the first uses of prayer to confront the inequity and impact of mountaintop removal happened near the coal camp of McRoberts in Letcher County, Kentucky, which had not experienced a severe flood since 1957. Beginning in 2000, it suffered five major floods in a period of 18 months. Lucius Thompson lived about 1,000 feet from the blasting site at the head of Little Tom

Biggs Hollow in McRoberts. The mining company sometimes used a supercharge of dynamite to loosen the rock, and the blast tremors caused an addition on his trailer to separate from the main structure. When it rained, Lucius put buckets throughout his house to catch the water dripping through the cracks caused by the blasting of mountaintop removal.

One day, three of his great-grandchildren, the oldest seven years of age, were playing in front of the house when a heavy thunderstorm sent the children running inside. A moment later, a torrent of water rushed down from the strip site, flushing debris and mud from the hillside with a force so powerful that any child or elderly person could have been swept away.

"If you don't live the life, you don't know what it's about," lamented Lucius. In response, the mining company claimed it operated within the law, and only God could send rains causing floods.

With little economic or political power to confront the coal interests, the religious community responded with the only true force it had: prayer and symbols. At the time, I served as the coordinator of the Peace and Justice Commission for the Catholic Diocese of Lexington, Kentucky. In collaboration with the Rev. Steve Peake, pastor of the Corinth Baptist Church in Fleming-Neon, I organized a prayer service to invoke God's healing for the damage caused by mountaintop removal to both the human and natural communities. We invited the Associated Press to attend the event.

We chose December 10, 2002, the United Nation's International Human Rights Day, to link human rights with the right to a safe and healthy environment. I wrote a proclamation that was signed by all four Catholic bishops of Kentucky, read during the service and later published in *Origins*, the documentary service of the Catholic Church.[3] Today it represents the only pronouncement on mountaintop removal that has been issued by the Catholic hierarchy.

The day of the service was overcast and windy, an uninviting day for public prayer, but we assembled at the Rev. Peake's church

to caravan up the mountain. We wound up narrow twisty roads until we reached a spot overlooking McRoberts in the valley below.
The site appeared like a moonscape of disturbed gray dirt, slate
and rocks awaiting the eventual hydro-seeding that would pass for
reclamation.

Liturgical churches are strong on sacraments and symbols, elements that give insight to the numinous and the mystery of the
divine. This service incorporated a song, readings, prayer and a
closing symbolic action. To end the service, I gave everyone a handful of wildflower seeds and proclaimed, "For the glory of God and
the restoration of community, let's take back the mountain!"

Given the weather, I predicted that the participants would fling
the seeds, jump in their cars, and head to the valley for the hot
soup and coffee awaiting us at the nearby community center. Yet in
a matter of minutes, the 60 participants dispersed over the mountain like people with a mission. Folks took time and intention
to plant their seeds where the ground cried for life — in a cranny,
near the edge of the ridge, behind a rock. These witnesses talked in
whispers as they consulted with each other about where to plant
their seeds.

Catherine Odem, a senior citizen of McRoberts, pondered the
scene as she walked among the rocks and dirt. A lifelong resident
of the area, she finally paused where she thought she would have
the best view of the mountain. Then with a symbolic gesture of
hope and determination, she scattered her handful of wildflower
seeds and said, "I'm sowing my community back!"

The Associated Press ran a story on the McRoberts prayer service, and one angry Catholic called the nearby parish in Hazard,
Kentucky, to protest the involvement of Catholic leaders in mountaintop removal. Scattering wildflower seeds on a strip mining site
exemplified a David-versus-Goliath gesture in this battle that has
significant impacts on the health of both ecological and human
communities.

The EPA's Clean Air Task Force found that fine-particle pollution from coal-fired power plants causes more than 30,000 pre-

mature deaths a year.[4] A National Academy of Sciences study estimates that more than 60,000 American babies could be overexposed in utero to mercury from coal-fired plants, possibly causing poor academic performance later in life.[5]

Erica Urise of Grapevine, Kentucky, testified before a panel of religious leaders that she bathed her three-year-old daughter in water highly contaminated with arsenic before she realized the danger. Health experts have traced the higher rates of nausea, diarrhea, vomiting and shortness of breath experienced by the children of Letcher County, Kentucky, to the sedimentation and dissolved minerals in the drinking water.[6] The cheap energy derived from coal-fired electrical plants results in serious unintended consequences.

In terms of climate change, every mining operation releases quantities of methane into the atmosphere. This greenhouse gas contributes to global warming, but it disperses in the atmosphere within a single decade. Carbon dioxide, a more troubling greenhouse gas emitted from coal-fired electrical plants, persists for many decades or even centuries in the atmosphere.[7]

At the time James Watt patented his steam engine in the late 1700s, the concentration of carbon dioxide in the atmosphere was roughly 280 parts per million (ppm). By 1900 it had risen to 300 ppm, and today, as noted in Chapter 3, it stands at nearly 390 ppm.[8] Keeping coal cheap through mountaintop removal encourages greater reliance on coal-fired plants for electricity, which only adds to the larger problem of global warming.

Going to the Mountaintop to Pray

The coal industry has rarely felt comfortable dealing with moral and religious principles, emphasizing instead arguments based on employment, economics and engineering. The Kentucky Coal Association states on its website: "Under most circumstances, we are of the opinion religion should not play a role in political debate. Recently, however, we've learned some religious leaders are railing against mountaintop mining..."[9] The statement then encourages dissenters to reflect on Isaiah 40:4, 5 (NAB): "Every valley shall be filled in, every mountain and hill shall be made low...."

In 2003, Bishop Walter Sullivan, moderator of the Catholic Committee of Appalachia, decided that he wanted to see mountaintop removal up close. As bishop emeritus of the Diocese of Richmond, he encouraged the Catholic bishops of Lexington and Knoxville to accompany him and asked me to oversee the tour. The bishops, with their staff and representatives from leading Catholic organizations, wanted to hear both sides of mountaintop removal. So I contacted a group of coal executives from St. Francis Catholic Church in Pikeville who had previously complained to the bishop about my writings on mountaintop removal.

Shortly thereafter, a representative from the Kentucky Coal Association sent word about bringing a PowerPoint presentation and a video to the feedback forum scheduled for the second day of the bishops' tour. I responded to my Pikeville contact that the forum was designed for open dialogue, not a public relations blitz for industry, and I needed to withdraw any invitation to that representative. "The important part is your testimony," I wrote to my friend in Pikeville. "So tell honestly how you feel the church should or should not respond to community needs."

The tour had scheduled a series of flyovers in a four-seater plane to view mountaintop removal from the air. We arrived at the Hazard airport, which the coal industry boasted was built on a reclaimed mountaintop removal site, but wind gusts that day grounded the small plane. Still, mountain roads around the area allowed views of vistas filled with scars while heavy mining equipment created plumes of dust that rose off a coal bench in the distance. Later, the Rev. Peake showed the 25 participants the highwater mark in his church from the latest flood in McRoberts. That night a stream of local residents gathered at the Hindman Settlement School and recounted stories of polluted water and cracked foundations due to mountaintop removal.

During the feedback forum the next morning, coal executives, religious leaders and academics made statements about mountaintop removal, especially from a theological or moral perspective. The Rev. Jim Sessions, a former executive director of the Commission on Religion in Appalachia, addressed the bishops and made an impassioned plea for the abolition of mountaintop removal and all strip mining. Several others from Catholic organizations reminded the bishops of the justice issues surrounding mountaintop removal.

Then, when the appointed time came for the coal executives to speak, an uninvited guest from the coal industry took the floor. As a Catholic from Lexington, the man may have thought he could talk convincingly to the bishops. In reality, he had crashed the forum, and without his slides and charts, he could only stammer about the economic and social dimensions of employment and reclamation. His arguments imploded with no reference to the social justice questions raised by others. Instead, he kept repeating, "There's another side to this issue; there really is another side."

Bearing Witness to Mountaintop Removal

While many Christians have denounced mountaintop removal, those who see the destruction firsthand often find greater authority to speak out. To that end, I have organized tours that bring religious leaders to the mountain. In 2007 I helped to develop "The Religious Leaders' Tour of Mountaintop Removal" for 22 religious leaders, which was featured in the *Renewal*[10] DVD broadcast on numerous PBS stations. This tour included a flyover, visits to backcountry mining sites and a panel of local citizens. The climax of the experience took place when participants signed a proclamation on a mountain site 200 feet above an active strip mining site.

During the last day, the participants hiked a mile up a steep grade to a spot overlooking a panorama of destruction. Our musician began playing "Amazing Grace," and people's hearts sank as they saw the feverish mining activity around them. Before the second verse, every head turned to see an explosion below and a puff of smoke rise from the loosened rock. "This is idolatry!" one said.

Participants saw firsthand the power needed to mine the coal that kept their lights on.

In an instant the witnesses grasped the reality of their pledges in the proclamation: "First, each of us will examine our own wasteful and extravagant lifestyle that causes the destruction of the mountains by demanding cheap energy from coal." Those people of faith recognized that the culprit was frivolous consumption and corporate greed, not the workers toiling below for the good of their families.

The experience sparked the indignation to speak truth in congregations and community gatherings, as promised in the proclamation: "Second, we pledge voice and vote against mountaintop removal. Our voices will retell the testimony we have heard and the destruction we have seen through our sermons, our writings and our conversations."

Subsequently many attended contentious public rallies, with strident and threatening counter-demonstrators nearby. When I mention mountaintop removal in my own sermons, depending on the parish and the political climate, occasionally people get up and walk out. It seems coal offers comfort and convenience, and many people expect the same from the church and its religious leaders.

Prayer Brings Conversion through the Way of the Cross

These experiences using prayer to address mountaintop removal coalesced in The Cross in the Mountains service, which involved a traditional prayer format pliable enough to integrate the issues of the mountains. The ancient *Via Crucis*, or Way of the Cross, could incorporate reflections about mountaintop removal, drugs, violence, the environment, sustainable jobs and other issues affecting the health of Appalachian communities. Made popular in the late Middle Ages, the Way of the Cross traces the last hours of the life of Jesus in 14 stations, from his condemnation by Pilate to his burial and resurrection. Just as the Way of the Cross invites believers to relive the hours of torture and crucifixion of Jesus, we recalled the torture of Earth and its possible death as we walked from station to station.

At the first station ("Jesus is condemned to death"), we remembered the legal instrument that separated surface rights from mineral rights leading to strip mining: "The broad-form deed condemned the land." The fifth station ("Simon of Cyrene helps Jesus to carry his cross") noted how people of faith can follow the role of Simon carrying the cross with Christ (Matthew 27:32, Mark 15:21, Luke 23:26): "Religious leaders and friends of creation speak out." During the eighth station ("Jesus consoles the women of Jerusalem"), we recalled that "Mothers and spouses weep over the death of miners." By the eleventh station ("Jesus is nailed to the cross"), we reflected that "Drug and alcohol addiction nail many, especially the young, to a cross for life."

Slowly and reverently, the participants followed a large processional cross from station to station. Each person held a smaller white cross with a sin against creation written on the crossbeam: "470 Mountains Leveled," "Water Pollution," "Destruction of Land." While most of the crosses highlighted offenses against the human community, a number of them spoke directly to the environment: "Ozone or Particle Pollution" and "Endangered Species of Plants and Animals." Participants chose a cross of sin from 30 themes as their personal prayer for reparation. Many chose their theme based on an aspect of destruction that had an impact on their daily lives. The physical scars of the mountains gripped their attention, and the growing awareness of coal's consequences on the health of human communities also called for conversion.

Coal wrapped in barbed wire

The prominent symbol used during The Cross in the Mountains service was, of course, the cross. As a symbol, the cross speaks to the Appalachian religious culture as the sign of salvation. The Cross in the Mountains also became a play on words: mountaintop removal was "the cross" the mountains had to bear. Seen in this

Christians carry the cross during an ecumenical prayer service for the renewal and protection of Appalachian communities. Photo courtesy of Fr. John S. Rausch.

way, a cross could unite Christians with people of faith from other religious traditions who care for creation.

Larry Sloan, a local artist from Knott County, Kentucky, designed and crafted the seven-foot-tall cross, which weighed 25 pounds and featured a lump of coal crudely shaped like a heart, wrapped in barbed wire, and affixed to the center of the crossbeam. During the procession, three participants carried the cross and then held it upright at each station. At the last station ("Jesus is laid in the tomb"), commemorating the resurrection, the cross stood upright on the property's edge with the fleeting mountain mist revealing the scars of Black Mountain in the background.

Coal wrapped in barbed wire offered an artist's expression of critical contradictions in Appalachia. Coal supplies nearly half of America's electricity, but black lung currently kills 1,500 former coal miners each year.[11] The coal industry pays some of the highest wages in Appalachia, but coal counties remain some of the poorest. Coal is known as a cheap form of energy, but residents near coal mining sites live in fear of flooding and polluted water.

Requiem for the mountains

Sam Newton, a student from Maryville College, played two haunting melodies on the bagpipes to begin and end the service, the music stirring hearts as we asked for God's help. Equally captivating was the "Requiem for the Mountains," composed and sung in Latin by Dr. Hunter Hensley of Eastern Kentucky University. Dr. Hensley had performed his requiem several times in auditoriums for Earth awareness programs, but he told me that he always intended to sing it at a strip mining site. "I think the heavens just opened for you. You're gonna get your chance," I replied.

The prayer site for The Cross in the Mountains was a field that had been leveled when the highway department needed earth and rock to improve US 119 just outside of Whitesburg. The venue offered a panoramic view of Black Mountain and occasionally the faint sounds of earth-moving equipment stripping the mountain. A small pavilion equipped with battery-powered microphones allowed participants praying silently to hear Dr. Hensley chanting his requiem even at the most distant station.

A requiem seemed most appropriate for the service. More than 500 mountains in Appalachia have been destroyed by mountaintop removal and more than 1.2 million acres of hardwood forest cleared.[12] Two-thirds of the native songbirds are in decline,[13] and the cowbird, a prairie species, has begun nesting on strip sites. Life as assigned by God is dying or being altered, and a requiem reminded us of the ultimate questions of life and death.

Mountaintop removal is the subjugation of creation. In Genesis God looked over creation and found it "very good" (Genesis 1:31), signifying its inherent worth. The text doesn't say that God found it "very useful." God so loved the world that God joined it (John 3:16), and sent the Son not "to condemn the world, but in order that the world might be saved through him" (John 3:17). After the resurrection, Christ needed creation, represented by his body with nail prints and side wound (Luke 24:39–43), to demonstrate God's power over death *and destruction.* Christ is called the "first-born of all creation" (Colossians 1:15), so seemingly at the end of time, creation won't be thrown away like a useless piece of paper. In reality, all creation awaits its own freedom from corruption and a share in the redemption of Christ (Romans 8:21; Colossians 1:20).

A simple meal and fellowship

This entire prayer service took approximately 50 minutes, with the last part hurried by the brief rain that greeted us at the fourteenth station. Under the pavilion, we raised our hands and blessed the mountains to indicate our solidarity with creation before the last dirge from the bagpipes. In the distance people looked toward the cross, which stood at the edge of the property against the background of moving mist and the scars of Black Mountain.

After prayer, the participants gathered for a time of mingling, food and conversation. Sliced apples and pears, Monterey Jack and cheddar cheese, humus and crackers made a light lunch that captivated folks when the McDonald's in Whitesburg was only two miles away. Part of the prayer encouraged simple living and appropriate lifestyle changes.

The sad reality is that coal continues to reign as king. With less than 5 percent of the world's population, the United States consumes more than 22 percent of all electricity generated in the world.[14] Coal will be used for decades until we account for the full cost of the health and environmental consequences.

A Closing Call for Mountain Justice

As faith communities use prayer and symbols to open people's eyes to these injustices and effect a conversion, there will be pushback from the power structures. When the local television news reporter from Hazard, Kentucky, an epicenter of mountaintop removal, covered The Cross in the Mountains, the slant emphasized that religious people are against mountaintop removal because more coal exists in deep mines than in strip mines, and deep mines employ more workers. The media switched the focus from a moral and religious analysis to an economic and social one, and no one in the viewing audience was offended. Even with symbols and prayers, the references to moral principles can be usurped.

So what shall we say to people of faith about the call for mountain justice? Mountaintop removal represents one small note in the song of creation, yet it is utterly graphic, unlike the disappearance of a species that we hardly miss or the rise of carbon dioxide that we seldom notice. Photos, tours and stories about mountaintop removal reveal our economic inefficiency, quest for profits and idolatry of growth like few other environmental efforts. The unsustainable nature of our current lifestyle produces chasms of destruction and exacerbates the impacts of climate change on all God's creatures.

My own struggle against mountaintop removal has raised my awareness of the spirituality inherent in the web of life. In the context of scriptural teachings, the beauty of creation described by numerous Psalms inspires a contemplation of God's handiwork in the mountains that rekindles my human spirit. While God creates in abundance, I also recognize my call to bear the cross of asceticism and not overuse the bounty intended for everyone, both now and in subsequent generations.

My spirituality compels me to join my voice with those who speak out to revere creation. I need contemplation from the beauty in nature, and I feel bloated when I overconsume. I feel purpose when I act with care beyond my own self-regard. To disregard this internal compass is, for me, to lose direction in my life. This insight has shifted my understanding from a focus on humans to one of humanity-in-creation, from dominance to mutual interdependence. For me the challenge now remains to transform thinking within the church from a pyramid with humanity on top to a circle that puts humanity within the web of life guided by the mystery of God.

In the end, The Cross in the Mountains crystallized nearly a decade of public prayer by using a traditional devotion. It combined elements of a demonstration, a celebration, and a time of prayer that meant conversion for some and a deeper commitment for others. The way to the heart seldom seems paved with facts and figures. That path appears filled with spiritual moments that, with the help of public prayer and symbol, deepen the presence of God among us.

○ ○ ○

FATHER JOHN S. RAUSCH, a Glenmary priest, is the director of the Catholic Committee of Appalachia and lives in Stanton, Kentucky.

justice

Speak out, judge righteously,
defend the rights of the poor and needy.

PROVERBS 31:9

He loves righteousness and justice;
the earth is full of the steadfast love of the Lord.

PSALM 33:5

CHAPTER 10

Faith and Flight

Immigration, the Church and the Climate

JILL RIOS

Jesus began his earthly journey as a migrant
and as a displaced person.

From "A Priest's Views of Immigration"[1]

I WORSHIP AT La Capilla de Santa Maria, a predominantly Spanish-speaking faith community of immigrants from Latin America. I am a mother raising a bilingual child, an environmental educator and an instructor of English as a Second Language (ESL) in western North Carolina. My life is lived at the intersection of immigration, the church and climate justice. I experience profound sadness as communities adopt and enforce punitive policies toward immigrants—and defend those policies with anger and fear. As I accompany close friends through the deportation process, I have felt deep disappointment, fear for my loved ones and a sense of loss.

Just as North Carolina was not planning to prepare coastal communities to deal with a rise in sea levels, it is fair to say that this state was also unprepared for the arrival of thousands of immigrants from Mexico and Central and South America.[2] As demographic trends have changed this region, climate change has also arrived and will continue to transform this state and nation. People of faith have a moral obligation to advocate for forward-thinking

167

plans that account for the significant movement of human populations as climate change reshapes the world. Indeed, in the Christian tradition, "Jesus began his earthly journey as a migrant and as
a displaced person."[3]

Many of our parishioners at La Capilla come from the state of
Michoacán, Mexico, the overwintering site for monarch butterflies
that migrate through the United States. Environmental and economic forces influence the movement of both human and nonhuman populations across geographic regions, especially in the face
of climate change. The migration of the monarch butterfly (*Dan-
aus plexippus*) provides a stepping stone for exploring the concept
of environmental refugees and the response of La Capilla to the
local realities of immigration.

As Christians, we have an ethical obligation to care for creation,
seek justice and welcome the stranger. To that end, this chapter
uses migration as a lens to explore the journey of the monarch butterfly, the movement of human populations due to climate change
and the story of La Capilla as a congregation. My hope and challenge is that religious communities will provide a prophetic voice
to welcome strangers into our communities in ways that reflect
our Christian values and protect God's Earth.

The Monarch Butterfly: A Talisman for Migration

The monarch's extraordinary migration is unrivaled in the insect
world, as it migrates twice each year for a total journey of nearly
3,000 miles. I have marveled at monarch migration since working
as a college intern at Mosquito Hill Nature Center near my childhood home in northern Wisconsin. This winged beauty is a non-
threatening and powerful symbol that has become a talisman for
me as I continue to understand population movements.

In 2010, the *Asheville Citizen-Times* reported that the numbers of
migrating monarchs had declined by 75 percent in one year alone,
in part because of changing weather and vegetation patterns resulting from climate change.[4] In Michoacán, Mexico, both legal and
illegal deforestation of the fir forests also threatens the overwinter-

ing sites, and therefore the long-term survival of monarch populations, as well as human populations.

As a migratory group, the monarch is under considerable threat from both climatic extremes and human activity. In 2010 the World Wildlife Fund included the monarch on its annual list of the most threatened species in the world, along with charismatic megafauna such as the polar bear and the giant panda, all species threatened by climate change and habitat loss.[5] Frequent storms and unseasonable weather, such as unusually cold spells and hailstorms, have sometimes caused the loss of millions of butterfly lives.

A *National Geographic* feature article and corresponding television series document animal migratory journeys that inspire awe in humans and ensure the survival of species. David Quamman writes, "There's another reason why the long-distance journeys of wildebeests, sandhill cranes, monarch butterflies, sea turtles, and so many other species inspire our awe. One biologist has noted the 'undistractibility' of migrating animals. A nonscientist, risking anthropomorphism, might say: Yes, they have a sense of larger purpose."[6]

I have also come to appreciate the extraordinary journeys of human migrants who are from the same region where the monarch butterfly overwinters in Mexico. By using the metaphor of the monarch, I am not suggesting that the majority of immigrants from Latin America migrate to the United States solely for environmental reasons. However, I do believe that environmental degradation has become one of the root causes of migration across the world. As the book *The Age of Migration* reveals, "Human beings have always migrated in search of new opportunities, or to escape poverty, conflict or environmental degradation."[7]

One Sunday, as my husband and I drank our morning coffee before heading to church to worship among immigrants, we read an article in the local *Hendersonville Times-News* announcing the arrival of the monarchs en route to Mexico, a journey celebrated each season as the butterflies return through the Blue Ridge

Mountains to the endangered oyamel fir forests in the mountains of Michoacán.

The article stated, "People think the Parkway is the only place to see monarchs, but any soccer field in Buncombe or Henderson Country is a good place to see them."[8] We commented on the irony of this comment in the newspaper—in a town where many of our parishioners have been detained due to their immigration status.

The article continued with suggestions for tracking "this natural wonder through the Blue Ridge" and yet made no connection between the phenomenon of human migrants and monarchs. The article *did* mention that if you go to any soccer field in this region, you will likely see "them"—monarchs. It did not mention that you will see our Mexican brothers and sisters on any soccer field as well—many of whom have migrated from the same high-elevation forests.

Environmental and Climate Refugees

In February 2010, severe storms during the dry season and excessive logging resulted in mudslides that killed at least 34 people in the town of Angangueo, Mexico, near the largest and most pristine monarch butterfly sanctuary, Sierra Chincua.[9] Many of the displaced people from this community remain environmental refugees. *The World Disasters Report*, published by the International Federation of Red Cross and Red Crescent Societies, maintains that more people are now forced to leave their homes because of environmental disasters than war, with an estimated 25 million people who could currently be classified as environmental refugees.[10]

Environmental refugees or migrants are defined as people forced to migrate away from their homeland due to sudden or long-term changes to their local environment. One of the leading scholars of environmental migration, Norman Meyers of Oxford University, predicts that the number of environmental refugees due to climate change will increase six-fold over the next 50 years to 150 million.[11] Climate refugees are people forced to migrate due to sudden or gradual changes in their natural environment related to the impacts of global warming.

Environmental refugees and environmental migration are concepts that remain controversial. In its conventions, the United Nations currently has no formal recognition of environmental refugees as a group with a rightful claim to protection and sanctuary. As *The Economist* reports, climate change creates a new underclass of travelers for whom "the classic definition of refugees—tossed between states by war or tyranny—is outdated. Eco-migrants will be paperless paupers, whose multiple woes are hard to disentangle."[12]

Climate justice involves alleviating the unequal burdens created by climate change. The church's response to climate justice must include preparing for an increase in climate refugees throughout the United States and helping communities adapt to changing environments. Climate change and climate refugees are at our coastlines, borders, doorsteps and the narthexes of our churches. Are we prepared for the conversion?

Discernment: Understanding and Prioritizing Adaptation to Climate Change

Discernment involves prayerful reflection leading to an understanding of God's call.[13] To discern right actions in the face of a warming planet, we must first remember that loving and welcoming the stranger is at the very heart of Christian discipleship. Second, it is important to understand two concepts: *mitigation* and *adaptation*.

Mitigation

The International Panel on Climate Change (IPCC) defines mitigation as "an anthropogenic intervention to reduce the sources or enhance the sinks of greenhouse gases."[14] In lay terms, this means reducing carbon emissions through such basic energy conservation efforts as replacing incandescent light bulbs with compact fluorescents in our sanctuaries and our homes.

It may also mean participating in the Interfaith Power &
Light (IPL) campaign's Carbon Covenant project. Through this
program, faith communities in the United States express solidarity with those on the front lines of climate change. By restoring
deforested lands in Ghana or planting three million trees on Kili-
manjaro, people of faith are enhancing sinks of greenhouse gases.
In addition to storing carbon, these projects introduce alternative
livelihood schemes to the unemployed and promote integrated environmental approaches, such as organic farming strategies.[15]

Adaptation

Mitigation is critical, but climate change has already arrived. Unless
the church wishes to be in the business of full-time disaster relief,
we must aggressively adapt for climate change. Dramatic changes
have already been set in motion, and impacts cannot be avoided,
even through the most ambitious mitigation efforts. Adaptation
therefore aims to alleviate the worst impacts of global warming
and is defined by the IPCC as "initiatives and measures to reduce
the vulnerability of natural and human systems against actual or
expected climate change effects."[16] I recall a domestic adaptation
strategy advertised on a well-worn T-shirt belonging to a friend
who was displaced from New Orleans by Hurricane Katrina. It
read, "Make levees, not war." Adaptation projects such as building
higher levees in New Orleans do not change climate variability
but make vulnerable communities more resilient. For example, in
areas where flooding is a natural phenomenon, but is becoming
more frequent due to global warming, adaptation efforts might include upgrading urban wastewater systems or creating watershed
restoration projects.

Study after study concludes that the cost of inaction in planning for the unavoidable impacts of climate change will be much
higher than the cost of action. As the largest historical emitter of
greenhouse gases, the United States has a moral responsibility to
fund adaptation, at home and around the world. However, adaptation allocations, domestic and international, represented only

three percent of a theoretical financing mechanism for the American Clean Energy and Security Act that passed the US House of Representatives in 2009, and the Kerry-Lieberman American Power Act (which never made it to the floor for a vote in the US Senate).

While adaptation may seem like an abstract concept in proposed legislation, it becomes real in the stories of those living with the daily realities of climate change. In my former role as director of North Carolina Interfaith Power & Light, I attended a national event in Washington, DC, on International Women's Day 2010 that focused on international adaptation. I joined a delegation of 100 female leaders and climate witnesses from around the globe as part of Oxfam's Sisters on the Planet program, an initiative that brings together American leaders to raise awareness about women and climate change, and to help vulnerable communities adapt to the crisis. I was profoundly affected by the presence and stories of women living on the front lines of climate change.

Particularly moving was the opportunity to lobby Senator Kay Hagan from North Carolina. I had visited the freshman senator on several occasions to discuss the IPL campaign's key priorities for climate and energy legislation, including increased financing for international adaptation. On this day, I joined several Oxfam staff members, Secretary of the California EPA Linda Adams, and Constance Okot, a climate witness from Uganda. Constance spoke about the climate variability in her village and how, before Oxfam had arrived and began to talk about "this climate change thing," she had assumed God was punishing the villagers. She talked about how seasons are no longer predictable in her village and how the subsistence crops perish in extreme drought or wash away in floods. Without adaptation in her community, Constance will be forced to migrate to an urban area to survive.

Dressed in traditional clothing, including a white felt hat, Marisa Marcavillaca was another Oxfam climate witness at the gathering. A farmer and indigenous women's organizer from Peru, Marisa had a quiet presence about her, but when she spoke, she

Climate witness Marisa Marcavillaca speaks at Oxfam's Sisters on the Planet Climate Leaders Summit. Photo by Ilene Perlman /Oxfam America.

did so with an authority that rivaled that of any leading climate scientist. (Even former Vice President Al Gore has quoted Marisa in his public speeches about climate change.) She described the Quechua-speaking communities that have farmed the steep Andean mountain slopes for generations.

Now the impacts of climate change threaten their livelihood and indigenous identity in the high altitudes of Peru, where climate variability has resulted in colder temperatures and changes in rainfall patterns. "Our seeds are degenerating, which means that our yields are down, and we are losing our livelihoods," she said. "Our cultural identity is being lost. And our Andean cultural identity is the most important thing we have."[17] This kind of profound loss is difficult to comprehend for those of us who are used to buying a sack of potatoes at the grocery store or local co-op.

La Capilla de Santa Maria

I have experienced the most poignant impacts of migration in my home congregation, La Capilla de Santa Maria, in Hendersonville, North Carolina, or *en la boca del lobo*. Many frequently use this nickname, *in the wolf's mouth*, to refer to Henderson County because it has adopted and enforced a local immigration policy called 287(g), similar to the immigration legislation in Arizona. La Capilla is the faith community where my daughter Aja has grown up and where I have felt closest to God. My husband, the Reverend Austin Rios, has served as the rector of this Episcopal parish since 2007. The story of La Capilla reflects how the church has adapted, reinvented its ministry in response to human migration and connected environmental sustainability with population movements.

At La Capilla, most parishioners live on the economic fringes, working several jobs to support their families in western North Carolina and in Mexico. The congregation provides a safe space for gathering together, and as a parish family, we have created programs aimed at environmental and economic sustainability such as a church garden for parishioners to grow vegetables, a cob oven as a baking micro-enterprise, a weatherization project to decrease the church's utility bills and ESL lessons to build fluency in English. Women in the church have used the kitchen at a nearby Episcopal church to make tamales, which they sell at church functions as a fundraiser. We are working with a local renewable energy company to explore funding the installation of solar panels for the church.

In the midst of these innovative projects, church members live daily with the fear of deportation. Several years ago, our senior warden was deported. He was forced to sign a voluntary departure after being denied political asylum. Each November at La Capilla de Santa Maria, the mutual realities of loss and resilience in response to immigration are palpable during our annual Day of the Dead celebration. Our congregation has a tradition of making a candlelit pilgrimage of the Stations of the Cross along a wooded path on the property. We stop at each station to speak aloud the names of the hundreds who died that year attempting to migrate to the United States for a better life. In response to the names of the dead—mostly unidentified bodies—we respond, "*Estamos presentes*" or "We are present!" At each station, we reflect on the realities of our broken immigration system and those impacted by it.

Parishioners at La Capilla de Santa Maria participate in the annual Day of the Dead service to grieve those who have died during border crossings. Photo by Marc Mullinax.

One of the area's Spanish-language newspapers, *La Voz Independiente*, reported that since its implementation in July 2008, the local immigration program had served to identify 820 undocumented immigrants in Henderson County, a figure that includes two of the most faithful members of La Capilla and another one of my closest friends.[18] Proponents of local and state immigration enforcement claim that these programs make our communities safer, with a goal to target violent and serious crimes such as drug trafficking and gang violence and not minor crimes and infractions such as traffic violations.[19] However, critics of these local enforcement programs report racial profiling and human rights abuses, the erosion of trust between the Latino community and law enforcement, and disproportionate arrests for civil immigration offenses and misdemeanors. Each of my loved ones was detained on a traffic violation—driving without an operator's license—and then forced to leave the country.

At a May 2010 meeting of the Henderson County Board of Commissioners, my husband presented concerns about the implementation of the local immigration program, as protesters and counter-protestors took to opposite sides of the street outside the historic courthouse. Throughout the meeting, Sheriff Rick Davis, who is responsible for oversight of the program within the county, continued to refer to anyone who opposed the immigration program as "pro-criminal." An exhaustive study published by the University of North Carolina, Chapel Hill, however, finds "no evidence that Hispanic population growth or greater rates of immigration in North Carolina counties are associated with higher crime rate."[20] Michelle Bedard, mother of two and local opponent of the program, interrupted the sheriff at one point to declare, "We are not criminals!" She was removed from the courtroom by law enforcement officers.

A few months earlier, an honor roll student from the local high school stood behind the pulpit during the morning mass at Immaculate Conception Catholic Church in Hendersonville. She spoke passionately about her arrival in this country from Mexico as a three-year-old, about her graduation from high school with honors and about the lack of opportunities to continue her education because of her immigration status. As she told her story, Sheriff Davis, who was attending the service with his family, rose and shouted, "What about the criminals?" He gathered his family and left the church.

My friends who have been forced to migrate back to their native villages in the state of Michoacán, Mexico speak about the violent drug cartels, impunity and lawlessness throughout that region. More than a year after resettling in Michoacán, one friend still has been unable to find consistent work. The downturn of the US economy, combined with strict immigration enforcement programs, has reduced the amount of cash transfers, or remittances, entering Mexico from family members living in the United States.[21] As the average minimum wage in Mexico hovers around five dollars per day, this loss of outside income is significant.

These factors, combined with worsened environmental conditions, will likely increase migration of desperately poor Mexicans into the United States. As Mexico and neighboring countries to the south are particularly vulnerable to climate change, the United States should expect increased streams of migration. A Princeton University study predicts that a reduction in crop yields alone caused by climate change could mean that up to 6.7 million additional Mexicans will immigrate to the United States by 2080.[22]

Transformation Through Adaptation: A Moral Obligation and Call to Action

At its best, the church prioritizes the needs of the poor and has been at the front lines of the great social movements such as women's suffrage, the civil rights movement and the environmental justice movement. Today, sea levels are on the rise, and it is predicted that port cities around the globe will experience massive coastal flooding, especially those in the developing world and with the largest populations.[23] Marginalized populations in the United States—and the poorest countries around the globe—will suffer the worst impacts of climate change and be least able to cope with its devastating impacts. As climate change penetrates our daily lives, people of faith are faced with a narrative that reads differently from justice struggles of the past—but which nevertheless, harks back to the core message of justice in the gospel. Our faith communities must take concrete action to confront the realities of climate change, environmental refugees and immigration. We must respond through policy and practice, advocacy and action.

Responding to climate change and climate refugees

Christian denominations throughout the world, including Roman Catholic, Eastern Orthodox, evangelical and mainline Protestant, have all adopted statements on climate change. In many cases these statements read like the nature poetry of Mary Oliver and offer biblically based moral witness to climate change as well as strong calls to action. Most urge action toward emissions reduction or mitigation and also recognize that the poorest will be the hardest hit by the impacts of global warming. In addition to mitigation, adaptation strategies should be part of the funding and hands-on projects of faith communities who aim to transform written statements and formal commitments into acts of justice. People of faith in this country also must continue to advocate for strong climate and energy legislation.

As the United Nations Development Program states, "The impact of climate change in the lives of the poor is not the result of natural forces. It is the consequence of human actions. More specifically, it is the product of energy use patterns and decisions taken by people and governments in the rich world."[24] Because the developed world bears the brunt of the responsibility for climate change, Christians especially should honor a moral obligation to the developing world for the adverse effects those countries will bear.

Though it will be a hard sell, the United States must recognize those displaced by climate change as a separate category of refugee. In a country that frequently refers to the whole of the immigrant community as "aliens, criminals and illegals" and is still widely populated with outspoken skeptics (and political critics) of climate change, it will be an uphill battle to change the hearts and minds of the American public to accept more newcomers to our country as climate refugees. However, if there is any institution that can cut through the caustic immigration debate and recognize climate scientists as modern day prophets, it will be the church.

Meanwhile, people of faith must also urge the US government to work with the United Nations toward appropriate recognition of climate refugees, through new or existing conventions. The United Nations Framework Convention on Climate Change, with 194 parties, has near universal membership and is the parent treaty of the 1997 Kyoto Protocol. In 2010, the Cancún Adaptation Framework was established as part of this convention.[25] A clear step forward, this framework establishes better planning and implementation of adaptation projects in developing countries through increased financial and technical support.

Welcoming the stranger

We must recognize that anti-immigrant policies promote division, not unity, and create problems, not solutions, in our communities. Our faithful voices should serve as reminders that mothers and wives do not want their children and husbands to risk—or lose—their lives in the desert. Families do not dream of crop failure, the loss of ancient subsistence livelihoods or separation from loved ones for decades. Religious leaders have taken stands against stringent immigration laws, such as legislation in Alabama that would require public school officials to check the immigration status of students and make it illegal to transport an undocumented person. In the Bible Belt, faith leaders joined a coalition of civil rights groups to file a federal lawsuit that challenged Alabama's immigration law, stating that the law criminalizes Christian acts of hospitality.[26] Throughout the country, many people of faith remain hopeful that immigration reform will make such lawsuits unnecessary.

In this often toxic environment, cultural exchanges organized by the church could address root causes of migration and help deepen cultural understanding between migrant-sending and migrant-receiving communities. For example, congregations in the migrant-receiving community of Henderson County, where I worship, could prioritize companion relationships in the migrant-sending state of Michoacán, Mexico. Youth groups and adult mission trips alike could participate in regionally relevant adaptation efforts, such as tree-planting, wastewater improvement and watershed restoration projects.

A Journey Toward Justice for All

As divisive interactions poison our communities, violent and unseasonable storms destroy our beloved crops, homes and communities. North Carolina and the nation have trended toward punitive enforcement programs for human migrants, even as we mourn grim statistics about the monarch butterfly population. At large, we celebrate the migratory phenomenon of the winged international traveler, but fail to honor the root causes of human migration. Nonhuman or human, the migrants have in common a resilience and fierce instinct for survival.

As a person of faith, I risk believing the science of climate change, preparing for its impacts and marveling at the natural instincts of human migrants to survive and their sense of a larger purpose in the face of one of the greatest challenges before us. As we consider the transformation necessary to deal with the sweeping changes brought about by climate change, including increased immigration, we are faced with a challenge to adapt and to survive, and to help others do so as well. There are clear ethical obligations, as well as legal and practical solutions, to guide us through this conversion.

At my home congregation, La Capilla, we will develop a butterfly garden to provide nourishment for the monarchs along their increasingly broken nectar corridor. Regardless of the anti-immigrant sentiment and immigration enforcement programs that exist just beyond the church's entrance, we will continue to be a sanctuary for human migrants who arrive and resettle in our community. The garden will symbolize our commitment to restoring the Earth in the midst of crisis and working toward justice for all—including those who arrive by wing as well as climate refugees who arrive no less miraculously.

● ● ●

JILL RIOS teaches English as a Second Language in western North Carolina and has a master's degree in environmental education from Lesley University. With her husband, the Reverend Austin Rios, and daughter Aja, she worships at La Capilla de Santa Maria in Hendersonville, North Carolina. She served for two years as director of North Carolina Interfaith Power & Light, a program of the North Carolina Council of Churches.

CHAPTER 11

For the Health of All

Faith Communities and Environmental Justice

Peggy M. Shepard

The environment is where we live, work,
play, pray and learn.

WITH A FULL-TIME JOB and three young children, Lauren
Smith[1] was living with her elderly mother and children in
a cramped Washington Heights apartment in northern Manhattan. One Saturday afternoon she overheard her neighbor talking
about lead poisoning with Ana Parks, who was conducting a lead-
dust sampling in the apartment. Ana works as the Healthy Homes
Initiative Coordinator for WE ACT for Environmental Justice, a
community-based organization with a mission to build healthy
communities by assuring that people of color and low income
participate meaningfully in creating policies and practices for environmental health.[2]

Lauren's experience with an inattentive landlord had convinced her that lead exposure from old paint was something she
would have to endure because she didn't have the money to move.
After consulting with Ana, however, she decided to have her home
tested, as the family was especially vulnerable due to her young
children and mother.

When Ana later returned to test for lead dust and mold exposure, she observed the disparities between the neighborhoods she
drove through, such as the stench of garbage and sight of diesel-

183

bus depots concentrated near public housing. Indeed, testing of Lauren's apartment indicated a high toxin level of 600 ppm (parts per million), which posed a serious health threat to the household.[3] Ana explained that Lauren needed to safeguard her children from neurological damage and her elderly mother from respiratory allergens. With a referral to a social worker at the Montefiore Medical Center, Lauren and her family were able to move to a lead-safe home until lead levels in their apartment were abated, enabling them to live in a toxin-free environment.

Environmental Justice

Environmental Justice (EJ) is the perspective that all communities deserve equity in environmental protection, enforcement of existing laws, siting of noxious facilities and consultation in the development of government policies and regulations. In New York City, communities of color and low-income residents enjoy few environmental amenities such as parks and waterfront access but bear the brunt of the disproportionate permitting and siting of polluting facilities. As a result, these communities—and residents like Lauren Smith and her family—face escalating health disparities in rates of asthma, diabetes, cancer, obesity, developmental delays and low birth weight.

The environmental justice frame is a precautionary one: it seeks to prevent environmental threats before they occur and to shift the burden of proof to the polluter. Environmental justice places human health at the center of environmental struggles, understanding that communities of color and the poor are home to more susceptible populations, that multiple and cumulative environmental exposures must be addressed and that children are more vulnerable to environmental exposures.

Too many children in low-income communities inhale diesel fumes while riding in school buses and live in "food deserts," with greater access to chicken nuggets than to fresh vegetables. Many of the contaminants in low-income neighborhoods are known or suspected asthma triggers, such as polycyclic aromatic hydrocarbons

(PAHs) and fine particles emitted in diesel exhaust and the combustion of fossil fuels, nitrogen oxide, cockroach and mice allergen, and mold. In northern Manhattan and the South Bronx, rates of asthma mortality and morbidity are still the highest in New York City and nationwide.[4]

Environmental justice provides a broad context for examining the specific impacts of climate change on the environmental health of communities. As such, this chapter looks at the concept of climate justice and reflects on the collaboration between WE ACT and churches in their advocacy for healthy communities for all. The inequities in northern Manhattan reveal the significant need for faith communities to work for the health of God's people, especially as we face a changing climate.

Climate Justice

Climate researchers report that vulnerable communities, even in the most prosperous nations, will be the first and worst hit by climate change.[5] In the United States, those most impacted will be communities of color, indigenous peoples and low-income communities, disproportionately burdened by poor environmental quality and least able to adapt to a changing climate. They will be the first to experience extreme heat events, respiratory illness, vector-borne infectious diseases, food insecurity and natural disasters.

Consider the case of Juan Rios,[6] who has a son at the Morningside Heights School, and whose apartment building was cited for 127 public health violations before it burned down. Juan and his family had to move to another apartment with more deplorable conditions, where he was not allowed to buy an air conditioning unit because it would cause the building's power to shut off. The family was "going crazy" from the excruciating heat in the apartment. "My dad lives with us, and he's a senior citizen," Juan explained. "Still, they don't let us get AC." Extreme weather events connected with climate change will affect us all, but will exacerbate existing environmental injustices.

Climate justice reflects the need to develop policies and interventions that address the ethical and human rights dimensions of global warming, the disproportionate burden of pollution, the unsustainable rise in energy costs for low-income families and the impacts of energy extraction, refining and manufacturing on vulnerable communities. Climate change is the most significant social and political challenge of this century. Carbon dioxide emissions caused by human activity will continue to impact the Earth's natural systems through global warming and sea-level rise for generations to come.

In these early years of the 21st century, we bear witness to a constant increase in the number of severe weather events impacting communities in the United States: hurricanes Katrina and Rita, the mighty Mississippi River rising along the shores of the Midwest, record-breaking tornados in Mississippi and Kentucky and the droughts experienced in Georgia, Tennessee and Alabama. With the predicted increase in extreme weather events, we are likely to implement a portfolio of adaptation and mitigation measures that can reduce the risk of climate change. As regions across the world experience the negative impacts, however, they will compete for control of diminishing resources, especially agricultural and grazing land, water and food. Such conflicts for the fundamentals of life can result in violence, displacements, migrations and deaths.

Since the first report of the Intergovernmental Panel on Climate Change in 1990, political will has dampened after flawed climate legislation, which focused on a cap-and-trade mechanism, died in the US Senate in 2010. Activists within the environmental justice movement argued that the legislation would raise energy costs to the consumer, create windfall profits to polluters, fail to generate enough revenue or meet targets for carbon emissions reduction and hurt the most vulnerable communities by creating hot spots and the trading of copollutants. Rather than a cap-and-trade mechanism, many advocates, scientists and economists believe that a tax on the polluter is the best strategy for establishing a price on carbon.

WE ACT and EJ groups across the country have initiated a campaign to influence federal climate change policy. Called the Environmental Justice Leadership Forum on Climate Change, it calls for democratic dialogue on climate change that is inclusive of all communities and sectors of our economy. We have come together over the past four years to acknowledge and communicate the impacts that New Orleans and Alaska communities and tribes are experiencing and to participate in determining the future of our economy and our environment.

The forum is working to effect just policies and legislation that would
- achieve significant, identified reductions in carbon emissions
- protect the most burdened and vulnerable communities
- reduce copollutants that exacerbate adverse public health outcomes
- promote the reduction of hotspot pollution in overburdened communities
- offset higher energy costs to low-income consumers
- shift from a fossil-fuel economy to a new green economy, providing training for workers in green jobs.[7]

This is our challenge, expressed well by Dr. Wangari Maathai, founder of the Greenbelt Movement in Kenya, as she accepted the Nobel Peace Prize in 2004: "There can be no peace without equitable development, and there can be no development without sustainable management of the environment in a democratic and peaceful space."[8]

A Legacy of Community Organizing: Congregations and WE ACT

Addressing climate justice will require community groups such as WE ACT and congregations to draw on their shared commitments, values and history in community organizing for justice. In 1968, *Time* reviewed a book of essays, *Christianity: Underground Manifesto*, and quoted the Rev. Robert W. Castle's essay, "Litany from the Underground":

O God, whose name is spik, nigger,
ginny, and kike,
Helps us to know you...
O God, who is children in the grave,
burned in the tenement fire,
Help us to hear your cry...
O God, who is tired of His church
and its ministers and priests, irrelevant
and unbloody,
Help us to join you.[9]

Eighteen years later, in 1986, Father Castle arrived at St. Mary's Episcopal Church in West Harlem, with experience that included leading congregations in Jersey City, New Jersey, hosting the Black Panther Breakfast Program in church basements and being arrested for civil disobedience for protesting against slumlords, drugs and racism. (Father Castle's philosophy and values were later documented by his cousin, Hollywood director Jonathan Demme, in the film *Cousin Bobby*.) A generous man, gentle and feisty, Father Castle began rebuilding a dwindling congregation drawn mostly from nearby Grant and Manhattanville Houses, two large public-housing developments.

The congregation of African American and Puerto Rican parishioners reflected the demographics of the community at that time, and St. Mary's, a landmark church founded in 1823, was steeped in the city's history. As the first "free pew"[10] Episcopal church in the city, its congregants have included veteran patriots and Tories, Alexander Hamilton's widow, African American abolitionists and Mayor Daniel F. Tiemann.

The arrival of Father Castle coincided with my own move to West Harlem and my election as West Harlem's Democratic Party assembly district leader. I had witnessed the vast disparity in the distribution of benefits and burdens in our city while serving as the public relations coordinator for the New York City campaign of the Reverend Jesse Jackson's historic run for the US presidency.

As an insurgent, I was elected in a Harlem assembly district that was so politically entrenched that not even the Association of Community Organizations for Reform Now (ACORN) or the Reverend Al Sharpton ran organizing activities in Harlem.

My new neighbors and Democratic Club members who attended St. Mary's introduced me to Father Castle, who had begun a renovation of the church rectory and a rejuvenation of its congregation. He invited community activists to "preach" from the pulpit on important community struggles, and the church became a well-known site for progressive organizations to hold meetings and events. Within the next two years, he founded a coalition of eight churches in West Harlem called Harlem Valley Churches, mostly Episcopal and Catholic, which worked to create drug-free zones near schools and later partnered with WE ACT to organize against the proliferation of diesel-bus depots in West Harlem. The support and activism of priests fueled the growth of progressive political leadership in West Harlem, the birth of WE ACT and the

WE ACT hosts a press conference in 1997 to launch a campaign against the Metropolitan Transportation Authority — "If You Live Uptown, Breathe at Your Own Risk" — with Father Robert Castle at podium and Peggy M. Shepard on right. Photo by Karl Crutchfield.

development of the environmental justice movement in northern Manhattan.

WE ACT in Northern Manhattan Neighborhoods

In 1988, WE ACT was founded as a result of community struggles around the use of northern Manhattan as the dumping ground for the downtown elite. As a cofounder and its first executive director, I worked with West Harlem residents in an eight-year organizing campaign around the operations of the North River sewage treatment plant, whose odors and emissions were exacerbating respiratory disease among residents. WE ACT's first victory for government accountability was achieved by mobilizing community support to retrofit the North River plant and filing a lawsuit — *WE ACT v. New York City Department of Environmental Protection* — that resulted in a $55 million odor-abatement plan and a $1.1 million environmental benefit fund for the West Harlem community. In 2000, under the Civil Rights Act of 1964, WE ACT filed a Title VI Administrative Complaint with the US Department of Transportation against the Metropolitan Transit Authority over the disproportionate burden of hosting one-third of the largest diesel-bus fleet in the nation: of the six diesel-bus depots in Manhattan, five are in northern Manhattan communities.

Northern Manhattan, the focus of WE ACT's work, is home to 630,000 residents who are primarily low-income African Americans (44 percent) and Latinos (44 percent). With four neighborhoods — East Harlem, Central Harlem, West Harlem and Washington Heights/Inwood — northern Manhattan is a densely populated area of New York City spread over 7.4 square miles. With a median household income of $32,000 in parts of West Harlem and $18,000 in Central Harlem, 44 percent of the population receives income supports, including public assistance and Medicaid.[11] There are multiple environmental exposures, a high proportion of learning disabilities, low birth weight and excess mortality rates from asthma, cancer and heart disease. In addition, Manhattan is a nonattainment area for clean air standards and is ranked number one in cancer risk from air toxics by the EPA.[12] To prioritize and assess its work in this area, WE ACT uses eight indicators of a healthy community: clean air and climate change; affordable, equitable transit; waste reduction, pests and pesticides; toxic-free products; good food in schools; sustainable land use; open and green space; and healthy indoor environments.

For the past 12 years, WE ACT has engaged in research to identify environmental exposures of mothers and children in West and Central Harlem, Washington Heights and the South Bronx and translate findings into improved policy and legislation for healthy communities. We have worked as a community partner with the National Institute of Environmental Health Sciences Center for Environmental Health and co-investigator with the Columbia Center for Children's Environmental Health, both part of the Mailman School of Public Health at Columbia University.

As a part of this collaboration, Columbia Center for Children's Environmental Health's *Mothers and Newborns Cohort Study* found that prenatal exposure to environmental toxins can alter the development of the fetus and thereby increase the risk of cancer in both childhood and later adulthood.[13] In this study, pregnant mothers in northern Manhattan and the South Bronx wore personal air monitors to measure their exposure to carcinogenic PAHs that result from the combustion of fossil fuels. Research at the center also revealed that a fetus is more at risk from atmospheric carcinogens than an adult.[14]

The WE ACT partnership with the Mailman institutes has resulted in air monitoring studies published in peer-reviewed journals, training courses for community leaders on environmental health topics, educational forums for community residents and input into policy decisions that have addressed diesel exhaust exposure in northern Manhattan and use of pesticides in indoor environments. The conversion of New York City's bus fleet to include hybrid diesel and compressed natural gas (CNG) and the installation of diesel retrofits on every bus in Harlem were two of the most significant outcomes of this partnership.[15]

Working With Faith Leaders For Environmental Justice

At a sidewalk café on busy Malcolm X Boulevard in Harlem, Lisa Sharon Harper shared with me the roots of her evangelical faith and her work for justice. Tall, dynamic and thoughtful, she discussed her book, *Evangelical ≠ Republican or Democrat*,[16] before departing the next day to begin work as director of mobilizing for Sojourners in Washington, DC. Raised in California, she lived in New York City for several years and was the inspiration for NY Faith and Justice, an ecumenical group of 200 pastors meeting bimonthly to address poverty in the city.

Her only regret in moving from New York, she said, was leaving colleagues like Charles Callaway, WE ACT's lead organizer, whom she had met four years earlier at a meeting that brought together faith leaders to discuss the serious environmental issues confronting Bronx residents. Several organizers at the meeting were startled when the pastors asked, "What is environmental justice?" Lisa and Charles seized the opportunity to educate and support the faith leaders in developing an action plan to address environmental justice in their congregations and communities. At a follow-up meeting in Manhattan, the organization Faith Leaders for Environmental Justice was born. According to Lisa, the role of this group "was not to lead but to upgird community leaders and bring issues to a tipping point." Her vision was to "expose and educate faith leaders, then you [advocates] give us the marching orders!"

For many years, WE ACT had hoped to collaborate with faith-based groups but had not been successful; in 2008, that situation changed when Charles and Lisa realized their profound impact if they worked together. Today, the collaboration includes more than 100 representatives from faith-based and environmental institutions across the five boroughs of New York. The core leadership includes New York Lawyers for the Public Interest, New York Theological Seminary, Ecologies of Learning Interfaith Center of New York, New York Divinity School, Interfaith Voices Against Hunger/ Feed the Solution, Hazon and St. Mary's Episcopal Church.

Charles also acknowledged the power of the two organizations working in collaboration: "Without the teamwork between NY

Faith and Justice and WE ACT, we wouldn't have been able to create this network of vital contacts and would not have been able to have an impact on faith leaders." Through partnerships, WE ACT has been able to make environmental and climate justice issues relevant in the eyes of the faith leaders so they can introduce these issues and take action with their congregations.

One of the most enthusiastic ministers in the group is Dr. Paul deVries, president of the New York Divinity School and the founder of both the Community Service Office at the University of Virginia and the Center for Applied Christian Ethics at Wheaton College. Dr. de Vries has developed a curriculum for green sermons, which he has shared with fellow members at the quarterly breakfast meetings. He views the faith leaders group as a gathering that fosters synergy between religious leaders of different traditions.

Faith Leaders for Environmental Justice provides a platform for its members to address the impact of climate change, toxic dumping and food deserts in New York City's most vulnerable populations through three working groups. The climate justice working group coordinates a dialogue on the effects of climate change on populations and how to get congregations ready for such events including sea-level rise. Its lessons revolve around decreasing energy consumption, switching to more sustainable energy options and greening communities. The toxics working group rallies around eliminating toxins such as lead paints and certain ethnic beauty-care products within the home, and ensuring safe disposal of waste within neighborhoods.

The food justice working group brings awareness of food politics and the barriers to healthful eating in low-income and minority areas such as the area above 125th Street, which has gained the reputation as one of American's worst urban food deserts. Involving owners of local bodegas, or markets, and national governmental leaders, the working group is dedicated to bringing healthful options to communities, teaching the importance of buying nutritious food and instilling good eating habits from an early age. In 2010, the Faith Leaders for Environmental Justice held a Food, Faith

and Health Disparities Summit that drew more than 200 members
of the community to implement a course of action against food
injustice. Among the outcomes was an Adopt-A-Bodega plan to
upgrade healthful food choices in these Latino-run convenience
stores.

Riverside Church

An active participant in the Faith Leaders for Environmental Justice Collaboration, the historic Riverside Church has been a pio-
neer for the past 80 years in raising awareness and cultivating activism around critical issues such as nuclear conflict, disarmament,
war, racial injustice, health care and civil rights. In the early 1990s,
rising threats from global warming made environmental stewardship and justice a salient issue for congregation members. In 1994,
the Riverside congregation drafted a *Statement of Commitment to
Become a Sustainable Earth Community Congregation*, which emphasizes the congregation's role as stewards of the Earth.[17] Riverside
Church acted on this commitment by assuming responsibility for
its use of resources, incorporating a green message in worship and
creating partnerships with environmental sustainability and justice organizations.

The Reverend Dr. Arnold I. Thomas, Riverside's minister of
education, ecumenical and interfaith relations, noted that the
church implemented environmental justice projects in more concrete ways due to the support and education provided to the congregation by both WE ACT and Faith Leaders for Environmental
Justice. He recalled the May 2011 Faith and Earth Summit, which
included workshops such as "Eco-Justice and Your Zip-Code," "Sea
Water Rise and Disaster Preparedness" and "Mobilizing Youth
Groups for the Sake of the Earth."

The Harlem Green Map has been one of the most visual outcomes from the collaboration with faith-based groups like Riverside Church. This map highlights both Harlem's green resources,
such as food co-ops, empty lots, gardens and parks, and its hazards,
including urban heat islands, waste sewage overflows and areas

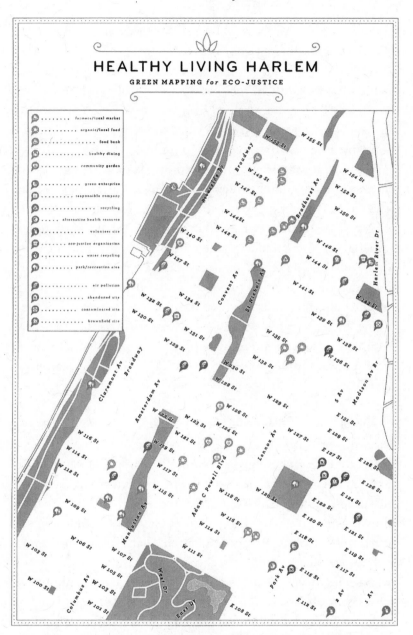

HEALTHY LIVING HARLEM
GREEN MAPPING *for* ECO-JUSTICE

Harlem Green Map Project, a product of Faith Leaders for Environmental Justice, shows the green areas and environmental hazards of Harlem. Photo courtesy of Green Map System and Greenmap.org.

exposed to asbestos.[18] Two churches, Riverside and Perfect Peace Ministries, coordinated youth to survey parts of northern Manhattan neighborhoods for the project. The community partners included Riverside Church, New York Theological Seminary's Ecologies of Learning Project, Faith Leaders for Environmental Justice, Center for the Study of Science and Religion at Columbia's Earth Institute, and the Green Map System.

The Green Map is not only useful as a tool for congregations but also provides solid evidence of environmental injustice and serves as a virtual toxic tour led by faith leaders and community residents. The Harlem Green Map is a tool to hold local and regional governmental officials accountable for institutionalized injustice. Inadequate access to quality food is reflected by the poorly stocked bodegas of low-income residential areas and also in the tax subsidies allocated to 13 fast-food joints in Manhattan, six of them located in Harlem and Washington Heights, by the Industrial and Commercial Incentive Program (ICIP).[19] Combined efforts like these draw attention to the potential impact of congregations in the environmental justice movement.

Challenges and Action for Faith Leaders

The work of Faith Leaders for Environmental Justice provides a model for engaging religious communities in climate justice, but many challenges remain, such as encouraging faith leaders to preach sermons on issues that affect the health of their congregations, including climate change. Although there are some religious institutions, such as Riverside Church, that give green sermons and dedicate programming to climate change, many still shy away from topics viewed as nontraditional. Indeed, faith communities must speak about personal salvation, but we also need religious leaders educated about climate change, toxic waste and food justice, which impact the health and safety of us all. To date, WE ACT staff has made presentations on environmental health and climate change at the invitation of eight churches in Harlem and developed a one-day briefing on environmental justice for Greenfaith's Fellowship program. (See Chapter 2.)

To build additional partnerships with congregations, WE ACT will continue to bring the perspectives of diverse grassroots communities into broad environmental coalitions where we work to craft consensus on environmental solutions and policies. Coalition-building is crucial to developing a community-generated vision and creating a space for collaborative problem-solving.

My own vision for the coming decade places communities at the center of dialogue, planning, action and change. My hope is to educate community members and congregations so they can better protect their families from dangerous exposures and play an active role in coordinated efforts to change policies that will help improve environmental conditions as we face the impacts of climate change. This approach will assist individuals in making behavior changes that can reduce the harmful exposures for their families, while community members can be trained to organize group actions to effect longer-term solutions.

Creating the political will and opportunities for all communities to engage in local, regional and national initiatives to address climate change with procedural and social equity is daunting, but it is needed now more than ever. Congregations understand that God created the Earth and called it good, assigned us to steward creation and charged us to love our neighbor as ourselves. The belief that God's creation is His temple can inspire people of faith to care about climate justice and act to ensure equal access to healthy environments for all communities.

● ● ●

PEGGY M. SHEPARD is the executive director and cofounder of West Harlem Environmental Action, Inc., also known as WE ACT for Environmental Justice. She received the 10th annual Heinz Award for the Environment and the 2008 Jane Jacobs Medal for Lifetime Achievement. She is a member of St. Mary's Church in Harlem, New York.

The author wishes to acknowledge the invaluable research assistance of Dianna Kim.

CHAPTER 12

Responding in Times of Disaster
Pray Without Ceasing

THE REVEREND MITCH HESCOX

Rejoice always, pray without ceasing, in everything give
thanks; for this is the will of God in Jesus Christ for you.

1 Thessalonians 5:16–18 (NKJV)

DURING THE EARLY morning hours of June 14, 2010, I walked in
darkness to the fishing pier near Waveland, Mississippi. I paid
a dollar, strolled onto the wharf, and chatted with the anglers who
had spent the night trying their luck for a prize catch. Unlike these
men, I had not come to Mississippi for the fishing. I was in search
of people, community members affected by the explosion of the
British Petroleum (BP) *Deepwater Horizon* deep-sea drilling platform and the subsequent oil spill that began April 20, 2010. Millions of gallons of crude oil had poured into the Gulf of Mexico.
As a leader in the creation care movement, I felt heartbroken for
Gulf residents wounded only five years after the disaster of Hurricane Katrina.

At the end of the pier, I gazed at the rising sun that cast a glow
throughout the sky. As the sun rose over the Gulf, I also saw the
remnants of Hurricane Katrina: uncompleted roadwork, churches
under construction, vacant lots and destroyed jetties that gave

199

testimony to a world in continual recovery. Bowing in prayer, I thanked God for His creation, asked for His grace and justice and remembered why I was standing more than a thousand miles from home.

Climate Change: A Matter of Life in Coal Country

Ansted, West Virginia, May 8, 2010

One month before traveling to the Gulf Coast, I had begun a 300-mile walk from Ansted, West Virginia, to Washington, DC, in support of creation care. The purpose of this journey was to educate local churches on our overdependence on fossil fuels and the impacts of climate change on the poor. The town of Ansted is the headquarters of Christians for the Mountains, a grassroots organization dedicated to the fight against mountaintop removal coal mining. (See Chapter 9 for more information on mountaintop removal.) This pilgrimage interwove a focus on fossil-fuel addiction, sustainable energy and the core theme of the Evangelical Environmental Network: "Creation Care: It's a Matter of Life." For many evangelicals, stewardship of God's creation is a pro-life issue, carrying measurable human costs if we fail to care for God's world.

Before the Creation Care Walk began, I gathered with other Christians on nearby Kayford Mountain, the family home of Larry Gibson, also known as "Keeper of the Mountain." Larry's family has lived near Kayford Mountain since the 1700s. In 1996, mountaintop removal mining began to destroy most of Kayford Mountain. To date, this mining practice has demolished 12,000 acres of scenic beauty surrounding this family home in "wild and wonderful" West Virginia.[1]

The Gibson family believed their ownership of Kayford Mountain covered more than 500 acres. However, shortly after mountaintop removal began, a title search revealed that in the early 1900s, the vast majority of the tract had changed hands for only a few dollars through the broad-form deeds common throughout the 19th and 20th centuries in these resource-rich Appalachian Mountains. The transactions occurred with the Gibson family signature recorded only as a mark on paper. With no living witnesses to refute the claim, Larry had no legal recourse.

Today Kayford Mountain exists as a 50-acre Garden of Eden surrounded by leveled mountains, filled valleys, destroyed streams, polluted groundwater and bullet holes. In a state whose economy relies on coal and petrochemicals, many are willing to take drastic actions to protect that livelihood. West Virginia is the second-largest coal-producing state in the United States. The coal industry supports approximately 30,000 jobs and produces 144 million tons of coal each year.[2] Although the state has lost almost 100,000 jobs to mechanization over the past 50 years, West Virginia remains a one-industry economy. This dependence on coal mirrors our national dependence on oil and fossil fuels.

As President George W. Bush stated in his 2006 State of the Union address, "Here we have a serious problem: America is addicted to oil."[3] In his book *Addiction and Grace*, Dr. Gerald May describes addiction as a deep-seated form of idolatry. "The objects of our addictions become our false god," he writes.[4] Addicts almost never see their illness as a problem, whether the addiction is to alcohol, drugs, sex or food. In my role as a church pastor for almost 20 years, I saw the signs and symptoms of addiction and heard these painful phrases: "It doesn't affect my job" or "I can stop any time." Such excuses allow addicts to escape reality and responsibility while those around them are devastated. Abuse, divorce, ruined families and destroyed careers are just a few of the consequences of addiction.

Our culture's addiction to fossil fuels, however, affects not only our families but also all of God's family; indeed, it affects all of creation, as reflected in the unjust destruction of 136 mountains, 352,000 acres of land and 2,000 miles of streams in West Virginia.[5] In addition to destroying diverse natural habitats, mining contaminates all forms of life, nearby and far away. In water sources near mining operations, the toxic levels of selenium commonly result in reproductive failure of fish and birds. Selenium, sulfur, iron, calcium and other chemicals associated with coal preparation pollute groundwater and streams long after the end of mining operations.[6] In many areas of West Virginia, it is unsafe for humans to drink their own tap water.

My own playgrounds as a child were the strip mines of Cambria County, Pennsylvania, where I lived in fear of hearing the fire siren in town during daylight hours. That sound signified an underground mine accident, often in the coal mine where my grandfather worked. Both my grandfathers eventually died from black lung disease. As an adult, I spent 14 years working with coal-fired utilities, and I recognize the entrenched role of coal in our society. I believe that alternative and renewable energy is our hope for providing energy security and justice and protecting God's creation.

Shenandoah Mountain, May 15, 2010

Traveling from West Virginia into Virginia on the Creation Care Walk, I reached the summit of Shenandoah Mountain and then followed the headwaters of the Shenandoah River toward Harrisonburg, Virginia. Under a shining sun and blue sky, two recreational anglers enjoyed fly-fishing in the river. I stopped and took a photo of the men basking in the beauty of God's creation, a sight that momentarily relieved the shin-splint pain that had cursed me for two days. Then I noticed a warning sign posted on a utility pole: "FISH ADVISORY: Do Not Consume More Than One Catch Per Month."

All 50 states have mercury consumption advisories, and with good reason. Coal-fired electric generating and industrial boilers, which emit mercury and pollute the US's fresh water, account for 87 percent of the domestic mercury pollution that mandates such warnings. Exposure to mercury levels correlates with developmental disabilities, threatening one in six unborn children in the United States.[7]

Currently the United States is the world's leading oil consumer, though it holds only two percent of the world's proven reserves.[8] To meet our demand, we attempt to feed our addiction with increasingly dangerous oil drilling methods, in spite of the growing recognition that fossil fuels are not sustainable. Meanwhile, more than half our oil imports come from areas of the world that are not friendly to the United States, and for security reasons, the US military is striving to end its dependence on fossil fuels.

Approximately half of all electricity generated in this country comes from coal combustion.[9] Coal is also the single largest source of the United States' greenhouse gas emissions, mercury pollution and acid rain.[10] Not only does the burning of coal pollute the air, the processing of coal also leaches heavy metals such as fly-ash and scrubber sludge into our waterways. (Fly-ash is the particulate matter removed from flue gases; scrubber sludge is the byproduct of sulfur removal designed to limit acid rain.)

We turn our faces from the health and environmental impacts of fossil-fuel consumption for fear of economic losses. Touted as the cheapest available energy source, coal is the most toxic and costly in terms of human health. Proponents of fossil fuels downplay the human costs of coal and exaggerate the economic costs of sustainable energy. As technology improves, however, the price of photovoltaic cells for solar energy continues to fall. Yet the energy industry spends less than 0.3 percent of its annual profits on research and development, compared to the pharmaceutical and electronic industries' reinvestment levels of 18.7 percent and 7.9 percent, respectively.[11]

Disaster in the Gulf: Planning a Response through Prayer

New Freedom, Pennsylvania, May 26–June 1, 2010
One morning during the Creation Care Walk, I conducted a telephone interview with a radio station in Florida. During the conversation, I described my prayer walk as a journey to draw attention to the impacts of our fossil-fuel addiction on the poor. The radio hosts shared their own fears surrounding the *Deepwater Horizon* explosion, a disaster that captivated the country in its massive scale of destruction. That discussion prompted the idea for a similar pilgrimage along the Gulf Coast, which I began planning after

completing the Creation Care Walk and returning home to New Freedom, Pennsylvania.

The spill had been pouring oil into the Gulf of Mexico for two weeks and qualified as the greatest environmental disaster ever to hit American shores. I began to plan the Gulf Coast Prayer Journey, with just one week of preparation, many prayers and the participation of staff members from the Evangelical Environmental Network, Dr. Galen Carey from the National Association of Evangelicals and several college students who accompanied me.

Since the explosion of the *Deepwater Horizon*, millions of well-intentioned people, both inside and outside the church, offered their assistance in any way imaginable. Unfortunately, the Gulf spill was not an ordinary disaster, if we can call any disaster ordinary. There was no need for traditional cleanup supplies, food, water or clothing, and only specially trained volunteers could deal with cleanup of wildlife. BP's offer to hire and train local fishers seemed to address the issue of oil removal from beaches and marshes. Many Christian relief agencies struggled to find a way to help.

Too many Christians forget the power that lies within prayer. Many years ago, as I prepared to enter ordained ministry, I delivered a sermon at my home church with this message: "For too long we have used prayer as the last gasp instead of our first hope." Scripture teaches that God created us in His image, not as gods ourselves. Each time we attempt to do something on our own without prayer, we repeat the fall from Eden and commit the greatest idolatry. Pride and arrogance underlie our separation not only from God, but also from the sustainable creation spoken through the Word.

Our pride also feeds our addiction to fossil fuels, consumerism and general disregard for God's creation. The Chronicler of long ago stated it well:

If my people, who are called by name, will humble themselves and pray and seek my face and turn from their wicked ways, then I will hear from heaven, and I will forgive their sin and will heal their land. Now my eyes will be open and my ears attentive to the prayers offered in this place.

2 Chronicles 7:14, 15 (NIV)

Prayer and other spiritual disciplines should be our first response, in everyday life and in times of disaster. Prayer begins with admitting our pride, placing us in right relation with our Creator and providing the opportunity for healing of all creation; it provides us with a channel for grace. No one understands how prayer works, but we know its power comes from our connection with God. As Paul tells the Thessalonians,

Rejoice always, pray without ceasing, in everything give thanks; for this is the will of God in Jesus Christ for you.

1 Thessalonians 5:16–18 (nkjv)

Prayer transforms us through the Holy Spirit, into the *imago dei* intended by the Creator. Jesus restores our lives in perfect relationship with God, each other and the entire creation. Prayer reflects the importance of inquiry before we attempt any action. When confronted with the oil spill, I prayed and inquired of the Lord, who dispatched me on this journey that I hoped would bring prayer to a people traumatized by crisis in the Gulf Coast.

Prayer Circles and Vessels of Opportunity in Mississippi

Pass Christian, Mississippi, June 14, 2010

The *Deepwater Horizon* oil spill closed Gulf waters to all fishing, from Texas to the Florida panhandle. By June 7, 2010, the no-fish area included more than 78,000 square miles — approximately 32 percent of all federally controlled water in the Gulf of Mexico.[12] By June 17, it had expanded to more than 81,000 square miles, roughly the area of Kansas. Thousands of people in the seafood industry were suddenly without work.

After prayer-walking several miles along the Mississippi coast, I paused at Pass Christian Harbor to hear the stories of local shrimpers and oyster folks at the start of their day. Hundreds of people stood around tables and awaited their sailing orders. The instructions came not from boat captains in search of fishing grounds but from BP contractors laying out grid patterns for the Vessels of Opportunity Program in search of oil.

In the words of one oysterman waiting on the wharf, "I'm fifty-nine years old, and I will never work in my chosen profession again." Fear permeated Pass Christian Harbor. While oil had not yet landed on Mississippi shores, the spill had impacted the hearts and livelihoods of the locals with connections to the water. "The oil is not on our shore, but it's sure in our business," said one oyster processor.

At its peak, the Vessels of Opportunity Program employed 3,200 boats and crews; as of August 14, just four months after the spill, its cost had topped 450 million dollars.[13] Hundreds of Gulf Coast boat captains found relief in the short-term work and income, but profiteers from across the southeastern United States also arrived to grab a piece of the action.

Since its inception, however, the program seemed to perpetuate inequality rather than justice. Vietnamese American shrimpers often lacked the language skills necessary to complete the registration requirements for the program and were largely ignored through the first two months of the spill. By January 2011, many shrimpers with years of proper documentation had received only one check from BP. The use of fishing boats instead of airplanes to search the Gulf waters for oil felt to many like a public relations ploy rather than an effective cleanup strategy.

Our cultural addiction to oil fueled the negligence that led to the *Deepwater Horizon* explosion. According to the official report of the commission investigating the spill for the government,

> [T]he Macondo blowout was the product of several individual missteps and oversights by BP, Halliburton, and Transocean, which government regulators lacked the authority, the necessary resources, and the technical expertise to pre-

vent.... What we nonetheless do know is considerable and significant: (1) each of the mistakes made on the rig and onshore by industry and government increased the risk of a well blowout; (2) the cumulative risk that resulted from these decisions and actions was both unreasonably large and avoidable; and (3) the risk of a catastrophic blowout was ultimately realized on April 20 and several of the mistakes were contributing causes of the blowout. [14]

Leaving Pass Christian, I walked along the white sandy beaches of southern Mississippi and glimpsed a Waffle House a mile or two up the road. After eating breakfast at this modern southern institution, I saw the battered remains of another jetty, poking out of the water like a sunken pirate ship. Every lot surrounding the Waffle House was barren, with weeds where buildings once stood. Almost five years after Katrina, the aftermath of the storm continued to scar the land and dim the hope of resurrection and justice.

The hopelessness expressed by many locals went beyond the oil spill and revealed a combined psychological impact of hurricanes and human-caused disaster. As climate change intensifies the hurricane season every year, Gulf Coast residents will continue to experience what falls under the moniker of post-traumatic stress. These emotional impacts may outweigh the economic burdens, and certainly have attributed to New Orleans's population loss after Hurricane Katrina. Today, the population of New Orleans remains 100,000 below the city's pre-Katrina population. [15]

Gulfport, Mississippi, June 14–16, 2010

I finished the first section of the Gulf journey in the town of Gulfport, Mississippi, and decided to drive to some local oyster houses. The first one I visited happened to be one of the BP staging areas on the coast. I noticed the guards and fences as I approached the facility but decided to drive through as if I were supposed to be there. I had the chance to visit with some of the families that depended on oyster farming for survival. Sylvia Cure and Ashley

An oysterman affected by the BP oil spill in the harbor of Gulfport, Mississippi. Photo by Rev. Mitch Hescox.

McClendon were a grandmother and granddaughter whose family had fished Bayou Caddy for five generations. They shared their stories with me and expressed their fears about the chemical dispersants used in cleaning the crude oil in the Gulf, which were believed by many to be toxic to the oyster beds.

For Sylvia and her family, oystering was "in our blood." Their entire oyster harvest was gone for this year and next, and some suggest it will be at least three years after the oil spill until oystering will resume at commercial levels.[16] As our conversation came to a close, Sylvia lamented, "We're not regular church people, but all there is left to do is pray." After we prayed together, she asked if I would call on another family-owned oyster house in more dire difficulties.[17]

Through the simple act of prayer and caring for another in crisis, something happened. At that moment, my belief was confirmed that prayer should be the first action to transform despair into hope. However, prayer and relationship must be authentic. Repeatedly, people shared their disappointment over church leaders who came to visit the site of the oil spill but ignored those living through the crisis. Many Gulf Coast residents I spoke with felt used because "church people came and took pictures and then went home."

Two days later, I was walking over a bridge in Biloxi, Mississippi, with a TV reporter and camera operator in tow when a local restaurant owner approached me. She wanted to pray, and her emotional outpouring testified to the responsive power of prayer. Everywhere I asked the question, "What can the church do?" The answer was always the same: "Please pray." As I toured oil-devastated marshes, a local fisher and boat captain stated, "If God is in control, we have hope." Another pastor put it this way, "God brought us through Katrina. He will bring us through an oil spill!"

> He has delivered us from such a deadly peril, and he will deliver us again. On Him we have set our hope that he will continue to deliver us, as you help us by your prayers. Then many will give thanks on our behalf for the gracious favor granted us in answer to the prayers of many.
>
> 2 Corinthians 1:10, 11 (NIV)

In mid-June 2010, the residents of the Gulf Coast desperately needed the hope that prayer ignites within all of us. The marshes were contaminated, the wildlife defiled and many of the people hungry, while crude oil continued to spew into the Gulf. For me, this journey was similar to traveling through a war zone, and the region may never recover from the economic losses. The *Deepwater Horizon* spill also claimed 12 human lives (11 on the drilling platform and one fisherman's suicide), 6,100 sea birds, 609 sea turtles and 100 dolphins.[18] Nearly 4,200 miles of coastline were hit by the spill. The total amount of the spill would have supplied 6 hours and 15 minutes' worth of our national daily consumption of oil.[19] It takes a genuine addiction for us to return to something that causes this much damage.

Port Sulphur and Grand Bayou, Louisiana, June 18, 2010

Later in my journey, in the Louisiana Delta, I met Bayou locals concerned that any day a summer hurricane would push oil farther up onto the coast. During a prayer meeting at Port Sulphur Baptist Church, Sister Ruby Ancar spoke of her passionate homecoming, years after Katrina. She described the joy of watching the Mennonite Disaster Services rebuild her home and her dreams for rebuilding the church. Her greatest fear was that another hurricane or contamination from the oil spill would force her to leave her home again.

At the same prayer meeting, Brother Lynn Rodrigue shared his concern for the hundreds of people who, because of the fishing ban, were forced to spend what little money they had buying food. Bayou locals have lived from creation for hundreds of years through fishing: they dipped nets and traps into the water for shrimp, crabs and other seafood. The *Deepwater Horizon* spill and subsequent fishing ban took those on the edge into starvation. Fortunately, churches banded together and brought assistance in the form of emergency food supplies.

Even if we can prevent permanent crude oil contamination, saving the Mississippi River Delta might not be possible. Since 1956, 23 percent of the delta has disappeared.[20] A generation ago, vast live oak forests stood where seawater and marsh grass now dominate the landscape. Since the mid-20th century, navigation channels, petroleum exploration and pipeline canals have permitted salt-water intrusion that destroyed the live oaks.

Without the root structures of the oak trees, soil erosion increases. Mississippi River flood control dams prevent fresh water and new sediments from being deposited into the bayou. Unable to retain soil and without new deposits, the bayous await their final blow—which could conceivably come from the projected sea-level rise associated with anthropogenic climate change.

Canals dug for fossil-fuel production caused the primary destruction of the Mississippi River Delta. Greenhouse gas emissions from burning those very fossil fuels might complete the damage. Additionally, the loss of the delta puts metropolitan areas like New Orleans at greater risk. Barrier islands, coastal forests and marshes have always been creation's own buffers against storm surges and hurricanes. Without them, the city becomes the front porch for a future with increasingly brutal hurricane seasons.

Native peoples such as the Atakapa-Ishak Tribe have inhabited the area in and around the Grand Bayou, Louisiana, for thousands of years with a subsistence culture that depends on fishing, shrimping and trapping. The Atakapa-Ishak culture may not be able to survive the loss of the Bayou to permanent damage from contamination and erosion. Yet the oil contamination affects food sources even now. During a later visit, I found that many members of the Atakapa-Ishak and United Houma Nation, two Native American groups, refused to eat local seafood months after the spill due to fears of both oil and dispersant contamination. They remained unsatisfied with EPA testing.

Brenda DarDar-Robichaux, former principal chief of the United Houma Nation, invited me into her home for a meal during this visit. She apologized for serving chicken gumbo instead of seafood. Her father, a lifelong shrimper, feared putting others at risk by fishing potentially contaminated seafood.

Mobilizing Prayer on a National Scale

Orange Beach, Alabama, July 17–18, 2010

After the Gulf Coast Prayer Journey, the staff at the Evangelical Environmental Network realized the Gulf Coast and the country needed a greater response from the church. In conjunction with the National Association of Evangelicals and the Christian Coalition of Alabama, we organized a National Day of Prayer for the Gulf on July 18, 2010. Congregations across the United States

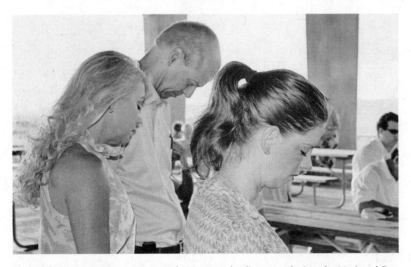

Dr. Randy Brinson, Pam Brinson and Mara Vanderslice pray during the National Day of Prayer for the Gulf in Gulf Shores, Alabama. Photo by Rev. Mitch Hescox.

joined our efforts. The oil flow stopped on July 15, 2010, three days before the National Day of Prayer for the Gulf. One little-known fact is that Congress introduced a resolution for the National Day of Prayer that same day, July 15. The oil stopped flowing one hour later.

The oil spill may have ceased, but our addiction continues. My greatest prayer is for a spiritual awakening that will end our addiction and dependence on our fossil fuels. With God's help, we can envision a new economy based on clean and renewable energy. Our past was never sustainable, and we must move beyond political diatribes into a future of sustainability. Our children and the world depend on us to take moral responsibility.

On July 17, 2010, after an interview with FOX News, I stood on the shores of the Gulf of Mexico with other faith leaders in Orange Beach, Alabama. A tearful woman approached and asked, "Can you help?" I learned that she lost her job as a restaurant server after tourism vanished due to the oil spill; for the same reason, her boyfriend had lost his maintenance position at a hotel. I thought of Peter and John's encounter with the crippled man in Acts 3, and I called out to Pastor Paul Smith from Romar Beach Baptist Church. We both offered to pray with her.

The woman agreed and burst into tears as we lifted her in prayer. After praying, we discussed her current situation and asked if she and her boyfriend had the resources to make it through the night. We then invited the couple to Romar Beach Baptist the next day for food and worship.

My wife and I arrived in the church's parking lot after our sunrise worship service for the National Day of Prayer. Admittedly, we were both surprised to find the couple standing in the parking lot. They looked fearful for their future and hesitant to enter the worship service. We greeted them and walked together into the church.

At the end of the service, Pastor Paul offered a traditional altar call. Within seconds, the Holy Spirit moved me. I reached for my wife's hand, and we approached the couple and invited them to the altar. Together we prayed for hope, new life and the love of Jesus.

After worship, the members of Romar Beach Baptist provided the couple with food and a Bible. Given the lack of tourism, one church member offered a vacant condominium for their use. The couple became active in the fellowship and on Labor Day 2010, they again entered the Gulf of Mexico. This time instead of being coated in oil that had cost them a way of life, they rose together in new life as baptized members in the body of Christ. This journey revealed to me that the Risen Lord can propel us to a sustainable life that ends our fossil-fuel addiction, limits climate change and gives all creation new life.

● ● ●

THE REVEREND MITCH HESCOX is the president/CEO of The Evangelical Environmental Network and publisher of *Creation Care Magazine*. His unique career path has included 14 years in the energy industry, 18 years as a pastor of a local church and extensive international travel.

On Earth as it is in Heaven

MALLORY McDUFF

It may be that when we no longer know what to do,
we have come to our real work,
And when we no longer know which way to go,
we have begun our real journey.
The mind that is not baffled is not employed.
The impeded stream is the one that sings.

Wendell Berry, "The Real Work"[1]

Let the heavens rejoice,
let the earth be glad; let the sea resound,
and all that is in it.

Psalm 96:11 (NIV)

THE CONSENSUS AMONG scientists sends an urgent message about the need to reduce carbon emissions, but it's hard for one person scanning the news headlines before work to know what to do to change the world. (And then there's the guilt if you have to drive to work.) In the face of climate change, however, we have a clear choice: we can choose to act in communion with others in a movement built on religious values of love and justice. We can choose sacred acts — holy acts dedicated to God — that protect people, places and the song of creation.

215

Sustaining momentum to address global warming is more likely in community with others who share a moral mandate to protect the Earth. When she saw the economic inequities in her Richmond, California, community, Michele McGeoy developed a green-jobs program that trained youth to install solar panels on churches and other buildings. The Rev. Fletcher Harper chose to talk about energy efficiency as both a financial and theological issue when he involved congregations in New Jersey to work with the interfaith coalition GreenFaith.

The contributors to this book show how Christians faced a Pentecost moment, a moment of choice and transformation, and acted on their vision of a world that many would describe as impossible to attain. What do we see when we imagine a world that stewards God's resources and provides justice for all? The four strategies of stewardship, spirituality, advocacy and justice reveal the breadth of actions taken by people of faith who are converting congregations to this end. And their stories are just a beginning.

Through stewardship, a farmer like Ragan Sutterfield sees Christians as tenants of the land and members of churches who grow, eat and preserve food together. Given the power of spirituality, a climate scientist such as Dr. Katharine Hayhoe sees believers harnessing both scripture and science for informed, passionate action. With a focus on advocacy, a nonprofit director like LeeAnne Beres sees people of faith who bear witness to their religious values in legislative offices and town hall meetings. Through justice, a community organizer like Peggy M. Shepherd sees Christians who work for healthy communities for all of God's people.

If we convened the contributors for a panel discussion, they would most likely disagree about the specific language to use when discussing climate change or the biblical passages to quote for inspiration. But here's the good news: it doesn't matter. We need them all and more for the task ahead.

With the diversity of perspectives, several common themes emerge in their stories that serve as signposts in the journey to address climate change. First, as Christians, we must recognize our historical legacy and involvement in societal transformation, even if we have come late to the table of climate justice. At this moment, our power as social organizers represents unrealized potential and a tipping point. The Rev. Bonnie Anderson, president of the House of Deputies of the Episcopal Church, states the challenge with clarity: "The church needs to be a movement. Right now we are an organization."[2] We don't have to write a mission statement for every congregation that joins us, because we all share God's covenant in the Bible to care for creation.

Second, religious communities bring joy and faith in the unknown, much needed assets for the climate justice movement. In the long term, hope is more powerful than guilt, faith more enduring than skepticism. Also, this hopeful focus on sustainable communities can reinvigorate the church, good news for congregations seeking to increase their relevance in today's world.

Lastly, people of faith must partner with other organizations, such as nonprofits and renewable energy companies, to seek solutions to the climate crisis. The success of many of the stories in the book resulted from partnerships with organizations like Interfaith Power & Light, WE ACT and Alachua Conservation Trust. Although it is a seemingly simple action, faith communities should invite groups to talk in Sunday school classes or brainstorm about partnerships at Wednesday night potlucks. Recruitment of collaborators is just as important as increasing the number of people in the pews (and it might have the same effect).

I witnessed these themes play out in my own life one afternoon when my daughters and I were interviewed on the local public radio station about my research on the religious environmental movement. Since I didn't have childcare that day, the host of the radio show and a member of our church, Carol Anders, decided to integrate the girls into the question-and-answer session.

We all donned headsets and crammed into the small radio booth as Carol posed questions to me, 12-year old Maya, and 5-year old Annie Sky, who didn't realize that nodding wasn't effective on radio. "So what did you learn from visiting all these churches with your mom?" Carol asked. As if reading from a script, Maya responded, "Before the trip, I thought you just went to church and came home. I didn't realize different churches across the country were all making a difference in the world."

I'd never heard this revelation before. During the visits to churches across the country, I was too busy taking notes and hoping the girls stayed quiet to debrief any deep lessons after the services. But by traveling to other houses of worship, Maya saw the church as bigger than her one congregation in Asheville, North Carolina. She understood that somehow individual churches shared a larger purpose.

In my twenties I experienced a similar expansion of my sense of church community during my initial months in the US Peace Corps in the village of Dekoa, Central African Republic. As I struggled with learning the national language of Sango, I began to consider the BBC announcers on my shortwave radio as close, personal friends. Finally, I followed my mother's advice for survival in any new city: I went to church. Indeed, I joined the choir of the Dekoa Catholic Church when I could speak only a few words of Sango. With every choir practice, I became more a part of a community and remained in that church family long after I had learned the language.

We will need to speak a common language to confront climate change. Church families exist across our towns, countries and the world. Our religious communities can model a language for building and sustaining communities, if we recognize our power to care for God's creation and the climate.

We can affect change if we can push past our comfort zones, remember our heritage of justice and join with others called to protect God's good Earth. People of faith are installing solar panels, praying at mountaintop removal sites, harvesting and canning food from church gardens, conducting energy audits, providing sanctuary for climate refugees and addressing childhood asthma in cities. We have begun the journey. There is momentum. Now let us pray and realize the kingdom of God, on Earth as it is in heaven.

The Power of Ideas

The Reverend Canon Sally Bingham

*Give us all a reverence for the earth
as your own creation, that we may use
its resources rightly in the service of others
and to your honor and glory.*

The Prayers of the People, *The Book of Common Prayer*, 388.[1]

To show our love for god, we don't destroy what God loves. To obey the commandment to love our neighbor, we don't destroy our neighbor's air, land or water. Human-induced climate change is harming God's good Earth and our neighbors, and our use of fossil fuels for energy is the culprit. Today we have reached a crisis: business as usual will not sustain the Earth or healthy human communities. We need the power of religion to bring a values-based message to the reality of climate change.

A Religious Response to Global Warming

My world changed drastically when I first recognized that religious voices were crucial to addressing climate change. As a stay-at-home mom, I had managed a household and raised three children. As a lifelong Episcopalian, I wondered why I wasn't hearing about pressing environmental issues within the church. To understand how people in the pews could impact climate change, I made what felt like a radical but rational decision. I returned to school to complete my undergraduate degree, attended seminary and served as a seminarian for three years, and then entered the ordination process.

Few, if any, religious leaders were making the connection between environmental stewardship and their call as ministers of the word. For me, it was the deepest of connections. After several years of trial and error, I honed a message that congregations should provide leadership around climate change. The message ultimately became "a religious response to global warming," which is now the tagline for the Interfaith Power & Light (IPL) campaign. This national network of diverse religious traditions uses religious values as a foundation for climate solutions.

When I was in seminary in 1993, I collaborated with fellow student Ben Webb to found The Regeneration Project with a mission to deepen the connection between ecology and faith. The Regeneration Project now serves as the fiscal agent for the Interfaith Power & Light campaign. Massachusetts IPL and Georgia IPL were two of the first affiliated programs in what is now a network in 38 states.

At its outset, The Regeneration Project established a national office, hired staff and set out to help congregations of all denominations lower their carbon footprints and lead congregants to do the same in their homes. The idea was not hard to sell given the number of congregations that adopted environmental stewardship as a priority. Within the first five years, 13 states had developed IPL organizations that promoted energy conservation, energy efficiency and renewable energy.

Now more than 14,000 congregations are engaged in state IPL programs and are taking action to address global warming. Our responsibility for stewardship of God's creation in the face of climate change has become a matter of faith for many clergy leading congregations. Nearly every mainstream denomination has issued a statement on climate change and taken action to reduce energy use and connect the impacts of global warming to poverty and care for the least among us.

Some churches have shown their concern for creation by retrofitting their buildings and focusing on energy efficiency, the cheapest and most efficient way to decrease carbon emissions. Others have built new energy-efficient houses of worship and parish halls or installed solar panels on rooftops. The examples in this book reveal the diversity of responses to climate change taken by congregations through stewardship, spirituality advocacy and justice.

The range of religious responses to a changing climate reflects a strong connection to place: what succeeds in Georgia may not work as well in Washington State. An initiative that thrives in one congregation may require a different emphasis in another. Interfaith Power & Light affiliates operate in individual states to support these diverse efforts, which might depend upon the politics, policies and people in each state. Local congregations often provide office spaces for IPL staff, such as the Washington IPL office located at St. John United Lutheran Church in Seattle and the Georgia IPL office at First Christian Church in Decatur. Funding for programming is varied also. It comes from foundations and individual grants, fundraisers, membership fees and even, in the case of Georgia IPL, federal stimulus money for weatherization of church buildings.

Within the Christian church our response to climate change has the potential to draw us together with other faith traditions that share that moral imperative to be stewards of creation. The organization Faith in Place supported the installation of a solar hot water system at the Mosque Foundation in Bridgeview, Illinois. Now Muslims at this mosque wash their hands before Friday prayers using water heated by solar panels.

The Jewish principle of *bal tashchit*—"do not destroy or waste"—influenced the design of the Jewish Reconstructionist Congregation in Evanston, Illinois. This congregation became the first in the world to reach LEED (Leadership in Energy and Environmental Design) certification at the highest level of Platinum by the US Green Building Council. At a time when religion is often seen as divisive and political, our response to climate change can unite people of faith from diverse religious backgrounds in powerful acts of redemption.

Meeting Challenges with Hopeful Action

The response of these congregations and thousands of others reflects the momentum behind this moral voice for sustainability. My experiences preaching a values-based message to congregations during the past 15 years have given me a strong sense of hope that we can and will solve this life-threatening problem. With few exceptions, people in the pews receive this message of stewardship with great enthusiasm. I have given hundreds of sermons in churches across the country, yet I have never heard a parishioner denounce the message of conservation.

Now, I have heard a variety of responses, such as "Creation was given to us to use." But I have never heard a person of faith say that we should plunder and destroy the Earth. I often hear people tell me, "I never thought about it [environmental stewardship] like this before." When one sermon or adult education class can inspire a group of people to form a creation care team in their congregation, I realize that people of faith are starving for this message.

The longer I preach and teach about climate change, the more committed I am to this ministry. I find increasing numbers of people seeking information about living out religious values through environmental stewardship. More clergy are looking for tools to inspire their congregations, and more lay people, too, want resources to inspire their clergy.

Confronting this important moral issue brings many challenges, such as the influence of skeptics or climate deniers. Another challenge is the lack of public knowledge about the science of global warming. Far too many people are listening to inflammatory talk-show hosts rather than to climate scientists. While this resistance proves frustrating, I have chosen to work with the 14,000 congregations that are ready to implement an idea that can help solve this crucial problem.

We are making a difference, but progress is painfully slow. Some people of faith are reluctant to embrace the environmental message for fear of appearing too liberal in their congregations. Climate change is real, but if naming it causes people to turn away, then we have to find another way. The reality is that the impacts of climate change will affect our food security, health, economy and life as we know it on this planet. The inspiring, truthful message is that addressing climate change is a response to God's call to us in Genesis to "till and keep the garden."

Often I wonder what it would be like to be a scientist, to understand that we are condemning our children to a dangerous future yet watch helplessly as people ignore scientific truths. My late friend, Dr. Stephen Schneider, was a climate scientist at Stanford University and a chief author of the Intergovernmental Panel on Climate Change report stating that human-induced climate change is real. We often talked about the role of both religion and science in confronting climate change, and I marveled at his perseverance as skeptics threw obstacles of false science and accusations at him. Indeed, he received death threats because of the implications of his scientific work on global warming.

Though I have never received a death threat, I once was called a communist in favor of "world government" when I first started preaching about climate. In the past two years, I have received unsigned hate mail from people who say that I don't know what I'm talking about. In response, I can only believe that IPL must be having an influence, and some people don't like what they are hearing.

I cannot predict our future, but I know that we cannot continue on this path of destruction. We are up against a powerful misinformation campaign funded by the fossil-fuel industries. Their tactics mirror the campaign of the cigarette industry that rebuked the science that smoking causes cancer. Eventually the truth prevailed.

I believe that we are on God's side if we embody His call to be stewards of creation. The Earth is a living planet in constant motion, and change is inevitable: we have to ensure that change remains consistent with God's plan and the natural world. We will lose if we continue to destroy our natural resources, and we will lose if we don't learn that our behaviors and beliefs must reflect loving God's Earth and loving each other.

A religious response to global warming began as an idea, and it has grown into a global movement. Every day, we are collecting new evangelists of the message. It has been worth every slow step of the way, especially given the moments of glory that sustain me and countless others. As people of faith addressing climate change, we line up with God and the call in Micah 6:3–13 to do justice, love kindness, and walk humbly with God.

● ● ●

THE REVEREND CANON SALLY BINGHAM is the founder and president of The Regeneration Project and Interfaith Power & Light campaign, a religious response to global warming that involves more than 14,000 congregations, mosques and temples in faith-based action to protect the Earth.

Notes

Introduction

1. Andy Crouch. "The Joyful Environmentalists: Eugene Peterson and Peter Harris." *Christianity Today*, June 17, 2011, christianitytoday.com /ct/article_print.html?id+92510 (accessed June 22, 2011).

2. The National Council of Churches is an ecumenical partnership of Christian denominations in the United States, including Protestant, orthodox, evangelical, traditional African American and living peace churches. The National Council of Churches represents 100,000 congregations and 100 million people. See ncccusa.org/about/about _ncc.html (accessed June 13, 2011).

3. Tyler Edgar and Lee Hu. *Climate and Church: How Global Climate Change Will Impact Core Church Ministries.* National Council of Churches Eco-Justices Program, 2008.

4. For a concise overview of climate change for faith communities see Peter Sawtell, "Eco-Justice Notes: Refresher Course," Feb. 26, 2010, eco-justice.org/E-100226.asp (accessed Feb. 27, 2010).

5. Bill McKibben. *Eaarth: Making a Life on a Tough New Planet.* Times Books, 2010.

6. Bill McKibben. "Climate Change: Just the Facts." *Sojourners*, March/April 2011 (vol. 40, 4), p. 19.

7. Editorial. "Climate Change Denial Becomes Harder to Justify." *The Washington Post*, May 15, 2011, washingtonpost.com/opinions/climate -change-denial-becomes-harder-to-justify/2011/05/13/AF44QQ4G _story.html (accessed May 16, 2011).

8. McKibben. "Climate Change."

9. Bryan Walsh. "The Greening of the American Brain." *Time*, March

9, 2011, time.com/time/printout/0,8816,2057979,00.html (accessed March 15, 2011).

10. Wendell Berry. "Seven Steps Toward Rescuing Earth From Human Destructiveness." *The Washington Post*, May 15, 2011, kentucky.com/2011 /05/15/1741181/7-steps-toward-rescuing-earth.html (accessed May 27, 2011).

11. Katharine Hayhoe and Andrew Farley. *A Climate for Change: Global Warming Facts for Faith-based Decisions.* FaithWords, 2009.

12. To calculate greenhouse gas equivalences, see US Environmental Protection Agency, "The Greenhouse Gas Equivalences Calculator," epa.gov/cleanenergy/energy-resources/calculator.html (accessed July 11, 2011).

13. Harvey Cox. *The Future of Faith.* HarperOne, 2009.

14. Mallory McDuff. *Natural Saints: How People of Faith are Working to Save God's Earth.* Oxford University Press, 2010, p. 189.

15. National Climate Ethics Campaign. "Statement of our Nation's Moral Responsibility to Address Climate Change." 2011, climate ethicscampaign.org/statement (accessed July 22, 2011).

Chapter 1

1. Robert Bailey. *Growing a Better Future: Food Justice in a Resource-Constrained World.* Oxfam, 2011, oxfamamerica.org/files/growing -a-better-future.pdf (accessed June 10, 2011).

2. Gerald Nelson is the author of a report titled "Climate Change, Agriculture, and Food Security: Impacts and Costs of Adaptation to 2050." He is quoted in the following source: Gerard David Biello, "Farmed Out: How Will Climate Change Impact World Food Supplies?" *Scientific American*, Sept. 30, 2009, scientificamerican.com/ article.cfm?id=how-will-climate-change-impact-world-food-supplies (accessed June 2, 2011).

3. Wendell Berry. "How to Be a Poet." Poetry, poetryfoundation.org /poetrymagazine/poem/30299 (accessed June 10, 2011).

4. Dietrich von Hildebrand. *Humility: Wellspring of Virtue.* Sophia Institute Press, 1997, p. 9.

5. Bernard of Clairvaux. *The Steps of Humility and Pride*, Trans. M. Ambrose Conway. Cistercian, 1989, p. 29.

6. Toby Hemenway and John Todd. *Gaia's Garden: A Guide to Home-Scale Permaculture*, 2nd ed. Chelsea Green Publishing, 2009.

Chapter 2

1. US Environmental Protection Agency. "ENERGY STAR for congregations." energystar.gov/index.cfm?c=small_business.sb_congrega tions (accessed June 4, 2011).

2. ecoAmerica and SRI Consulting. "American Environmental Values Survey." October 2006, ecoamerica.typepad.com/blog/files/ecoAmer ica_AEVS_Report.pdf (accessed Dec. 13, 2010).

3. The full listing of all seven principles is available at Unitarian Universalist Association of Congregations: "Our Unitarian Universalist Principles," May 2, 2011, uua.org/beliefs/6798.shtml (accessed June 4, 2011).

4. "The Interfaith Coalition on Energy." interfaithenergy.com (accessed June 4, 2011).

5. For a description of the program, see "Turning Houses of Worship into Religious Environmental Leaders: GreenFaith Certification Program," 2011, greenfaith.org/programs/certification/the-greenfaith -certification-program (accessed June 6, 2011).

6. Pastor Darrel Armstrong, Shiloh Baptist Church, personal communication, May 18, 2003.

Chapter 3

1. The Episcopal Church, USA. "Commemoration of the Dead." *The Book of Common Prayer.* Church Publishing, 1979, p. 382.

2. Mark Harris. *Grave Matters: A Journey Through the Modern Funeral Industry to a Natural Way of Burial.* Scribner, 2007.

3. McKibben. *Eaarth.*

4. "Understanding 350." 350.org/understanding-350#2 (accessed March 16, 2011).

5. James Hansen et al. "Target Atmospheric CO_2: Where Should Humanity Aim?" *Open Atmospheric Science Journal,* Vol. 2 (2008): pp. 212–231.

6. "Understanding 350."

7. Casket and Funeral Association of America and Federal Trade Commission, as cited in Prairie Creek Conservation Cemetery, "Frequently Asked Questions: What are the Environmental Impacts and Costs of Conventional Burial Practices vs. Conservation Burial Practices?" conservationburialinc.org/?page_id=11 (accessed July 7, 2011).

8. Cremation Association of North America and Federal Trade Commission, as cited in Prairie Creek Conservation Cemetery, "Frequently Asked Questions: What are the Environmental Impacts and Costs of Conventional Burial Practices vs. Conservation Burial Practices?" conservationburialinc.org/?page_id=11 (accessed July 7, 2011).

9. Harris. *Grave Matters.*

10. Ibid.

11. Jessica Mitford. *The American Way of Death Revisited.* Vintage, 2000.

12. For details on caring for the dead, state-by-state regulations and the modern funeral industry, see Joshua Slocum and Lisa Carlson, *Final Rights: Reclaiming the American Way of Death* (Upper Access Books, 2011). Note that Josh Slocum is the executive director of the Funeral Consumer's Alliance, a nonprofit organization dedicated to protecting a consumer's right to choose a meaningful, dignified and affordable funeral. Lisa Carlson is a leader of the Funeral Ethnics Organization and author of *Caring for the Dead* (Upper Access Books, 1998).

13. "Green Burial Council Standards/Eco-Rating System for Burial Grounds." 2011, greenburialcouncil.org/what-we-do/standards-setting/burial-grounds (accessed March 9, 2011).

14. US Funerals Online. "Planning an Affordable and Memorable Funeral." us-funerals.com/funeral-planning-guide.html (accessed March 16, 2011).

15. Land Trust Alliance. "Climate Change." landtrustalliance.org/policy/emerging-issues-climate-change/intro (accessed March 9, 2011).

16. Reed Noss. "Climate and Conservation: Land Conservation is Even More Essential and Urgent in a Time of Rapidly Changing Climate." March 4, 2011, conservationnw.org/wildlife-habitat/climate-change-intensifies-need-for-land-conservation (accessed March 9, 2011).

17. Mirele Goldsmith. "Nice Country for Camping, Not Fracking." *The Jewish Daily Forward.* March 18, 2011, forward.com/articles/135997/ (accessed March 14, 2011).

18. Slocum and Carlson. *Final Rights.* Harris. *Grave Matters.* Also see the website for the Funeral Consumers Alliance, 2010, funerals.org/ (accessed August 17, 2011).

Chapter 4

1. P. Foukal, C. Frohlich, H. Spruit and T. Wigley. "Variations in Solar

Luminosity and their Effect on the Earth's Climate." *Nature,* 442 (2006): pp. 161–166.

2. R. Pachauri, A. Reisinger et al. *Climate Change 2007: Synthesis Report. Contribution of Working Groups I, II and III to the Fourth Assessment Report of the Intergovernmental Panel on Climate Change.* IPCC, 2007.

3. T. Boden, G. Marland and B. Andres. "Global CO_2 Emissions from Fossil-fuel Burning, Cement Manufacture, and Gas Flaring: 1751– 2008." Carbon Dioxide Information Analysis Center (CDIAC), 2011, cdiac.ornl.gov/trends/emis/overview_2008.html (accessed Aug. 31, 2011).

4. C. Le Quéré et al. "Trends in the Sources and Sinks of Carbon Dioxide." *Nature Geoscience,* November 17, 2009.

5. International Panel on Climate Change (IPCC), ed. S. Solomon et al. "Summary for Policymakers," *Climate Change 2007: The Physical Science Basis. Contribution of Working Group I to the Fourth Assessment Report of the Intergovernmental Panel on Climate Change.* Cambridge University Press, 2007.

6. It's true that carbon dioxide and other heat-trapping gases make up no more than a tiny fraction of our atmosphere. How could such a small amount affect something as large as our atmosphere? An easy analogy helps to explain this common question: "It's just a small amount of poison. How could it affect something as large as my body?" Clearly, the amount of a substance doesn't matter; it's the potency that matters. And we are producing some very potent heat-trapping gases.

7. Unified Synthesis Product Team. *Global Climate Change Impacts in the United States: A State of Knowledge Report.* National Oceanic and Atmospheric Administration, Cambridge University Press, 2009.

8. Pachauri, Reisinger et al. *Climate Change 2007: Synthesis Report.*

9. National Climatic Data Center. "State of the Climate: Global Analysis for July 2011." NOAA Satellite and Information Service, August 2011, ncdc.noaa.gov/sotc/global/ (accessed Sept. 1, 2011).

10. Ibid.

11. Brian Fagan. *The Little Ice Age: How Climate Made History, 1300–1850.* Basic Books, 2001.

12. G. W. Kling et al. "Confronting Climate Change in the Great Lakes Region: Impacts on Our Communities and Ecosystems." Union of

Concerned Scientists, 2003, ucsusa.org/greatlakes/ (accessed Aug. 31, 2011).

13. Katharine Hayhoe et al. "Emissions Pathways, Climate Change, and Impacts on California." *Proceedings of the National Academy of Sciences* 101 (2004), pp. 12422–12427.

14. K. Hennessy, C. Lucas, N. Nicholls, J. Bathols, R. Suppiah and J. Ricketts. "Climate Change Impacts on Fire-weather in Southeast Australia." CSIRO, 2006, p. 91, cmar.csiro.au/e-print/open /hennessykj_2005b.pdf (accessed Sept. 1, 2011).

15. T. Brown, B. Hall and A. Westerling. "The Impact of Twenty-First Century Climate Change on Wildland Fire Danger in the Western United States: An Applications Perspective." *Climatic Change*, 62 (2004), pp. 365–388.

16. Alaska Climate Research Center. "Total Change in Mean Annual Temperature (°F), 1949–2007." climate.gi.alaska.edu/ClimTrends /Change/TempChange.html (accessed February 17, 2009).

17. T.E. Osterkamp and V.E. Romanovsky. "Evidence for Warming and Thawing of Discontinuous Permafrost in Alaska." *Permafrost and Periglacial Processes* 10 (1999), pp. 17–37. doi: 10.1002/(SICI)1099– 1530.

18. ACIA. *Arctic Climate Impact Assessment.* Cambridge University Press, 2005.

19. A. Ansari. "Climate Change Forces Eskimos to Abandon Village." *CNN Tech*, April 24, 2009, cnn.com/2009/TECH/science/04/24 /climate.change.eskimos/ (accessed Sept. 1, 2011).

20. US Army Corps of Engineers. *Relocation Planning Project Master Plan: Kivalina, Alaska.* US Army Corps of Engineers, 2006.

21. World Glacier Monitoring Service. *Global Glacier Changes: Facts and Figures.* World Glacier Monitoring Service, 2008.

22. "Peru Bets on Desalination to Ensure Water Supplies." Reuters, March 11, 2008, reuters.com/article/environmentNews/idUSN 1161583720080312 (accessed Aug. 30, 2011).

23. California Office of the Governor. "Executive Order S-3-05." gov.ca .gov/index.php?/executive-order/1861/ (accessed Aug. 29, 2011).

24. J.L. Chen, C.R. Wilson and B.D. Taple. "Satellite Gravity Measurements Confirm Accelerated Melting of Greenland Ice Sheet." *Science*, 313 (2006), pp. 1958–1960.

25. I. Velicogna and J. Wahr. "Measurements of Time-Variable Gravity Show Mass Loss in Antarctica." *Science*, 311 (2006), pp. 1754–1756.

26. S. Rahmstorf. "A Semi-empirical Approach to Projecting Future Sea-level Rise." *Science*, 315 (2007), pp. 368–370.

27. J.A. Church et al. "Understanding global sea levels: past, present and future." *Sustainability Science* (2008): Special Feature: Original Article, doi:10.1007/s11625-008-0042-4.

28. G. McGranahan, D. Balk and B. Anderson. "The Rising Tide: Assessing the Risks of Climate Change and Human Settlements in Low Elevation Coastal Zones." *Environment and Urbanization*, 19 (2007), pp. 17–37.

29. "Climate Change and a Global City: An Assessment of the Metropolitan East Coast Region." Metropolitan East Coast Assessment. 2000, metroeast_climate.ciesin.columbia.edu/reports/assessment synth.pdf (accessed Sept. 2, 2011).

30. S. Dasgupt et al. "World Bank: The Impact of Sea Level Rise on Developing Countries: A Comparative Analysis." econ.worldbank.org /external/default/main?ImgPagePK=64202988&entityID=0000164 06_20070209161430&pagePK=64165259&theSitePK=469382&piPK =585673 (accessed Sept. 7, 2011).

31. The World Conservation Union. *Polar Bears: Proceedings of the 14th Working Meeting of the IUCN/SSC Polar Bear Specialist Group*. 2005, pbsg.npolar.no/export/sites/pbsg/en/docs/PBSG14proc.pdf (accessed Aug. 30, 2011).

32. S.W. Taylor, A.L. Carroll, R.I. Alfaro and L. Safranyik. "Forest, Climate and Mountain Pine Beetle Outbreak Dynamics in Western Canada." *The Mountain Pine Beetle: A Synthesis of Biology, Management and Impacts in Lodgepole Pine*, L. Safranyik and B. Wilson, eds. Natural Resources Canada, 2006, pp. 67–94.

33. Unified Synthesis Project Team. *Global Climate Change Impacts in the United States*.

34. E.J. Burke, Simon J. Brown and Nikolaos Christidis. "Modeling the Recent Evolution of Global Drought and Projections for the Twenty-first Century with the Hadley Centre Climate Model." *Journal of Hydrometeorology*, 7:5 (2006), pp. 1113–1125.

35. C.D. Thomas et al. "Extinction Risk from Climate Change." *Nature*, 427 (2004), pp. 145–148.

36. S. Arrhenius. "On the Influence of Carbonic Acid in the Air Upon the Temperature of the Ground." *The London, Edinburgh, and Dublin Philosophical Magazine and Journal of Science*, 5th Series v. 41(1896) n. 251.

37. Philip Shabecoff. "Global Warming Has Begun, Expert Tells Senate." *New York Times*, June 24, 1988, p. 1. Transcript available online at image.guardian.co.uk/sys-files/Environment/documents/2008/06/23 /ClimateChangeHearing1988.pdf (accessed Sept. 1, 2011).

38. M. R. Raupach et al. "Global and Regional Drivers of Accelerating CO_2 Emissions." *Proceedings of the National Academy of Sciences of the United States of America*, 104:24 (2007), pp. 10288–10293.

39. International Energy Agency (IEA). "CO_2 Emissions from Fuel Combustion." 2010, iea.org/publications/free_new_Desc.asp?PUBS _ID=1825 (accessed Aug. 29, 2011).

40. S. M. Gorelic. *Oil Panic and the Global Crisis Predictions and Myths.* Wiley-Blackwell, 2010.

41. "Sustainability Survey: Global Warming Cools Off as Top Concern." Nielson, 2011, nielsen.com/us/en/insights/press-room/2011/global -warming-cools-off-as-top-concern.html (accessed Aug. 31, 2011).

42. Gallup Social Series Environment Poll. 2011, gallup.com/poll/1615 /environment.aspx (accessed Sept. 1, 2011).

43. National Climatic Data Center. "State of the Climate: Global Analysis for July 2011."

44. C. Borick, E. Lachapelle and B. Rabe. "Climate Compared: Public Opinion on Climate Change in the United States and Canada." *Issues in Governance Studies* (2011), p. 39.

45. Gallup Social Series Environment Poll.

46. B. Johnson. "Half of GOP Caucus are Climate Zombies, Four Members Admit Science is Real." ThinkProgress, 2011, thinkprogress.org /green/2010/11/03/174833/climate-zombie-caucuse/ (accessed Sept. 7, 2011).

47. "A Deeper Partisan Divide Over Global Warming." Pew Research Center, 2008, people-press.org/2008/05/08/a-deeper-partisan-divide -over-global-warming/ (accessed Sept. 2, 2011).

48. L. Bengtsson, V. Ramanathan et al. "Fate of Mountain Glaciers in the Anthropocene: A Report by the Working Group Committee Commissioned by the Pontifical Academy of Science." Pontifical Academy of Science, 2011, catholicclimatecovenant.org/wp-content

/uploads/2011/05/Pontifical-Academy-of-Sciences_Glacier_Report
_050511_final.pdf (accessed Sept. 1, 2011).

49. L. Wilson. "Anglicans, Episcopalians Issue Statement on Climate Justice, Form Commitments." 2010, episcopalchurch.org/79425_126183
_ENG_HTM.htm (accessed Aug. 29, 2011).

50. David Roach. "Lifeway Research Finds Increase in Pastors' Skepticism About Global Warming." April 18, 2011, lifeway.com/Article
/LifeWay-Research-finds-increase-in-pastor-skepticism-about-global
-warming (accessed Sept. 7, 2011).

51. "Famine In Africa: Bono, Anderson Cooper, K'naan Call For Famine Solution." *Huff Post Impact*, August 13, 2011, huffingtonpost.com/2011
/08/13/famine-africa-anderson-cooper_n_926173.html (accessed
Sept. 7, 2011).

52. Religious and faith-based divisions over climate change may certainly reflect theological divergences on other issues, including which sources or authorities we rely on to frame our attitudes and perspectives about social and justice issues; but in most cases, with the exception of some Dominionists who interpret the admonition to "subdue" the earth as advocating rampant exploitation, I do not believe that the reason for the religious divide over climate change lies in our basic theology about the physical world that surrounds us.

53. "List of Christian Thinkers in Science." Wikipedia, en.wikipedia.org
/wiki/List_of_Christian_thinkers_in_science (accessed Sept. 7, 2011).

54. Robert Fay. "Science and Christian Faith: Conflict or Cooperation?"
Pursuit of Truth: A Journal of Christian Scholarship, csslewis.org
/journal/?p=10 (accessed Sept. 7, 2011).

55. F. Turner. "The Victorian Conflict Between Science and Religion: A Professional Dimension." *Isis*, 69 (1978), pp. 356–376.

56. "Warming World: Impacts by Degree." National Academy of Sciences, National Research Council, 2011, dels.nas.edu/materials/book
lets/warming-world (accessed Sept. 7, 2011).

57. Unified Synthesis Product Team. "Global Climate Change Impacts in the United States." F. Bender, V. Ramanathan and G. Tselioudis. "Changes in Extratropical Storm Track Cloudiness 1983–2008: Observational Support for a Poleward Shift." *Climate Dynamics* (2011): doi: 10.1007/s00382-011-1065-6.

58. Unified Synthesis Project Team. "Global Climate Change Impacts in the United States."

59. "Amid Heat Wave, Senator Talks 'Global Cooling.'" ABC News, July 23, 2010, abcnews.go.com/Politics/amid-heat-wave-senator-talks -global-cooling/story?id=11237381 (accessed Sept. 1, 2011).

60. *Global Warming: A Scientific and Biblical Exposé of Climate Change.* DVD. Answers in Genesis and Coral Ridge Ministries, 2008.

61. *Resisting the Green Dragon.* DVD. Cornwall Alliance for the Steward-ship of Creation, 2010.

62. G. Jeffries. *The Global-Warming Deception: How a Secret Elite Plans to Bankrupt America and Steal Your Freedom.* WaterBrook Press, 2011.

63. "Koch Industries: Still Fueling Climate Denial." Greenpeace, 2011, greenpeace.org/usa/en/campaigns/global-warming-and-energy /polluterwatch/koch-industries/ (accessed Aug. 29, 2011).

64. J. Hoggan and R. Littlemore. *Climate Cover-Up: The Crusade to Deny Global Warming.* Greystone Books, 2009.

65. N. Oreskes and E. Conway. *Merchants of Doubt: How a Handful of Scientists Obscured the Truth on Issues from Tobacco Smoke to Global Warming.* Bloomsbury Press, 2010.

66. Ibid.

67. "Skepticism About Skeptics" (sidebar of "Climate of Uncertainty"). *Scientific American*, October 2001, web.archive.org/web/20060823 125025/sciam.com/page.cfm?section=sidebar&articleID=0004F43C -DC1A-1C6E-84A9809EC588EF21 (Aug. 29, 2011).

68. P. Doran and M. Kendall Zimmerman. "Examining the Scientific Consensus on Climate Change." *EOS* 90, 2009, p. 20.

69. National Research Council. *Surface Temperature Reconstructions for the last 2,000 years.* National Academies Press, 2006.

70. National Science Foundation, Office of Inspector General. "Close-out Memorandum, Case Number A09120086," August 2011, nsf.gov /oig/search/A09120086.pdf (accessed Sept. 2, 2011).

71. Arrhenius. "On the Influence of Carbonic Acid in the Air Upon the Temperature of the Ground." G.S. Callendar. "The Artificial Produc-tion of Carbon Dioxide and Its Influence on Temperature." *Quar-terly Journal Royal Meteorological Society*, 64 (1938), pp. 223–240.

72. "Psychology and Global Climate Change: Addressing a Multi-faceted Phenomenon and Set of Challenges." *Report of the American Psychological Association Task Force on the Interface Between Psychol-ogy and Global Climate Change.* American Psychological Association,

2009, apa.org/science/about/publications/climate-change.aspx (accessed Aug. 29, 2011).

73. Katherine Hayhoe and Andrew Farley. *A Climate for Change: Global Warming Facts for Faith-based Decisions*. FaithWords, 2009.

74. We can't say whether Katrina occurred because of climate change. We do expect some stronger hurricanes in the future, but we can't pin any one event on climate change. I am simply using it here as an example of the potential for socially disparate consequences of disaster-related impacts.

75. H. Rodriguez. "There is No Such Thing As a Natural Disaster: Race, Class, and Hurricane Katrina" (review). *Social Forces*, 86 (2008), pp. 1360–1362.

76. "Climate Change Response Initiative." World Vision International, 2011, wvi.org/wvi/wviweb.nsf/maindocs/C799F54BADDD6FA188257 4BF007F82CB?opendocument (accessed Sept. 2, 2011).

77. Panel (a) is based on the data provided by the World Resources Institute's EarthTrends: earthtrends.wri.org/ (accessed Sept. 6, 2011). The data for the panel (b) is interpolated to individual nations from the Climate-Demographic Vulnerability Index analysis by J. Samson, D. Berteau, B. McGill and M. Humphries: "Geographic disparities and moral hazards in the predicted impacts of climate change on human populations," *Global Ecology and Biogeography*, doi 10:1111/j.1466-8238.2010.00632.x, 2011.

78. Global Humanitarian Forum. "The Anatomy of a Silent Crisis: Human Impact Report." GHF, 2009, ghf-ge.org/human-impact-report .pdf (accessed Sept. 1, 2011).

79. The Green Patriot Working Group. *50 Simple Steps to Save the Earth From Global Warming*. Freedom Publishing Company, 2008.

Chapter 5

1. In *Scripture, Culture, and Agriculture: An Agrarian Reading of the Bible* (Cambridge University Press, 2009), Ellen F. Davis shows convincingly that our reading of the Bible, and thus also our understanding of God, is impoverished when we forget the agricultural context that both framed Israelite life and shaped their shared imagination.

2. Terence Fretheim has developed this theme of the dynamic

relationship between Creation and creation in *God and World in the Old Testament: A Relational Theology of Creation* (Abingdon Press, 2005).

3. For an excellent discussion of Genesis 1, see Davis's *Scripture, Culture, and Agriculture*, pp. 42–65, along with William P. Brown's *The Seven Pillars of Creation: The Bible, Science, and the Ecology of Wonder* (Oxford University Press, 2010).

4. Psalm 65 extends this image beautifully by describing God as a farmer come to his fields: "You visit the earth and water it, you greatly enrich it; the river of God is full of water; you provide the people with grain, for so you have prepared it. You water its furrows abundantly, settling its ridges, softening it with showers, and blessing its growth. You crown the year with your bounty; your wagon tracks overflow with richness. The pastures of the wilderness overflow, the hills gird themselves with joy, the meadows clothe themselves with flocks, the valleys deck themselves with grain, they shout and sing together for joy" (vv 9–13).

5. For further treatment of the theme of Sabbath delight see my book *Living the Sabbath: Discovering the Rhythms of Rest and Delight* (Brazos Press, 2006).

6. I have developed some of the practical and cultural implications that follow from this view in *The Paradise of God: Renewing Religion in an Ecological Age* (Oxford University Press, 2003).

7. An excellent place to begin is Louis Dupré's *Passage to Modernity: An Essay in the Hermeneutics of Nature and Culture* (Yale University Press, 1993).

8. For a description of some of the difficulties farmers will face on a warming planet see McKibben's *Eaarth: Making a Life on a Tough New Planet* and Lester R. Brown's *World on the Edge: How to Prevent Environmental and Economic Collapse* (W.W. Norton & Company, 2011).

9. James Gustave Speth. *The Bridge at the Edge of the World: Capitalism, the Environment, and Crossing from Crisis to Sustainability*. Yale University Press, 2008, p. x.

10. J.R. McNeill. *Something New Under the Sun: An Environmental History of the Twentieth-Century World*. Yale University Press, 2000, particularly chapter 1.

11. For an inspiring account of how one church community developed a community garden as a witness to God's nurturing and reconcil-

ing ways with the world, see Fred Bahnson's article "A Garden Becomes a Protest," *Orion*, July/August 2007, orionmagazine.org/index
.php/articles/article/312/.

12. See James B. Martin-Schramm's book *Climate Justice: Ethics, Energy,
and Public Policy* (Fortress Press, 2010) for a lucid description of policy options and their ethical and theological significance.

13. Celia Deane-Drummond's *Seeds of Hope: Facing the Challenge of Climate Justice* (CAFOD, 2009) provides a very helpful, non-technical
treatment of theological resources that can guide us in responding
to the many challenges associated with climate change.

Chapter 6

1. W. H. Auden. "For the Time Being: A Christmas Oratorio." *Collected
Poems: Auden*. Vintage, 1991.

2. Stanley Hauerwas. *Matthew: Brazos Theological Commentary on the
Bible*. Brazos Press, 2007.

3. Anglican Communion Office. "Mission – The five marks." 2011
anglicancommunion.org/ministry/mission/fivemarks.cfm (Accessed
May 19, 2011). The Anglican Communion is a worldwide association
of churches that trace their roots to the Church of England. The
Episcopal Church is a member of the Anglican Communion.

4. Thomas Merton. *New Seeds of Contemplation*, revised edition.
Shambhala Publications, 2003, p. 31.

5. Wendell Berry. *Jayber Crow*. Counterpoint, 2001, p. 160.

Chapter 7

1. Environmental Priorities Coalition, environmentalpriorities.org (accessed April 11, 2011).

2. Washington State Department of Ecology and State of Washington
Department of Community, Trade and Economic Development.
*Washington State Greenhouse Gas Inventory and Reference Case Pro-
jections, 1990–2020*. Dec. 2007, ecy.wa.gov/climatechange/docs/WA
_GHGInventoryReferenceCaseProjections_1990-2020.pdf (accessed
April 11, 2011).

3. Eric de Place. "Centralia's Coal Emissions In Context." *Sightline
Daily*, May 20, 2010, daily.sightline.org/daily_score/archive/2010/05
/20/centralias-coal-emissions-in-context (accessed April 12, 2011).

4. Alan H. Lockwood et al. *Coal's Assault on Human Health: A Report*

from Physicians for Social Responsibility (Executive Summary). November 2009, psr.org/assets/pdfs/coals-assault-executive.pdf (accessed April 11, 2011).

5. Dixon H. Landers et al. *The Fate, Transport, and Ecological Impacts of Airborne Contaminants in Western National Parks (USA)*, EPA/600/R -07/138. US Environmental Protection Agency, Office of Research and Development, NHEERL, Western Ecology Division, February, 2008, nps.gov/olym/parknews/airborne-contaminants-study-released .htm and nature.nps.gov/air/Studies/air_toxics/docs/2008Final Report/WACAP_Report_Volume_I_Main.pdf (accessed April 11, 2011).

6. Jennifer Langston. "Coal Cuts: Oregon vs. Washington." *Sightline Daily*, January 8, 2010, daily.sightline.org/daily_score/archive /2010/01/08/curbing-coal-pollution (accessed April 12, 2011).

7. US Environmental Protection Agency. "Human-Related Sources and Sinks of Carbon Dioxide." epa.gov/climatechange/emissions/co2 _human.html (accessed April 12, 2011).

8. Pew Center on Global Climate Change. *Addressing Emissions From Coal Use in Power Generation: Congressional Policy Brief*. Fall, 2008, pewclimate.org/docUploads/Coal.pdf (accessed April 12, 2011).

9. Ted Nace. *Climate Hope: On the Front Lines of the Fight Against Coal*. Coal Swarm, 2010.

10. James E. Hansen. "Letter to Kraig R. Naasz." November 21, 2007, columbia.edu/~jeh1/mailings/2007/20071121_NMAletters.pdf (accessed April 11, 2011).

11. Sierra Club. *Mountaintop Removal Coal Mining: Destroying Appalachia One Mountain At A Time*. sierraclub.org/coal/mtr/downloads /brochure.pdf (accessed April 11, 2011).

12. Lockwood et al. *Coal's Assault on Human Health*.

13. Paul Sheldon, Emily Evans and Nick Sterling. *Coal Plants in Transition: An Economic Case Study*. Natural Capitalism Solutions, January 23, 2010, natcapsolutions.org/CoalPlantsinTransition.pdf (accessed April 11, 2011).

14. Steve Weiss. *Bright Future*. NW Energy Coalition, March, 2009, nwenergy.org/resources-publications/studies/bright-future/ (accessed April 11, 2011).

15. Felicia Reilly. "Moving Washington Beyond Coal." *Faith and Envi-

ronment Network, August 22, 2010, faithandenvironmentnetwork
.org/2010/08/22/moving-washington-beyond-coal/ (accessed April 12,
2011).

16. Earth Ministry. "Historic Agreement Reached to Phase Out Coal-
burning in Washington." March 5, 2011, earthministry.org/press-room
/press-releases/coal-agreement (accessed April 12, 2011).

17. Governor Christine Gregoire. "Gov. Gregoire Announces Agreement with TransAlta." March 5, 2011, governor.wa.gov/news/news
-view.asp?pressRelease=1664&newsType=1 (accessed April 12, 2011).

Chapter 8

1. David Roberts. "An Interview with Van Jones, Advocate for Social
Justice and Shared Green Prosperity." March 20, 2007, grist.org/news
/maindish/2007/03/20/vanjones/ (accessed June 1, 2011).

2. Commission for Racial Justice, United Church of Christ. "Toxic
Wastes and Race in the United States: A National Report on the Racial and Socio-Economic Characteristics of Communities with Hazardous Waste Sites." 1987, ucc.org/about-us/archives/pdfs/toxwrace87
.pdf (accessed June 2, 2011).

3. "Rosie the Riveter—World War II Home Front National Historical
Park." nps.gov/rori/index.htm (Accessed June 2, 2011).

4. "A History of the Richmond Shipyards." rosietheriveter.org/shiphist
.htm (accessed June 1, 2011).

5. "2005 Murder Rate in Cities." infoplease.com/ipa/A0934323.html (accessed June 6, 2011).

6. "Wealth Holdings Remain Equal in Good Times and Bad." stateof
workingamerica.org/charts/view/206 (accessed June 6, 2011).

7. "State of the Dream—Austerity for Whom?" faireconomy.org/files
/State_of_the_Dream_2011.pdf (accessed June 4, 2011).

8. For a discussion of power purchase agreements and funding of solar
projects for faith-based organizations, see Mallory McDuff's book
Natural Saints: How People of Faith are Working to Save God's Earth
(Oxford University Press, 2010), pp. 156–161.

9. "How Does TVA 'Green' Power Benefit the Environment?" Dec. 24,
2002, mensetmanus.net/windpower/tva-foia/green-claims.shtml (accessed June 17, 2011).

10. "In 2008, MONDRAGON provided 3.6% of the Basque Autonomous

Community's total GDP and 6.6% of its Industrial GDP." Dec. 4, 2009, mondragon-corporation.com/ENG/Press-room/articleType /ArticleView/articleId/1377.aspx (accessed June 4, 2011).

11. Sarah Anderson, John Cavanagh, Chuck Collins, Sam Pizzagat and Mike Lapham. "Executive Excess 2008: How Average Taxpayers Subsidize Runaway Pay." Aug. 25, 2008, faireconomy.org/files/executive _excess_2008.pdf (accessed June 4, 2011).

12. Demian Bulwa. "California Violent Crime Rate Drops for 2010." May 27, 2011, articles.sfgate.com/2011-05-27/news/29589333_1_violent -crime-police-officials-and-criminologists-homicide-rate/2 (accessed June 17, 2011).

13. 2009 Bay Area Solar Installations Report. July 14, 2010, norcalsolar .org/docs/BASI_2009.pdf (accessed June 17, 2011).

14. "United Nations Climate Change Impact Report: Poor Will Suffer Most." April 6, 2007, ens-newswire.com/ens/apr2007/2007-04-06-01 .asp (accessed June 12, 2011).

15. "Quote Library—Buddha." beliefnet.com/Quotes/Relationships/B /Buddha/Like-a-caring-mother.aspx?q=Love (accessed June 17, 2011).

Chapter 9

1. Appalachia Catholic Bishops. "This Land is Home to Me: 1975 Pastoral Letter of the Bishops of Appalachia." catholicconferencewv.org/ (accessed June 7, 2011).

2. Ronald D. Eller. *Uneven Ground: Appalachia since 1945.* The University Press of Kentucky, 2008, p. 200. See also Appalachian Landownership Task Force, *Who Owns Appalachia: Land Ownership and Its Impact.* The University Press of Kentucky, 1983.

3. Catholic News Service Documentary Service. "Mountaintop Removal Protested." *Origins,* 32, no. 30 (Jan. 9, 2003), p. 504.

4. Eric Reece. *Lost Mountain: A Year in the Vanishing Wilderness.* Riverhead Books: 2006, p. 25.

5. Ibid.

6. Ibid., p. 105.

7. James Fallows. "Dirty Coal, Clean Future." *The Atlantic,* 306, no. 5 (December, 2010), p. 66.

8. Ibid.

9. The Kentucky Coal Association. "Mountaintop Mining Issues and

Responses." kentuckycoal.org/index.cfm?pageToken=mtmIssues (accessed June 9, 2011).

10. The Renewal Project. *Renewal.* 2011, renewalproject.net/ (accessed June 9, 2011).

11. Steve James. "Black Lung Disease Seen Rising in U.S. Miners." *Reuters,* May 20, 2011, news.yahoo.com/s/nm/20110520/hl_nm/us_black _lung_1 (accessed June 9, 2011).

12. Appalachian Voices. "Mountaintop Removal 101." 2011, appvoices.org /end-mountaintop-removal/mtr101/ (accessed June 9, 2011).

13. Reece, *Lost Mountain,* p. 92.

14. I computed these numbers from data, available at and compiled by the US Energy Information Administration (accessed June 9, 2011). Total Electricity Net Consumption in 2008 (billion kilowatt hours): United States = 3,906.443 and world = 17,444.762. The percentage of US electrical consumption was 22.39 percent of the world's consumption. China ranks second with 19 percent of the world's electricity consumed.

Chapter 10

1. Tim Funk. "A Priest's View of Immigration." Jan. 22, 2011, faithin publiclife.org//content/news/2011/01/a_priests_views_of_immigra tion.html (accessed June 13, 2011).

2. The Latino population in North Carolina increased 111 percent in the past decade, from approximately 379,000 to 800,000. "North Carolina Latino Population Swells." Reuters, March 3, 2011, reuters.com /article/2011/03/03/idUS220181+03-Mar-2011+PRN20110303 (accessed June 24, 2011).

3. Funk. "A Priest's View of Immigration."

4. Mark Stevenson. "Reserve May Come Too Late for Monarchs." *Asheville Citizen-Times,* November 29, 2010, p. A8.

5. Kerry Zobor. "Tigers, Polar Bears and Blue Fin Tuna Among the Most Threatened Species in 2010, Says World Wildlife Fund." December 2, 2009, worldwildlife.org/who/media/press/2009/WWFPre sitem14481.html (accessed on June 13, 2011).

6. David Quamman. "Great Migrations." *National Geographic,* November, 2010, pp. 28–51.

7. Stephen Castles and Mark J. Miller. *The Age of Migration: International*

Population Movements in the Modern World, 4th ed. The Guilford Press, 2009, p. 2.

8. Beth Beasley. "Migrating Monarchs: Track This Natural Wonder Through the Blue Ridge. *Hendersonville Times-News*, September 12, 2010, pp. E1, E6.

9. Monarch Larva Monitoring Project. "Winter Storms in Mexico & Crucial Importance of MLMP." *Monarch Larva Monitoring Project Newsletter*, March 2010, docstoc.com/docs/43410156/Monarch-Larva -Monitoring-Project-2010-Newsletter (accessed June 24, 2011).

10. The International Federation of Red Cross and Red Crescent Societies (IFRC) comprises the 186-member Red Cross and Red Crescent National Societies. The world's largest humanitarian organization assists victims of disaster and promotes development. Increasingly, the IFRC addresses victims of the impacts of climate change. The Red Crescent is used in Islamic countries in place of the Red Cross.

11. Friends of the Earth Australia. *Friends of the Earth Citizens' Guide to Climate Refugees*. April 2007, foe.org.au/resources/publications /climate-justice/CitizensGuide.pdf/view (accessed June 24, 2011).

12. "A New (Under)class of Travelers." *The Economist*, June 25, 2009, economist.com/research/articlesBySubject/PrinterFriendly.cfm?story _id=13925906 (accessed June 13, 2011).

13. Carolyn Brock. "Discernment: Transformative Practice for a Prophetic People." 2009, cofchrist.org/discernment/articles/transform ative.asp (accessed on May 25, 2011).

14. "Climate Mitigation and Adaptation." global-greenhouse-warming .com/climate-mitigation-and-adaptation.html (accessed May 27, 2011).

15. Interfaith Power & Light. "Carbon Covenant." interfaithpowerand light.org/2009/12/carbon-covenant (accessed June 13, 2011).

16. IPCC. "Annex I: Glossary." ipcc.ch/pdf/glossary/ar4-wg3.pdf (accessed May 27, 2011).

17. Anna Kramer. "Speaking Out About Peru's Climate Crisis." April 9, 2010, firstperson.oxfamamerica.org/index.php/2010/04/09/speaking -out-about-perus-climate-crisis (accessed June 13, 2011).

18. Robert McCarson. "Expulsan a 614 Desde Henderson." *La Voz Independiente*, July 1, 2010, p. 6.

19. A similar immigration program called Secure Communities checks detainees' fingerprints against federal databases for criminal or immigration-status violations. Secure Communities exists in all 100 counties of North Carolina.

20. Mai Thi Nguyen and Hannah Gill. *The 287(g) Program: the Costs and Consequences of Local Immigration Enforcement in North Carolina*. The University of Chapel Hill, 2009, p. 9.

21. Manuel Roig-Franzia. "Mexicans Get Less Aid from Migrants." April 18, 2008. washingtonpost.com/wp-ddydyn/content/article/2008/04/17/AR2008041703786.html?nav=emailpage (accessed on June 13, 2011.)

22. David Biello. "Climate Change May Mean More Mexican Immigration." *Scientific American*, July 26, 2010, scientificamerican.com/article.cfm?id=climate-change-may-mean-more-mexican-immigration (accessed June 13, 2011).

23. Don Belt. "Buoyant in Bangledesh." *National Geographic*, May 2011.

24. United Nations Development Programme. "Fighting Climate Change: Human Solidarity in a Divided World." *Human Development Report 2007/2008*, hdr.undp.org/en/media/HDR_20072008_EN_Complete.pdf (accessed June 13, 2011).

25. United Nations. "UN Climate Change Conference in Cancún Delivers Balanced Package of Decisions, Restores Faith in Multilateral Process." December 11, 2010, unfccc.int/files/press/news_room/press_releases_and_advisories/application/pdf/pr_20101211_cop16_closing.pdf (accessed June 13, 2011).

26. Bob Allen. "Faith Leaders Join Challenge to Alabama's Immigration Law." Associated Baptist Press, July 13, 2011, abpnews.com/content/view/6559/53/ (accessed July 13, 2011).

Chapter 11

1. Not her real name.

2. WE ACT for Environmental Justice stands for the West Harlem Environmental Action, Inc.

3. National Center for Healthy Housing. "Testing for Lead in Consumer Items for Children." kdheks.gov/lead/download/NCHH_Fact sheet_Lead_Testing_Consumer_Products.pdf (accessed August 1, 2011).

4. Renu Garg, Adam Karpati, Jessica Leighton, Mary Perrin and Mona

Shah. *Asthma Facts*, 2nd ed. New York City Department of Health and Mental Hygiene, p. 16, May 2003, nyc.gov/html/doh/downloads /pdf/asthma/facts.pdf (accessed August 1, 2011).

5. Lenny Bernstein et al. *Climate Change 2007: Synthesis Report: An Assessment of the Intergovernmental Panel on Climate Change*. 2007, p. 65, ipcc.ch/pdf/assessment-report/ar4/syr/ar4_syr.pdf (accessed August 1, 2011).

6. Not his real name.

7. Larry Parker. "Statement from the Environmental Justice Forum on Climate Change." June 2, 2008, weact.org/Portals/7/Statement FromTheEnvironmentalJusticeForumOnClimateChange.pdf (accessed August 1, 2011).

8. Wangari Maathai. "Nobel Lecture." December 10, 2004, nobelprize .org/nobel_prizes/peace/laureates/2004/maathai-lecture-text.html (accessed August 1, 2011).

9. Robert W. Castle. "Christianity: Underground Manifesto." *Time*, March 29, 1968, time.com/time/magazine/article/0,9171,838120,00 .html (accessed August 1, 2011).

10. A "free pew" congregation is one that abolished pew rents, a system that allowed wealthy parishioners to rent or buy pews for worship.

11. "Northern Manhattan Improvement Corp. Building a Path to Prosperity." *New York Nonprofit Press*, Feb. 27, 2010, nynp.biz/agencies-of -the-month/2100-northern-manhattan-improvement-corp-building -a-path-to-prosperity (accessed August 1, 2011).

12. Brad Heath and Blake Morrison. "EPA Study: 2.2M Live in Areas Where Air Poses Cancer Risk." July 26, 2009, usatoday.com/news /nation/environment/2009-06-23-epa-study_N.htm (accessed August 1, 2011).

13. F. Perera. "Molecular Epidemiology, Prenatal Exposure and Prevention of Cancer." *Environmental Health*, June 2011, pp. 1–3, ccceh.hs .columbia.edu/pdf-papers/Perera2011.pdf (accessed August 1, 2011).

14. Ibid.

15. V.B. Vásquez, M. Minkler and P. Shepard. "Promoting Environmental Health Policy through Community-based Participatory Research: A Case Study from Harlem, New York." *Journal of Urban Health*, 83(1), Jan. 2006, pp. 101–110, ccceh.hs.columbia.edu/pdf -papers/VasquezUrbanHealthJan2006.pdf (accessed August 1, 2011).

16. Lisa Sharon Harper. *Evangelical ≠ Republican or Democrat.* The New Press, 2008.

17. "A Statement of Commitment to Become a Sustainable Earth Community Congregation." The Riverside Church, April 25, 2004, theriversidechurchny.org/about/files/sustainable.pdf (accessed August 1, 2011).

18. For a video of the mapping project and its relevance to congregations, see "Healthy Living Harlem: Green Mapping for EcoJustice," Faith Leaders for Environmental Justice, weact.org/Coalitions/Faith LeadersforEnvironmentalJustice/tabid/360/Default.aspx (accessed Aug. 8, 2011).

19. Scott M. Stringer. "Senseless Subsidies: A Report on Tax Benefits Under the Industrial and Commercial Incentive Program." 2008, mbpo .org/uploads/policy_reports/Senseless%20Subsidies.pdf (accessed July 25, 2011).

Chapter 12

1. Appalachian Voices. "Welcome to Kayford Mountain." ilovemoun tains.org/category/communities/c251 (accessed April 10, 2011).

2. West Virginia Office of Miners' Health, Safety and Training. "West Virginia Coal Mining Facts." July 26, 2010, www.wvminesafety.org /wvcoalfacts.htm (accessed April 10, 2011).

3. "President Bush's State of the Union Address" (transcript). *The Washington Post*, Jan. 31, 2006, washingtonpost.com/wp-dyn/content /article/2006/01/31/AR2006013101468.html (accessed April 10, 2011).

4. Gerald May, MD. *Addiction and Grace.* Harper Collins, 1988, p. 18.

5. Ross Geredien and Appalachian Voices. *Extent of Mountaintop Removal Mining in Appalachia* 2009. ilovemountains.org/reclamation -fail/details.php#reclamation_study (accessed April 10, 2011).

6. M.A. Palmer et al. "Mountaintop Mining Consequences." *Science*, 327, no. 5962, (January 8, 2010), pp. 148–149.

7. Kathryn Mahaffey, Robert Clickner and Catherine Bodurow. "Blood Organic Mercury and Dietary Mercury Intake." *Environmental Health Perspectives*, 112, no. 5 (April 2004).

8. US Energy Information Administration. "United States, Petroleum 2009." Oct. 28, 2010, eia.doe.gov/countries/country-data.cfm?fips=US (accessed April 15, 2011). US Energy Information Administration.

"World Proved Reserves of Oil and Natural Gas, Most Recent Estimates." March 3, 2009, eia.doe.gov/international/oilreserves.html (accessed April 15, 2011).

9. US Energy Information Administration. "What is the Role of Coal in the U.S.?" Feb. 25, 2010, eia.doe.gov/energy_in_brief/role_coal_us .cfm (accessed April 16, 2011).

10. Paul R. Epstein et al. Robert Costanza, Karin Limburg and Ida Kubiszewski, eds. "Full Cost Accounting for the Life Cycle of Coal in Ecological Economics Reviews." *Annals of the New York Academy of Sciences*, 2011, 1219, pp. 73–98.

11. Peter Coy. "The Other Energy Crisis: Lack of R & D." *Business Week*, June 17, 2010, businessweek.com/magazine/content/10_26/b4184029812114.htm (accessed April 10, 2011).

12. NOAA Fisheries Service. "Deepwater Horizon/BP Oil Spill: Size and Percent Coverage of Fishing Area Closures Due to BP Oil Spill." Jan. 31, 2011, sero.nmfs.noaa.gov/ClosureSizeandPercentCoverage .htm (accessed April 16, 2011).

13. Kimberly Kindy. "Fishermen Stake Shots at BP Skimming Program." *Washington Post*, Aug. 15, 2010, articles.boston.com/2010-08-15/news /29282162_1_fishermen-oil-spill-bp (accessed April 20, 2011).

14. National Commission on BP Deepwater Horizon Oil Spill and Offshore Drilling. *Deepwater: The Gulf Disaster and the Future of Offshore Drilling. Report to the President.* January 11, 2011, p. 115, purl.fdlp.gov /GPO/gpo2978 (accessed April 10, 2011).

15. Amy Liu and Allison Plyer. *The New Orleans Index at Five.* August 4, 2010, brookings.edu/reports/2007/08neworleansindex.aspx (accessed April 10, 2011).

16. Michael Hill. "Oil Spill Puts Gulf Oyster Industry on Ice." June 22, 2010, msnbc.msn.com/id/37856183/ns/business-us_business/t/oil-spill -puts-gulf-oyster-industry-ice/ (accessed May 2, 2011).

17. For more detail on the impact of the oil spill on oyster beds, see Charles Jacoba, "For Oyster Industry, Gulf Oil Disaster is Far from Over," Aug. 5, 2010, solveclimatenews.com/news/20100805/oyster -industry-gulf-oil-disaster-far-over (accessed May 1, 2011).

18. Earthjustice. "Deepwater Horizon Spill: By the Numbers." 2011, earthjustice.org/features/preventing-more-bp-type-oil-disasters (accessed April 16, 2011).

19. US Energy Information Administration. "Oil: Crude and Petroleum Products Explained." Oct. 28, 2010, eia.gov/energyexplained/index .cfm?page=oil_home#tab2 (accessed April 26, 2011). To calculate this number, I divided the US daily consumption of oil by the total amount of the oil spill.

20. B.R. Couvillion et al. "Land Area Change in Coastal Louisiana from 1932 to 2010." *US Geological Survey Scientific Investigations Map 3164*, 2011.

Conclusion

1. Wendell Berry. "The Real Work." americanpoems.com/poets/wendell -berry/14017 (accessed Aug. 11, 2011). This "poem" is an excerpt from the essay "Poetry and Marriage" in Berry's *Standing by Words* (Counterpoint, 2005), p. 97.

2. Episcopal News Service. "House of Deputies President Calls Church to 'Courageous Change.'" May 5, 2011, episcopalchurch.org/80263 _128254_ENG_HTM.htm (accessed May 5, 2011).

Afterword

1. The Episcopal Church, USA. "Prayers of the People." *The Book of Common Prayer*. Church Publishing, 1979, p. 388.

Index

About the Author

MALLORY McDUFF teaches environmental education at Warren Wilson College, a unique liberal arts school in Asheville, North Carolina that combines academics with work and service. A lifelong Episcopalian, she grew up on the Gulf Coast in Fairhope, Alabama, where her parents connected faith to environmentalism through actions such as giving up driving for Lent.

Mallory has a Ph.D. in wildlife ecology and conservation, with a focus on environmental education. She is the author of *Natural Saints: How People of Faith are Working to Save God's Earth*. She lives on the campus of Warren Wilson College with her two daughters, Maya and Annie Sky.

If you have enjoyed *Sacred Acts,*
you might also enjoy other

BOOKS TO BUILD A NEW SOCIETY

Our books provide positive solutions for people who want to
make a difference. We specialize in:

**Sustainable Living • Green Building • Peak Oil
Renewable Energy • Environment & Economy
Natural Building & Appropriate Technology
Progressive Leadership • Resistance and Community
Educational & Parenting Resources**

New Society Publishers

ENVIRONMENTAL BENEFITS STATEMENT

New Society Publishers has chosen to produce this book on recycled paper made
with **100% post consumer waste,** processed chlorine free, and old growth free.
For every 5,000 books printed, New Society saves the following resources:[1]

28	Trees
2,551	Pounds of Solid Waste
2,807	Gallons of Water
3,661	Kilowatt Hours of Electricity
4,638	Pounds of Greenhouse Gases
20	Pounds of HAPs, VOCs, and AOX Combined
7	Cubic Yards of Landfill Space

---

[1]Environmental benefits are calculated based on research done by the Environmental Defense
Fund and other members of the Paper Task Force who study the environmental impacts of the
paper industry.

For a full list of NSP's titles, please call 1-800-567-6772 *or check out our website* at:

www.newsociety.com

new society
PUBLISHERS